Romantic Complexity

Romantic Complexity

Keats, Coleridge, and Wordsworth

Jack Stillinger

UNIVERSITY OF ILLINOIS PRESS

Urbana and Chicago

© 2006 by the Board of Trustees
of the University of Illinois
Manufactured in the United States of America
c 5 4 3 2 1

⊛ This book is printed on acid-free paper.

Library of Congress Cataloging-in-Publication Data
Stillinger, Jack.
Romantic complexity : Keats, Coleridge, and Wordsworth / Jack
Stillinger.
p.   cm.
Includes bibliographical references and index.
ISBN-13: 978-0-252-03062-8 (cloth : alk. paper)
ISBN-10: 0-252-03062-1 (cloth : alk. paper)
1. English poetry—19th century—History and criticism.   2. Keats,
John, 1795–1821—Criticism and interpretation.   3. Coleridge, Samuel
Taylor, 1772–1834—Criticism and interpretation.   4. Wordsworth,
William, 1770–1850—Criticism and interpretation.   5.
Romanticism—Great Britain.   I. Title.
PR590S75   2006
821'.709145—dc22   2005034422

Contents

Part III: Romantics and the Classroom

Preface

THIS BOOK PRESENTS A SELECTION of shorter writings mainly from the 1980s and 1990s, with three pieces from 2000–2003 and one going back to 1970–71. They exemplify a wide array of original sources and formats—book chapters, articles in scholarly journals, contributions to edited collections, plenary addresses at international conferences, papers delivered at Modern Language Association sessions, an introduction to a scholarly text, an electronic publication on a website dedicated to Romanticism, and, at the end, a bit of personal reminiscence—and were written with a considerable range of audiences in mind. While they also represent a variety of subjects, they collectively address some of the questions and topics that have interested me most during the latter half of my five-decades-long career as a Romantics scholar.

An anonymous reader for the University of Illinois Press has conveniently summarized "several themes of great importance" running through these essays. They include "the multiplicity of meanings produced by 'complex adaptive systems'; the strategic instability of meaning in Romantic poems as the mark of 'modernity' in English language poetry; the measure of this instability or 'complexity' as a means for making aesthetic judgments on poetry; the complicated intersections between the two generations of Romantic poets; the relationship of all these issues to theoretical models, past and present, of reading, teaching, and writing about poetry." Above all, the essays underlie, or branch off from, three interconnected longer studies that I published in the 1990s: *Multiple Authorship and the Myth of Solitary Genius* (1991), *Coleridge and Textual Instability* (1994), and *Reading "The Eve of St. Agnes"* (1999). These books focus cumulatively on what I have called, in the subtitle of the most recent of the three, "the multiples of complex literary transaction." In order, progressing from the left side to the right, each takes up one of the three elements in a standard graphic representation of the process of written communication—

Author—Text—Reader

—and argues for the *multiple* character of that element. Works routinely assumed to have been written by the single author named on the title page frequently are multiply authored (as in the well-documented collaboration of T. S. Eliot and Ezra Pound that produced the twentieth century's most influential poem in English, "Eliot's" *The Waste Land*). Works usually studied in isolated single versions almost always exist in multiple variant texts, sometimes with drastic differences among them (for example, the eighteen recoverable versions, all by Coleridge, of *The Rime of the Ancient Mariner*). And almost always there are multiple productive ways of reading and understanding these works, even when some of the ways directly oppose some of the others (for example, Porphyro as Romantic hero versus Porphyro as cruel seducer in *The Eve of St. Agnes*). In the present collection, I set forth these ideas most elaborately in chapters 6 and 12, which in effect propose fifty-nine different ways of reading first *The Eve of St. Agnes* and then *Ode on a Grecian Urn.* But multiplicity and the complexity resulting when the multiples conflict with one another show up, or at least hover in the background, in many of the other chapters, starting with the explanation in chapter 1, "What Keats Is About," that describes "the rich complexity" produced by a continuous tug-of-war between visionary and down-to-earth tendencies existing simultaneously in Keats's best poetry.

The phrase "Romantic complexity" in my title points to this complexity deriving from conflicting multiples. I take it to be a signature characteristic of three of the most admired writers of the British Romantic period, and I begin with a Keats section, in mild defiance of historical chronology, because Keats's poems offer the clearest illustration of the quality. Coleridge and Wordsworth come next in my organization as two slightly earlier writers who helped pass complexity on to modern (twentieth-century) poets. Modernist poetry, I believe, is categorically definable in terms of this same complexity that I see beginning with the Romantics. There is less of the quality in the three other Romantics deemed most major—Blake, Byron, and Percy Shelley—who, to me, are more dependent on history for their strong positions in the canon. I have long considered Keats, Coleridge, and

Wordsworth as the principal male writers of the period in terms of their continuing appeal. None of the other Romantics so effectively *captures* modern readers—in the way the Mariner captures the Wedding-Guest, "He cannot choose but hear"—and the modern readers I'm talking about include twenty-first-century undergraduates in my survey courses at the University of Illinois covering the second half of British literature.

My first scholarly essay, explaining a handful of allusions in Keats's letters, appeared in 1956. My most recent, on some problems in representing discrete textual versions in the apparatus of J. C. C. Mays's new edition of Coleridge's poems, is scheduled for some time in 2005, a mere forty-nine years later. No doubt I shall write some more before I hang up my laptop. In the theoretical line, I should like to put together a piece on "canonical simplicity," a concept that connects with the already-established "canonical complexity" (as in chapters 6 and 12 in the present volume and at greater length in *Reading "The Eve of St. Agnes,"* 120–29) to further explain a basic characteristic of our longest lasting and most admired literary works. Canonical simplicity, as I would develop it, refers to a significant element in a canonical work about which there is unanimous interpretive consent— a *single* way of reading it that everyone agrees on, rather than the fifty-nine (or fifty-nine hundred) ways that I propose for *The Eve of St. Agnes* as a whole. Canonical simplicity can be an element of plot—"With my cross-bow / I shot the Albatross," where there are no questions concerning who did the shooting, what the weapon was, or what kind of bird the victim was, even while these same facts raise innumerable critical questions concerning the Mariner's motive and the symbolic significances of the action, the weapon, and the bird. Such simplicity can be a matter of the plainness of language—"The Rainbow comes and goes, / And lovely is the Rose"—a bit of unambiguously beautiful nature description, part of the "glory" that "hath past away . . . from the earth" in one of Wordsworth's most complicated shorter poems. It can be an element of theme—the youth growing pale and specter-thin and dying in Keats's *Nightingale,* or the bold lover who never, never can kiss, though winning near the goal, in *Grecian Urn,* where there is no interpretive doubt about these characters' condition of mortality, even in the face of numerous questions about the poems' structures of attitudes and recommendations concerning their situations. I think that complexity alone may not be a sufficient condition to explain the essential quality of these passages and that some contrasting simplicity is necessary, especially as a framing or structuring device, to produce the totality of the effects that we respond to. In this new piece I would recommend practical testing by teaching poems in a two-part exercise consisting of (1) Where's the complexity? and (2) Where's the simplicity?—with the ideas that both elements are present and identifiable in a good poem and that focusing on just one of them to the neglect of the other doesn't guarantee sufficient grasp of the whole.

In the extremely practical line, I would like to do a short piece titled "The Multiple Harvard Editions of Keats's Poems" with the aim of clearing up a growing misunderstanding concerning the two editions of Keats's complete poems that I published in 1978 and 1982. The earlier of these, titled *The Poems of John Keats,* is an elaborate scholarly presentation, some 770 pages of introduction, texts, apparatuses, textual notes, and half a dozen appendixes. It was favorably received from the beginning, and for two and a half decades it has been the American (and usually the British) standard for scholarly use and citation in Romantics studies. The later of the two, for which the usual bibliographical citation is *John Keats: Complete Poems,* is a spin-off from the earlier work, a 490-page "reading edition" in smaller format using the same texts with an accompaniment of critical introduction and commentary but without the various textual apparatuses at the foot of the page and in the back that were a feature of the larger parent edition. The misunderstanding I would correct is the confusion of the two editions—in scholarly citation and, more seriously, in scholars' minds. Increasingly, new publications on Keats, as well as manuscripts that I evaluate for journals and university presses, cite the two editions as if they were a single work, with frequent discrepancies of title, date, and page reference. There are historical reasons for this. Harvard University Press removed the separate title-page dates, 1978 and 1982, in subsequent issues and from the beginning used the two dates together ("© 1978, 1982" on the verso of the title) as the copyright date for the 1982 edition because it repeated the texts of the earlier. Around 1990, Harvard (perhaps making the same mistake that scholars themselves are repeating more recently) let the textual edition go out of print, filling orders for "the Harvard edition of Keats's poems" with the paperback reading edition and even, in recent years, using comments from reviews of the textual edition ("the first reliable edition," "the first completely authoritative text," "our standard for a long time to come," and so on) in advertising the reading edition. What worries me most, of course, is the idea of scholars doing serious work on Keats and *not* knowing, because they are using the reading edition, about the several hundred pages of textual information that were a part of the earlier work. Harvard is now interested in correcting the situation (the press has recently made the textual edition again available in its print-on-demand program of reissues). It will take time, though, for the news to get around.

But the imaginary pieces I just described are matters for the future. The essays in this collection are the ones I wish to reprint now. All fifteen have been revised to some extent, but none so drastically as to be unfaithful to the original circumstances of publication or delivery. I have updated many of the citations of Romantics scholarship and criticism but also have retained some early ones—for example, the references to Robert Langbaum, Morse Peckham, and Earl Wasserman in chapter 13—that seem, for historical purposes or their continued validity, worth keeping even though these critics' works were first published three or four decades ago. I have left in a few repetitions of statement and example (perhaps most awkwardly in a handful of paragraphs of chapter 6 that reappear in chapter 7) in order to preserve what I fancy is the separate integrity of the pieces in which they occur. The earliest of the selections, again chapter 13, going back to 1970–71, may seem overly simple in its wide-eyed prophecy of an accelerated interest in the historical contexts of Romanticism. I include it because I'm rather pleased, thirty-five years later, that it turned out to be right.

The source of each essay is detailed in the Notes section at the back of the book. I'm much obliged to the various editors and publishers for permission to use the pieces again on the present occasion. I'm also much indebted to Bill Regier and the University of Illinois Press for accepting these essays with such enthusiasm. Illinois published my first scholarly book, in 1961, which was a study of the original draft of John Stuart Mill's *Autobiography*—a wonderful manuscript (containing, among other things, Mill's wife's penciled revisions and queries up and down the margins) that came to the University of Illinois library in the same fall month of 1958 in which I joined the English faculty. I chose Illinois as my first publisher because I had a strong desire to be publicly identified with this campus, and I am happy to be an Illinois author again, toward the end of my career.

As for colleagues in the endeavor to understand the Romantics, I have obligation to many hundreds of individuals over the years—far too many to mention here—for their information, ideas, encouragement, and even occasional mistakes that led to better facts and ideas by way of correction. Off campus, I want to specially thank Hermione de Almeida, Neil Fraistat, Marilyn Gaull, Greg Kucich, Deidre Lynch, Paul Magnuson, Jim Mays, Jim O'Rourke, Don Reiman, Bob Ryan, Ron Sharp, Peter Shillingsburg, David Wagenknecht, Jim Weil, Susan Wolfson, and six of my best students over the years—Allan Chavkin, Beth Lau, Ron Primeau, Heidi Thomson, Chris Valeo, and Carol Walker. On campus I would single out, as especially valuable colleagues, Rick Powers, Ted Underwood, Leon Waldoff, and Gillen Wood.

My greatest debt of all, as always, is to Nina Baym, who by now should be considered coauthor of me as well as of these various essays.

Romantic Complexity

PART I

Keats Essays

1

What Keats Is About

THE FIRST AND MOST OBVIOUS FACT about Keats is how young he was. Born in London on 31 October 1795, dead in Rome at the age of twenty-five on 23 February 1821, he was a young man all his adult life. Of the half-dozen other most highly regarded British poets, only Spenser, who died in his later forties, did not live at least twice as long as Keats did. Chaucer and Shakespeare were alive in their fifties; Milton reached the age of sixty-five; Yeats and Wordsworth, dying at seventy-three and eighty, lived three times as long. These poets would be virtually unknown today had they stopped writing as early as Keats did (their most enduring works, collectively, would be *The Book of the Duchess, On the Morning of Christ's Nativity, An Evening Walk*, and *Descriptive Sketches*), and the same is true of our major writers in fiction and other forms. By contrast, between the ages of twenty-one and twenty-four Keats published three volumes of poetry— *Poems* (1817), *Endymion* (1818), and *Lamia, Isabella, The Eve of St. Agnes, and Other Poems* (1820). The last of these, containing among the "other poems" the five great odes and *Hyperion,* is universally regarded as one of the landmark volumes of British literature.

Paradoxically, for all this youthful productivity Keats actually made a late start as a poet and then progressed relatively slowly. The second fact for consideration here is what might be called the shape of his poetic career, in which the most prominent feature is the suddenness of his development to maturity. He wrote his first poem at the age of eighteen and produced another twenty or so occasional pieces during the next two years, while finishing an apprenticeship to an apothecary-surgeon at Edmonton and taking a year's course in medicine at Guy's Hospital in London. But he did not seriously embark on a career as poet until after he passed the apothecaries' examination toward the end of July 1816, three months before he turned twenty-one. His terminal illness (tuberculosis, which had killed his mother and his brother Tom) lasted more than a year, and he wrote almost no work of any consequence later than the final months of 1819. Thus, if we set aside the juvenile effusions, his entire writing career amounts to little more than three and a half years.

Within that span, Keats's major achievement comes only at the very end. There are 150 titles in a complete edition of his poems. If we number the items consecutively, the long "poetic romance" *Endymion,* which critics usually class among the youthful preliminary works and which Keats himself (in the preface printed with the poem) characterized as the product of "great inexperience, immaturity, and every error denoting a feverish attempt," is actually sixty-third in the chronological array. The serious shorter poems of the winter of 1817–18 are approximately in the middle of the list (*Welcome joy, and welcome sorrow* is seventy-fifth of the 150). *Isabella,* another poem that seems stylistically more like an earlier than a later work, is eighty-eighth. The fifteen poems written during the walking tour of the summer of 1818 (*Give me your patience* through *On Some Skulls in Beauley Abbey*) are numbers 91–105—and at this point, more than two-thirds through the list, Keats is still tuning up, still making his preparations to win immortal fame. *The Eve of St. Agnes,* which is the first of what we call the poems of Keats's maturity, is number 117. The works of 1819—the final thirty-four items minus *In after time a sage,* which is assignable to 1820— constitute an astonishing outpouring that includes some of the most famous poems in the language. And they are products of just the last few months of Keats's poetic life. The ripening between the "early" three-fourths (or even four-fifths) of the career and the mature remainder is a phenomenon unparalleled in literary history.

A third central fact has to do with an important aspect of Keats's charac-ter—a commonsense practicality that helped make him extraordinarily levelheaded, perceptive, and wise. This is difficult to convey in a single word, but all those who study Keats recognize its presence and significance. It is a quality that pervades the incidents of his daily life and the pages of his letters and obviously was a substantial element in the attraction that his wide circle of loyal friends felt toward him. Douglas Bush admirably depicts the quality in his introduction to Keats's *Selected Poems and Letters* (1959), commenting on a now outdated view of the poet as extravagant sensualist:

[T]hough Keats's name is identified with sensuous richness, he was never the aesthete or voluptuary of sensation that, to the later nineteenth century, he often seemed to be. For one thing, he was—except in genius—too normal and sensible: if we can imagine ourselves contemporaries, and in urgent need of wise advice, we would never think of consulting Shelley or Byron or Blake or Coleridge or even Wordsworth, but we would turn with confidence to Keats, the youngest of the lot. It is part of his fundamental wisdom that he was never carried away by ideological mirages or into misjudgments of other people or himself; along with a manly self-respect and high ambition, he had a healthy and humble capacity for self-criticism, an incapacity for self-deception. (Keats 1959, xii–xiii)

Keats also had a hearty sense of humor, and he was never the least bit stuffy. But the terms "normal," "sensible," and "fundamental wisdom" do approach the essence of the kind of person he was.

The fourth central fact that I would set down here (though its "factuality" resides primarily in the poems rather than in the poet's life) is Keats's prolonged concern, from almost the beginning of his career to the very end, with dreams, visions, and the kind of imagination that he took them to represent. Forms of "dream" as noun and verb (plus adjectives and adverbs such as "dreamy" and 'dreamingly") occur about 125 times in the poems, and "vision" and "visionary" another 40 times. Dreaming plays a part in all the narrative poems except *Hyperion;* it is fundamental to the plots of *Endymion, The Eve of St. Agnes, Lamia,* and *The Fall of Hyperion* and also figures significantly in *Isabella* and *La Belle Dame sans Merci.* In addition, we have the dreamlike or visionary situations of Bertha in *The Eve of St. Mark* and of the speakers in *Ode to Psyche, Ode to a Nightingale,* and *Ode on a Grecian Urn*—in some places the dreamlike character of the situation is just hinted at, while in others it is made more explicit with questions such as "Surely I dreamt to-day, or did I see . . . with awaken'd eyes?" and "Was it a vision, or a waking dream?" And there are numerous passages about dreaming in the lesser poems—for example, the "barren dream" of romance in *On Sitting Down to Read "King Lear" Once Again;* the descriptions of dreams and the theorizing about them in *Dear Reynolds, as last night I lay in bed;* the dreamlike unreality of the setting in *On Visiting the Tomb of Burns;* and the dream that Keats experienced after reading Dante as recreated in *As Hermes once took to his feathers light.* Keats also describes dreams in his correspondence with friends, and in the best-known of the early letters, to Benjamin Bailey, 22 November 1817, he likens the imagination to Adam's dream in *Paradise Lost:* Adam, he says, "awoke and found it truth" (*KL,* 1:185).

The earliest manifestation of dreaming in Keats's poems (apart from off-hand references to "fair dreams" before the "mind's eye" in *To Hope* and swans "dream[ing] so sweetly" in *Calidore*) takes the form of an interest in poetic trances and visionary flights—the result, apparently, of accepting seriously and literally a couple of the oldest motifs in literary tradition. We see this prominently in poems of the closing months of 1816, most notably the epistle *To My Brother George, Sleep and Poetry,* and *I stood tip-toe upon a little hill.* In these poems, thus early, Keats has already arrived at a basic metaphor: poetic flight to another, higher realm. With *Endymion,* the principal work of the following year, 1817, the extraworldly excursion becomes a main element of narrative plot, while dreaming becomes a major symbol (for visionary imagination) and the "authenticity" or truth of dreams is a major thematic interest. From this point on, characters in the poems (and sometimes Keats outside the poems, as in the letter to Bailey) puzzle over the reality of their dream experiences, become engrossed in other worlds that they have reached or created by means of their imagination, and sometimes go too far and cannot return to the real world from which they took flight. It is a most interesting paradox in literary history that Keats, the man of commonsense practicality, the one whom above all others we would seek out for wise advice, also appears to be the Romantic poet most concerned with dreams and visionary excursions into the unreal. It may well be that this paradox is itself a chief component of the rich complexity of Keats's best poetry: the visionary and down-to-earth tendencies frequently exist simultaneously, in an ongoing tug-of-war.

*   *   *

There is a basic Keatsian structure—a literally spatial conception of two realms in opposition and a mythlike set of actions involving characters shuttling back and forth between them—that appears in a great many of the poems and can usefully serve as a device for relating poems, passages, and situations one to another in a view of what Keats's work as a whole is preponderantly "about." This structure can be illustrated by means of a simplified cosmography of the poems.

Figure 1 is a diagram I have used many times in the classroom (and first published in a 1968 essay on the odes that is reprinted in *The Hoodwinking of Madeline*) to represent the typical lyric poem of Keats's time as a literal or metaphorical excursion and return. The horizontal line stands for a boundary separating the actual world (below) and the ideal (above). The two realms have many familiar labels—for example, earth and heaven, mortality and immortality, time and eternity, materiality and spirituality, the known and the unknown, the finite and the infinite, realism and romance, the natural and the supernatural. The ideal is represented above the line because it is, so to speak, a higher reality. Characteristically, the speaker in a Romantic lyric begins in the real world (A), takes off in mental flight to visit the ideal (B), and then—for a variety of reasons, but most often because he finds something wanting in the imagined ideal or because, being a native of the real world, he discovers that he does not or cannot belong permanently in the ideal—returns home to the real (A'). But he has not simply arrived back to where he began (hence A' rather than A at the descent). He has acquired something—a new understanding of a situation, a change in attitude toward it—from the experience of the flight, and for better or worse he is never the same afterward.

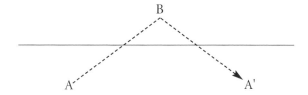

If we emphasize that the actual world is the realm of mortals and is associated with mutability, natural process, and death, while the ideal world is the realm of gods and fairies and is associated most significantly with permanence—the absence of all that mutability, process, and death imply—then the diagram becomes a type of map on which we can locate the characters and actions not only of Keats's lyrics but of the major narratives as well.

Thematically, the most serious problem that Keats's characters face is, at the outset, the painful half of the pleasure-pain complexity of mortal life. The characters—Endymion, Madeline in *The Eve of St. Agnes,* the knight at arms in *La Belle Dame,* the speakers in *Nightingale* and *Grecian Urn,* Lycius in *Lamia,* to list the most obvious examples—want to "unperplex bliss from its neighbour pain" (*Lamia,* 1.192), to separate the two so as to be able to get rid of the pain entirely and enjoy pure bliss. This is something that mortals, because of their mortal nature, cannot succeed in doing, as almost all the characters in the course of their experiences and meditations come to learn. Typically, the attempt to solve the problem takes the form of a mortal-nonmortal pairing—Endymion with the moon goddess, the knight at arms with the fairy Belle Dame, the ode speakers with the ode objects ("immortal Bird," the "eternity" of ancient Greece), Lycius with the serpent-woman Lamia—a pairing that promises bliss but turns out to be an ideal impossible of permanent realization. The action of a poem, whether narrative or lyric, involves first some kind of union between a mortal and the nonmortal ideal by means of a dream (or a visionary entrancement that is like a dream) and then a gradual or sudden end to the union as the dreamer awakens to reality. The conclusions of the poems are frequently ambiguous—they end in questions, doubtful circumstances, "wonderment"—but a new and more positive view of the pleasure-pain complexity is sometimes inferable: where there is no death there is no life; the complexity is better than no life at all.

Endymion is Keats's earliest and most literal embodiment of these thematic and narrative materials. Having become enamored of an unknown goddess who visits him in a dream, Endymion renounces the real world and sets forth to wander through caverns, under the ocean, and through the air (all realms that are out of the real world, therefore figuratively above the line in the diagram in figure 1) seeking reunion with his dream goddess. After numerous adventures (and numerous long speeches), he returns to the real world, meets and falls in love with an Indian maiden, and vows to abandon his search for the goddess. On several occasions while he is out of the world he laments his situation as a solitary, an alien, an "exil'd mortal" suffering "homeward fever," as in the speech at 2.302–32, ending, "let me see my native bowers! / Deliver me from this rapacious deep!" Much of books 1 and 4 focus on the question of the reality of the dream he is pursuing, and his renunciation toward the end of his wanderings has an impressive fervency:

> I have clung
> To nothing, lov'd a nothing, nothing seen
> Or felt but a great dream! O I have been
> Presumptuous against love, against the sky,
> Against all elements, against the tie
> Of mortals each to each. . . .
> . . . so my story
> Will I to children utter, and repent.
> There never liv'd a mortal man, who bent
> His appetite beyond his natural sphere,
> But starv'd and died. . . .
> . . . gone and past

Are cloudy phantasms. Caverns lone, farewel!
And air of visions, and the monstrous swell
Of visionary seas! No, never more
Shall airy voices cheat me. . . .

(4.636–54)

The action of the poem accords with the structure outlined above until the very end, when, in the final thirty lines, the Indian maiden reveals to Endymion that she is his dream goddess in disguise, and the two are blissfully and permanently united, vanishing "far away." This of course represents a last-minute reversion to the realm of the ideal, but the conclusion was inherent in the legend that Keats was retelling. The emphasis in his elaboration, since so many lines are given to it, would seem to fall on the necessity of Endymion's coming to terms with the real world and human existence.

Almost all of the subsequent major poems have at least partial elements of this basic structure. In *The Eve of St. Agnes,* the hostile castle, Porphyro, physical love, and the icy storm are various aspects of the reality below the line; Madeline's ritual and dream state, as unnatural as a rose that can "shut, and be a bud again," are the realm of the ideal, and the consequences of her attempt to attain this ideal are, in some interpretations of the poem, first isolation, then deception by "stratagem," and finally possibly even death. There is a similarly isolated character in *The Eve of St. Mark,* which, although it is only a fragment, presents a clear contrast between the everyday reality of the town (and the church and churchgoers) and the separation from this reality represented by Bertha's indoor confinement and her "captive" absorption in the "curious volume" containing the life of St. Mark. The mortal knight at arms in *La Belle Dame* is still another instance of dreamer separated from reality. His enthrallment to a beautiful fairy lady who sings, feeds him, and takes him to her "elfin grot"—again, figuratively above the line—results in a nightmare "horrid warning" by "pale kings, and princes . . . Pale warriors, death pale," and he awakens in a barren landscape, seemingly paralyzed by the outcome of his excursion into the ideal.

The odes have a place in this scheme as well. Psyche's "fane / In some untrodden region" of the speaker's mind is an ideal realm somewhere above the line; and so are the supernature of the nightingale's forest, the art world of the Grecian urn's piper, lovers, trees, and sacrificial procession, and (though they are referred to only in a single line) the "songs of spring" in *To Autumn,* while the mortal speaker in each case makes an imaginative excursion and return. (*Ode on Melancholy,* the shortest of the odes, advises against the excursion, tells what to do instead, and explains why.) Lamia's palace is still another ideal realm, and the mortal Lycius lingers there contentedly until "a thrill / Of trumpets" reminds him of the claims of "the noisy world almost forsworn," whereupon he holds a wedding-feast at which the piercing eye of his old tutor exposes his beloved Lamia as a serpent and causes her to vanish. Lycius falls dead, too engrossed in his dream to survive such a precipitous return to reality.

Many lesser poems embody elements of the basic structure. I have already mentioned the trances and visionary flights to a higher realm in the long poems of Keats's first volume—the epistle *To My Brother George, Sleep and Poetry,* and *I stood tip-toe*—each of which prefigures significant actions in *Endymion,* which in turn prefigures much of the rest. The structure of excursion and return shows up in a variety of types of poem, some less serious than others—for example, *Lines on the Mermaid Tavern* and *Robin Hood* (in both of which the speaker makes brief contact with an ideal realm of the past, fully aware at the same time that the poets are "dead and gone," the days "gone away"), *God of the meridian* ("worldly fear . . . when the soul is fled / Too high"), *Dear Reynolds* (on the dangers of seeing both "beyond our bourn" and "Too far into the sea"), *There was a naughty boy* (a whimsical excursion "to the north" to find out that Scotland is after all much the same as England), *There is a joy in footing slow* (sober depiction of "the gentle anchor" of mortality bringing man back to "the sweet and bitter world"), and the *Bright star* sonnet (imaginative flight to a situation of "lone splendor . . . aloft," followed by descent to "earth's human shores" and "my fair love's ripening breast").

Although this scheme identifies a basic structure in Keats's poems, it must be modified to accommodate some special difficulties. There are two complications in particular that cannot be ignored. One of them has to do with Keats's intermittent interest in the dividing line or space *between* the two realms. There are a great many images of midwayness in the poems—bourns, brinks, bars, edges, and boundaries. In lines 185–92 of *I stood tip-toe,* "the invisible world," an "unearthly" region that is beyond "our mortal bars," is equated with "the *middle* air," which may or may not be the same as the "middle air" in which Endymion is said to be lost when he comes to a dispirited halt early in his travels outside the world (2.653, 656). Endymion's life in the mortal world is described as a journey "through this middle earth" (1.723). The epistle *Dear Reynolds* speculates on a halfway situation in which the imagination is "brought / Beyond its proper bound, yet still confined,— / Lost in a sort of purgatory blind," so that it "Cannot refer to any standard law / Of either earth or heaven." Madeline appears to enter some sort of state between worlds when she falls asleep and is "Blissfully haven'd both from joy and pain . . . Blinded alike from sunshine and from rain." The knight at arms may be similarly immobilized between realms. Having awakened from his dream in La Belle Dame's "grot," he still seems unable to rejoin the real world (the richness suggested by the squirrel's full granary and the completed harvest, in contrast to the knight's bleak surroundings "On the cold hill's side"). In *Ode on a Grecian Urn*, the sacrificial procession is stopped forever midway between source and destination. The "space of life between" (Keats's phrase in his preface to *Endymion*) sometimes constitutes a third realm that a two-realm scheme does not sufficiently recognize.

The other complication is more strictly a matter of ideas than of imagery or structure. In the oppositions between reality and the hypothetical ideal, the values attributed to the ideal—most often the permanence that, if only it were possible, would exempt mortals from time, change, and mortality—are clear enough. But the values attached to the contrasting realm of reality are not always so readily graspable. This is the source of some serious problems of interpretation. One likes to think of Keats as a poet who ultimately affirmed reality and disapproved of fanciful and impossible attempts to escape. Yet in many of the poems there seems to be something wrong with the reality. Consider just three instances. In *The Eve of St. Agnes*, the sought-after perfection lies in the ritual that Madeline practices and the dream that it produces. Unlike Madeline (until too late), we are allowed to see some faults of the alternative to reality—the ritual is an old wives' tale, Madeline is said to be "hoodwink'd," Porphyro displays some of the characteristics of a Peeping Tom and cowardly seducer, and he and Madeline are last seen fleeing "into the storm." But where, exactly, is a clearly contrasting reality? The chapel in the opening stanzas is freezing cold and is full of associations with death, and the Beadsman is an old man who has renounced life and is about to die. The revelers, Madeline's kinsmen and the warrior-guests, are "barbarian hordes," "bloated wassaillers," who are later punished with nightmares of witch, demon, and coffin worm. Porphyro not only is the worker of a "stratagem" but (in the imagery of speeches and description) is associated with fairy lore, witchcraft, and sorcery. Angela is morally as well as physically decrepit (she too dies before the night is over). Madeline's room is a scene of deception and, when she awakens, dismay. The nature outside the castle is ominously dark, icy, and gusting. It may be that there is no genuinely attractive reality anywhere in the poem.

Then we have the curious circumstance that in *Ode to a Nightingale*, the real world that the speaker wishes to escape in stanza 3—the world of weariness, fever, fret, and so on—has an entirely different set of references from the real world that, after he imaginatively succeeds in escaping, he longs to return to in stanza 5. In stanza 3 the transient reality is depicted exclusively in human terms (old men, youth, Beauty, Love). In stanza 5 it is conveyed in images of nature (flowers, trees, the season, grass, summer flies). If the two are combined in a concept that rejects weariness, fever, and fret while retaining the flowers and flies, it may be that the "reality" of the poem is just as unreal, and just as impossible of attainment, as the timeless perfection represented by the "immortal Bird." And where, to turn briefly to the third example of complication, is the reality in *Lamia?* It is clear that Lamia's palace and its furnishings are (in the words of the quotation from Burton printed at the end of the poem) "no substance but mere illusions." But the "world almost forsworn" is clamorous; Lycius's prideful nature in part 2 is singularly unattractive; the Corinthians at the wedding-feast are a "gossip rout" and a "herd"; and the exposer of the illusion, Apollonius, is not admired by anybody in the poem, including the narrator. There are other notable instances of the problem, as in the "heart high-sorrowful and cloy'd . . . burning forehead . . . parching tongue" of human passion in *Ode on a Grecian Urn* and the final situation ("among her cloudy trophies," an image of defeat) of the burster of Joy's grape in *Ode on Melancholy*. Possibly Keats was of a divided mind about reality in these poems. When his images and attitudes are translated into ideas, the results are sometimes puzzling in their inconsistency.

*   *   *

Keats is not, however, primarily a poet of ideas. His letters, reflecting not only the happenings of his outward life but some of the most important events of his day-to-day mental progress, do teem with ideas about life and poetry. He writes to Benjamin Bailey, on 22 November 1817, about sensation, thought, and "the authenticity of the Imagination"; to his brothers, in late December 1817, about "Negative Capability" in philosophy and literature; to John Hamilton Reynolds, on 3 February 1818, about egotism in modern poetry; to John Taylor, on 27 February 1818, about his "Axioms" in poetry; to Reynolds again, on 3 May 1818, about Wordsworth and Milton, "axioms in philosophy," and human life as a "Mansion of Many Apartments"; to Richard Woodhouse, on 27 October 1818, about the "poetical Character"; to George and Georgiana Keats, 14 February–early May 1819, about life as "a continual allegory," the ideal of disinterestedness, and the world as a "vale of Soul-making." These letters (and many more by Keats) are among the most readable and most admired in English literature. The ideas in them have pervaded our intellectual culture, and they surface everywhere—in theology and philosophy, literary criticism, novels, plays, detective fiction, even crossword puzzles. But the ideas are not central in his best poems. They form a background to the poetry, part of a context in which the poems were written, but are not themselves the explicit or implicit content of the poetry.

The content of Keats's best poems, if reduced to their themes, would be, just as with the best work of Shakespeare and Dickens, quite banal (life is very difficult, the imagination is not to be relied on, everybody has to die, nature consoles). But Keats's concerns with dreaming, illusion, problems of time and mortality, and the pleasure-pain complexity of life should not be translated in this way. They give a pleasurable and requisite seriousness of content to the poems, but they cannot be taken as the equivalent of the poems. The same may be said of the most characteristic tensions in the poems—the conflicting claims of human and immortal realms of existence, the opposition of attitudes toward the actual and the ideal. These provide structure and dramatic conflict, but they are not the equivalent of the poems either. And the ideas and tensions cannot be invoked to account for Keats's sudden rise to greatness in the poems of the last nine months of his career, because they are in his work all along, from late 1816 to the end. Something else is needed to explain the excellence of his mature poetry.

That something else, I suggest, is Keats's style. This is a topic that was comprehensively considered in the 1940s (by Walter Jackson Bate and Richard Harter Fogle in particular) but has been relatively slighted in more recent decades, possibly because critics have become increasingly aware of the methodological difficulties seemingly inherent in stylistic analysis of a literary text. Nowadays there is a great deal of argument about what "style" is and where it resides, if at all, in literary works. But it is still practically useful, while the debate goes on, to retain a concept of style in the old-fashioned sense of "mode of expression," referring to such things as choice of words and images, sentence structure, rhythms and sound patterns, and figures of speech. These fundamentals are, or used to be, taught in a freshman Introduction to Poetry course, with a textbook such as James R. Kreuzer's *Elements of Poetry* or Laurence Perrine's *Sound and Sense.* It would be a mistake, even if we cannot precisely describe or account for their effects, to underestimate the importance of these elements in literary art. All works have subject matter, themes, structures, incidents, ideas, and feelings. It is ultimately the language in which these are contained and transmitted that makes some works more pleasing and more moving than others.

Below are three passages of description that are characteristic of Keats's writing at its best. I propose that these passages are self-evidently excellent as poetry and that their excellence lies not in their content—interesting as that may be (our first view of the deposed monarch Saturn, the atmosphere both outside and inside Madeline's castle, and the sights and sounds of autumn)—but in various components of their style: the sounds of the words, the rhythmical variations played upon the basic iambic pattern, the concreteness and textural density of the words and images, and some special qualities deriving from the character of the speaker or narrator (or, to be more accurate, Keats himself speaking through these). The first passage was written sometime toward the end of 1818. The second and third belong to January and September 1819.

> Deep in the shady sadness of a vale
> Far sunken from the healthy breath of morn,
> Far from the fiery noon, and eve's one star,
> Sat gray-hair'd Saturn, quiet as a stone,
> Still as the silence round about his lair;
> Forest on forest hung above his head
> Like cloud on cloud. No stir of air was there,
> Not so much life as on a summer's day
> Robs not one light seed from the feather'd grass,
> But where the dead leaf fell, there did it rest.
> A stream went voiceless by, still deadened more
> By reason of his fallen divinity
> Spreading a shade: the Naiad 'mid her reeds
> Press'd her cold finger closer to her lips.
>
>   Along the margin-sand large foot-marks went,
> No further than to where his feet had stray'd,
> And slept there since. Upon the sodden ground
> His old right hand lay nerveless, listless, dead,
> Unsceptred; and his realmless eyes were closed;
> While his bow'd head seem'd list'ning to the Earth,
> His ancient mother, for some comfort yet.
>   (*Hyperion*, 1.1–21)

> St. Agnes' Eve—Ah, bitter chill it was!
> The owl, for all his feathers, was a-cold;
> The hare limp'd trembling through the frozen grass,

And silent was the flock in woolly fold:
Numb were the Beadsman's fingers, while he told
His rosary, and while his frosted breath,
Like pious incense from a censer old,
Seem'd taking flight for heaven, without a death,
Past the sweet Virgin's picture, while his prayer he saith.
(*The Eve of St. Agnes*, 1–9)

Where are the songs of spring? Ay, where are they?
Think not of them, thou hast thy music too,—
While barred clouds bloom the soft-dying day,
And touch the stubble-plains with rosy hue;
Then in a wailful choir the small gnats mourn
Among the river sallows, borne aloft
Or sinking as the light wind lives or dies;
And full-grown lambs loud bleat from hilly bourn;
Hedge-crickets sing; and now with treble soft
The red-breast whistles from a garden-croft;
And gathering swallows twitter in the skies.
(*To Autumn*, 23–33)

Though his friend Woodhouse once commented on how badly he read his own poetry aloud, Keats obviously heard well enough when he was composing. The lines in these passages abound in both repetition and variation of vowel sounds and consonants. We can say, without specifying why, that they are pleasing to listen to, even when one pays no attention to the meanings of the words (they would be musically pleasing to auditors who knew no English). Keats is reported to have had a theory about "melody in Verse . . . particularly in the management of open & close vowels" (*KC*, 2:277), but of course the contrasts and interchanges originated spontaneously, according to ear rather than principle. The same is true of the rhythmical qualities of the lines. Departures from the metrical norm occur almost everywhere (there are only two or three regular iambic pentameter lines in the opening paragraph of *Hyperion* and very few in the other passages). Caesuras and enjambments—the rhetorical pauses within lines and the run-on continuations of sense from one line to the next—are similarly varied. One can count up and tabulate these things (the percentage of caesuras occurring after the fourth syllable in the line, the percentage after the fifth, and so on), but the results never explain, except in the bare fact of its existence, how or why such variation creates pleasure. There is, however, no denying the pleasure.

Two of the chief qualities of the diction and imagery in these passages are particularity and concreteness. On a rough scale that runs from the abstractness of Shelley's "loftiest star . . . , / Pinnacled dim in the intense inane" (where there is no pinnacle in sight, and "star" and "dim" are only very faint visual images, which is just what Shelley intended) to the specificity of Shakespeare's "engiṇer / Hoist with his own petar" (a clear picture, with sound effects, of an artilleryman being blown up by his own bomb), Keats is definitely "with Shakespeare." This is not to say that his lines contain no abstractions. The first line of *Hyperion* refers to a vale's "sadness" and the second to the vale's distance from "the healthy breath of morn." But even here the words "Deep," "shady," and "Far sunken" give a topographical spatiality and particularity to the abstractions that create a picture even while the primary emphasis is on tone. Consider the progression from concreteness to abstraction and back to concreteness in the fourth and fifth lines of the second paragraph of the same work: "nerveless" and "listless" are both physical description (terms, say, in a medical report at Guy's Hospital); "dead" is partly physical (motionless) and partly abstract (referring to the state of being dead); "Unsceptred" is both literal (the hand has no scepter) and abstract (Saturn is no longer king); "realmless" is almost fully abstract, but then "eyes were closed" returns to purely physical description. In these two lines, which may serve to epitomize the large results of Keats's strong lines generally, we get extremely sharp pictorial effects, political implications, and a moral tone all at once. The physical quality in these opening paragraphs of *Hyperion* is sometimes called "sculpturesque," referring to the three-dimensional solidity of "Forest on forest," the dead leaf falling and then not moving, the Naiad pressing her finger to her lips, the large footprints ending at Saturn's feet, and the implied massiveness of his bowed head. But there is almost as much physicality in the images of cold and silence in the second of the passages above and in the many sounds, shapes, and motions of the third.

The textural density of the imagery in these passages is again Shakespearean (and not Shelleyan). There is a striking quantity of *things* in the lines, things that can be visualized or that stimulate the auditory and other senses. The last five lines of the opening stanza of *The Eve of St. Agnes,* for example, contain seven distinct visual images (the Beadsman's fingers, his rosary, the action of fingering the beads, the vapor of exhaled breath, the vapor of burning incense, the censer, and the Virgin's picture), some tactile images (the numbness of the fingers, the sensation of fingers in contact with the beads), and a nonvisual notion of wafting upward in the words

"Seem'd taking flight for heaven." The fourth line from the end of *To Autumn* begins with the shortest possible compassing of a sheep's life span ("full-grown lambs"), creates a picture of sheep and the sound of their bleating, and then, with a camera-like zoom, distances them on hilly ground. It is surely this kind of textural density that Keats had in mind when he advised Shelley, in a letter of 16 August 1820, to "be more of an artist, and 'load every rift' of your subject with ore" (*KL*, 2:323). Keats's own lines at their best show a remarkable concentration in this way.

Obviously Keats had an exceptionally keen sensitivity to the minute particulars of objects, sounds (as well as various shades of silence), and motions in the world around him. He was also the least egotistical of all the Romantic poets, both in his life and in his poetry (even in the odes and other lyrics having a first-person speaker throughout), and on the basis of this personal trait he developed a now-famous theory about the "poetical Character," which, as he wrote about it to Woodhouse in a letter of 27 October 1818, "has no self—it is every thing and nothing—It has no character—it enjoys light and shade; it lives in gusto, be it foul or fair, high or low, rich or poor, mean or elevated—It has as much delight in conceiving an Iago as an Imogen. What shocks the virtuous philosop[h]er, delights the camelion Poet. . . . A Poet is the most unpoetical of any thing in existence; because he has no Identity—he is continually . . . filling some other Body." Woodhouse, telling Keats's publisher Taylor about this letter, comments, "The highest order of Poet will . . . be able to throw his own soul into any object he sees or imagines, so as to see feel be sensible of, & express, all that the object itself wo^d see feel be sensible of or express—& he will speak out of that object—so that his own self will . . . be 'annihilated'"—and he adds that Keats said he could conceive of a billiard ball's "sense of delight from its own roundness, smoothness volubility. & the rapidity of its motion" (*KL*, 1:386–87, 389).

The sympathetic imaginative activity that these quotations describe is responsible for the most peculiarly Keatsian characteristic of all, the ability to identify with an object perceived and convey to the reader—certainly to the reader who reads the poems imaginatively—what it feels like to *be* that object. The tenth line of *Hyperion* pictures a dead leaf at rest and simultaneously somehow, perhaps more than anything else by the sounds and rhythm of the line, gives a sense of the experience of falling, coming to a stop, and feeling contact with the ground (the final word "rest" has a dead-leaf crispness about it). The second and third lines of *The Eve of St. Agnes,* with clear visual images of the owl and the hare, carry a sense of what it is like to be cold inside a coat of feathers and to be limping and to put tender feet down, one at a time, on frozen grass. And there may be a further sensation of how frozen grass itself feels when it is walked upon. The density in these passages is the product of several different kinds of sensation coming simultaneously, and the reader makes very intimate contact with the objects depicted.

These are some of the most prominent qualities of Keats's mature poetic style, but pointing them out is not the same as explaining how Keats arrived at them or succeeded in bringing them all together in the final months of his career. One contributing factor, obviously, is that by the beginning of 1819 he had served a relatively long apprenticeship to poetry, had done his journeywork, so to speak, and had put his juvenilia and "transitional" works behind him. Another clear cause is his steady absorption of the works of the greatest writers who preceded him. When he first began writing seriously, his principal models included the eighteenth-century Spenserians and contemporaries and near-contemporaries such as James Beattie, Mary Tighe, Tom Moore, George Felton Mathew, and Leigh Hunt. But Keats matured as a reader as well as a writer. The better influences of Shakespeare, Milton, Wordsworth, and Dante certainly had their effect.

There is a third cause, however, largely independent of these, in Keats's intellectual and emotional experiences of the twelve-month period preceding his major achievement. The year 1818, which began with a somewhat reluctant rewriting and copying out of *Endymion* and what Keats characterized as "a little change . . . in my intellect lately" (*KL,* 1:214), was a year of accelerated growing-up. His shorter poems become more serious, more cognizant of the hardships of human life, and the narrative *Isabella,* along with flowery and sentimental stanzas describing adolescent love, attempts realistic psychological portrayal that in places is quite moving. The walking tour through the Lake District and Scotland gave Keats firsthand acquaintance with mountains, lakes, and other beauties of nature but also with the realities of rural poverty. He became ill with a sore throat and had to break off his travels to return home, where he took several weeks to recover. He nursed his brother Tom in a lengthy illness that ended with Tom's death on 1 December 1818, and as an added complication he met and fell in love with Fanny Brawne.

More than anything else, I think, it is this combined experience of suffering, death, and love all at once, against a background of serious conversation, reading, and thinking, that accounts for Keats's sudden rise to excellence in his poetry. He approaches 1819 with what Wordsworth in the last stanza of the Intimations ode called "an eye / That hath kept watch o'er man's mortality." Keats has arrived at a more sober view of the subjects and themes he was writing about. Now images of death pervade his descriptions ("dead leaf," "stream . . . still deadened more," "listless, dead," "soft-dying day," "light wind lives or dies" in the first and third of the passages quoted above, and the opening stanza of *The Eve of St. Agnes* leads into an account of the "sculptur'd dead" in the chapel and mention of the Beadsman's "deathbell"). There are many indications of sadness and discomfort ("shady sadness," "Far sunken," "fallen," "sodden," "bitter chill," "trembling," "wailful . . . the small gnats mourn," "lambs . . . bleat"). At the same time there are countering consolations: Saturn may be comforted yet; the owl and the hare will survive the night, and the Beadsman's prayer may get to heaven; the crickets, robin, and swallows are singing away. The mature Keats confronts the human predicaments implied in these passages— change, old age, and death, for none of which is there any practical solution—and by the stylistic expression of a complexity of attitudes and feelings, and with a steadfast honesty concerning the good and the less good aspects of reality, seems to make these human predicaments bearable and even ennobling.

Keats at one time quietly predicted that he would, after his death, be "among the English Poets" (*KL,* 1:394). An array of his complete poetical works in chronological order allows the reader to follow his poem-by-poem progress toward that end. Some of the pieces are today regarded as among the very best achievements in literary art in any language. Many others are much less successful and have to be considered of interest mainly because they are the work of the same poet who wrote the major narratives and the great odes. All told, there are nearly fifteen thousand lines of verse in his complete poems—an impressive quantity for so short a career.

2

Keats and Wordsworth

KEATS'S FIRST MEETING with Wordsworth, the occasion on which he recited the Hymn to Pan from his then unpublished *Endymion* and Wordsworth called it a "pretty piece of Paganism," is a famous anecdote in literary history. The meeting, arranged by a mutual friend, the historical painter Benjamin Robert Haydon, took place in the third week of December 1817 (around the sixteenth) at the house of Thomas Monkhouse, a cousin of Wordsworth's wife, in Queen Anne Street, Cavendish Square, London. Wordsworth, who was in town for several weeks on business, was forty-seven years old at the time and by far the most distinguished poet of his generation—author of ten volumes of verse, leading figure among the Lake school, and controversial proponent of widespread reform in the language and subject matter of poetry. Keats, at twenty-two, was nearly the *least* distinguished among living poets in Great Britain. He had published a single slim first volume, *Poems* (1817), which, as he said in a discarded preface to his next work, "was read by some dozen of my friends, who lik'd it, and some dozen whom I was unacquainted with, who did not" (*Poems of JK*, 739).

We have six nineteenth-century accounts of this meeting: by Leigh Hunt (in a book about Byron published in 1828), Walter Savage Landor (in a letter of 1837), Haydon (in a letter of 1845), Richard Monckton Milnes (in his biography of Keats published in 1848), Charles Cowden Clarke (in a magazine article of 1861), and the painter Joseph Severn (in a manuscript autobiography written in the 1860s or 1870s). Five of the six accounts are reports at second (or third or fourth) hand, and they contain various mistakes and embroiderings concerning date, place, and the number and identities of those present.[1] All, however, agree in condemning Wordsworth's bad behavior. Here is the version by Haydon, the only account by an actual witness, written twenty-eight years after the event:

> When Wordsworth came to Town, I brought Keats to him, by his Wordsworth's desire—Keats expressed to me as we walked to Queen Anne S[t] East where M[r] Monkhouse Lodged, the greatest, the purest, the most unalloyed pleasure at the prospect. Wordsworth received him kindly, & after a few minutes, Wordsworth asked him what he had been lately doing, *I* said he has just finished an exquisite ode to Pan—and as he had not a copy I begged Keats to repeat it—which he did in his usual half chant, (most touching) walking up & down the room—when he had done I felt really, as if I had heard a young Apollo—Wordsworth drily said
>
> "a Very pretty piece of Paganism—
>
> This was unfeeling, & unworthy of his high Genius to a young Worshipper like Keats—& Keats felt it *deeply*—so that if Keats has said any thing severe about our Friend; it was because he was wounded—and though he dined with Wordsworth after at my table—he never forgave him. (*KC*, 2:143–44)

Keats's wounded feelings on the occasion, rather like his supposed faintness in reaction to the harsh reviews of the published *Endymion* several months later, were assumed to be fact through much of the second half of the nineteenth century and the first six decades of the twentieth. They appear as late as 1963 in the biography by Aileen Ward, who writes that "Keats was stunned. . . . He suddenly stopped seeing Wordsworth in the last week of January" (157; the latter statement is certainly true—Wordsworth left London on 19 January). But the other modern full-length biographies of both Keats and Wordsworth—by Walter Jackson Bate, Robert Gittings, Andrew Motion, Mary Moorman, and Stephen Gill—are more circumspect. Bate, for example, suggests that Keats "may have been more surprised than hurt" and "in retrospect may even have found [Wordsworth's] remark an amusing revelation of character."[2]

The fact is that Keats's letters and other biographical documents (many of which became available after—in some cases many decades after—the first published accounts of this meeting with Wordsworth) tell a different story. There is evidence of a genial and rapidly growing initial acquaintance between the two poets. Keats saw Wordsworth again on 28 December, at the so-called immortal dinner at Haydon's, when Wordsworth, Monkhouse, Keats, and Charles Lamb made up the party, with several others dropping in afterward—the occasion on which Keats and Lamb, agreeing that Newton had destroyed the poetry of the rainbow, drank to "Newton's health, and confusion to mathematics!" Haydon's several-page record in his diary, written just after the event (and not, like his letter quoted above, nearly three decades later), describes a warm and festive affair, with lively conversation, uproarious jokes, and, for background, Haydon's huge painting *Christ's Entry into Jerusalem,* in which he had depicted both Wordsworth and Keats among the crowd of spectators. Haydon's conclusion gives no hint of unfriendly tension among the principals:

> There was something interesting in seeing Wordsworth sitting, & Keats & Lamb, & my Picture of Christ's entry towering up behind them, occasionally brightened by the gleams of flame that sparkled from the fire, & hearing the voice of Wordsworth repeating Milton with an intonation like the funeral bell of St. Paul's & the music of Handel mingled, & then Lamb's wit came sparkling in between, & Keats's rich fancy of Satyrs & Fauns & doves & white clouds, wound up the stream of conversation. I never passed a more delightful day, & I am convinced that nothing in Boswell is equal to what came out from these Poets. Indeed there were no such Poets in his time. It was an evening worthy of the Elizabethan age, and will long flash upon "that inward eye which is the bliss of Solitude." Hail & farewell! (Haydon 1960, 2:173–76)

Three days after this dinner party, on 31 December, Keats met Wordsworth again while walking on Hampstead Heath. On 3 January he called on Wordsworth at his temporary lodgings in Mortimer Street (near Monkhouse's), and on the fifth he dined with him there. Perhaps he was with Wordsworth on other occasions too, for by the twenty-third (four days after the older poet had left town) he had, as he told his friend the theological student Benjamin Bailey, "seen a good deal of Wordsworth" (*KL*, 1:212). The first note of disharmony in Keats's letters appears on 3 February, when, in an animated discussion of the egotism of modern poetry, he remarks to another friend, John Hamilton Reynolds, "I will have no more of Wordsworth" (*KL*, 1:224). But at this point, a month and a half after the "pretty piece of Paganism" incident, he is in the process of developing a theory of poetry in which the "wordsworthian or egotistical sublime" plays an important contrasting role. The earlier biographers were overly simple in seeing Keats's criticism of Wordsworth as a (delayed!) result of hurt feelings. Even at age twenty-two, Keats was very much his own person, and by 3 May, when he wrote down some of his most serious philosophical ideas in the "Mansion of Many Apartments" letter to Reynolds, with its extended comparison of Wordsworth and Milton, his stance toward Wordsworth had become that of a partner or fellow worker in the "grand march of intellect": "I will put down a simile of human life as far as I now perceive it; that is, to the point to which . . . we both have arrived at. . . . To this point [a compound threshold of "dark passages"] was Wordsworth come. . . . Now if we live, and go on thinking, we too shall explore them" (*KL,* 1:280–82).

In his attitude toward the influences acting on him and helping to shape his career, Keats was one of the least anxious writers in English literature. He wanted to be a poet in part because he so much admired poetry, and poetry to him was what the individual poets who preceded him had accomplished. His earliest pieces on poetry—for example, *Imitation of Spenser, To Lord Byron, Oh Chatterton, Ode to Apollo*—are acutely aware of the presence and achievements of older poets and are congratulatory, openly admiring, and not in the least envious. When he sits down to compose, as he says in a poem on this very topic of relationship with his predecessors (the sonnet beginning "How many bards gild the lapses of time"), the sounds and images of previous writers intruding on his consciousness produce "no confusion, no disturbance rude," but instead make "a pleasing chime . . . pleasing music." Almost at the beginning of his career he arrived at an idea, really a mental picture, of "laurel'd peers" (as in *Ode to Apollo* and the sonnet *To My Brother George*), a masquelike array of "mighty Poets" initially as spectators to whatever subject he happens to have at hand, including his own attempts in rhyme, and then as a kind of distinguished academy that he will one day, if all goes well, be invited to join. His fellow feeling toward the three most major of his predecessors in English literature—Spenser, Shakespeare, and Milton—is thoroughly documented in his poems, letters, marginalia, and the reminiscences of his friends. His quietly confident prediction in a journal letter to his brother and sister-in-law on 14 October 1818 that "I think I shall be among the English Poets after my death" (*KL,* 1:394)—which is the more impressive for coming just *before* the year in which he produced, one after another in astonishing succession, all the works for which he is now most admired—is the best known of several passages assessing his strength in relation to the "peers" who had gone before.

Keats's remarkable independence does not, however, mean that he was uninfluenced by the poets with whom he enjoyed this congenial fellow feeling. On the contrary, as is well known, he was profoundly influenced by all the major authors he read. He first discovered Spenser around the age of sixteen, going through *The Faerie Queene,* in his friend Clarke's description, "as a young horse would through a spring meadow—ramping" (Clarke and

Clarke 1878, 126), and the effects on his poetic style, especially in the luxurious physicality of his imagery, show up all through his career. His earliest and two latest works are in the Spenserian stanza, as is the narrative poem with which he initiated his most fruitful period of productivity, *The Eve of St. Agnes.* The next significant beneficial influence (to speak only of the best known among English writers) was Shakespeare, who was pictured in profile on the title page of Keats's *Poems* of 1817 (along with an epigraph from Spenser) and then served as spiritual "Presider" over the composition of *Endymion* and in one way or another over much of the rest of Keats's poetry. As chief exemplar of nonegotistic artistic imagination, Shakespeare was Keats's theoretical as well as practical ideal. The third major influence was Milton, a principal inspiration for the Hyperion fragments and more generally for various elements of theme and technique in many of Keats's poems. The fourth major influence, and unquestionably the most important and pervasive among Keats's living contemporaries, was Wordsworth.[3]

Keats's first references to Wordsworth in his extant letters come on 20 and 21 November 1816 (*KL,* 1:117–19), when he sends Haydon the sonnet beginning "Great spirits now on earth are sojourning" (specifying Wordsworth, Leigh Hunt, and Haydon among the "spirits . . . standing apart / Upon the forehead of the age to come") and then, at Haydon's request, writes out a second copy for the painter to forward to Wordsworth ("The Idea of your sending it to Wordsworth put me out of breath—you know with what Reverence—I would send my Wellwishes to him"). There is another general mention (again in a letter to Haydon) on 11 May 1817 (*KL,* 1:143), then a great many references to specific titles and passages by Wordsworth beginning in September, when Keats spent a month with Bailey at Oxford and the two men read and discussed Wordsworth almost daily. Probably *The Excursion* (1814) was the first of Wordsworth's works that Keats knew well. Both Leigh Hunt and Keats's friend George Felton Mathew, in magazine reviews of Keats's *Poems* (1817), point to its influence on Keats's idea of the origin of myths in the opening poem of the volume, *I stood tip-toe,* written in December 1816, and there are many echoes of it in Keats's principal accomplishment of the following year, the four thousand-line *Endymion.* On 10 January 1818 (in writing to Haydon) and again on the thirteenth (to his brothers), Keats named *The Excursion* first among the three most considerable works of genius "in the modern world" (*KL,* 1:203–5).

Other works that we can be sure he knew at least something about are Wordsworth's *Lyrical Ballads* (1798, 1800, 1802, 1805)—most notably *Tintern Abbey* and *The Idiot Boy,* first published in the original edition of 1798, and

The Old Cumberland Beggar, the Lucy poems, and the Matthew poems, first published in the second edition (1800)—and *Poems, in Two Volumes* (1807), containing, among other pieces, *Ode: Intimations of Immortality, Resolution and Independence, I wandered lonely as a cloud, The Solitary Reaper,* and a number of sonnets that Keats mentions or echoes. The contents of both *Lyrical Ballads* (minus the Coleridge items) and *Poems, in Two Volumes* were reprinted in Wordsworth's two-volume collected *Poems* of 1815. It is not certain which of these books Keats actually used. Possibly he read, on different occasions, in all of them. There is no doubt, however, that he knew the works, especially those such as *Tintern Abbey* and the Intimations ode that he repeatedly alludes to in his letters and poems.

The most immediately obvious results of Wordsworth's influence are the two hundred or more echoes and borrowings that scholars have detected in Keats's poems. A handful of random instances might include the brief description of "Startl[ing] the wild bee from the fox-glove bell" in Keats's first published poem, *O Solitude* (seeming to echo "bees . . . Will murmur by the hour in foxglove bells" in Wordsworth's sonnet beginning "Nuns fret not at their convent's narrow room"); the heart dancing with pleasure, "And always does my heart with pleasure dance," in *Specimen of an Induction to a Poem,* line 51 (compare Wordsworth's "And then my heart with pleasure fills, / And dances" in *I wandered lonely as a cloud;* the wording to express uncertainty of origin in "many a verse from so strange influence / That we must ever wonder how, and whence, / It came" in *Sleep and Poetry,* lines 69–71 (echoing Wordsworth's "A happy, genial influence, / Coming one knows not how, or whence" in *To the Daisy* ["In youth from rock to rock I went"], lines 70–71); and both the image of the ocean's bosom and the accompanying idea, "The blue / Bared its eternal bosom . . . But ye were dead" in *Sleep and Poetry,* lines 188–93 (echoing Wordsworth's "This Sea that bares her bosom to the moon . . . It moves us not" in the sonnet *The world is too much with us).*

Keats's first description of Glaucus in *Endymion* seems clearly indebted for several details to Wordsworth's first description of the Leech-Gatherer in *Resolution and Independence.* Here are some of Wordsworth's lines:

> I saw a Man before me unawares:
> The oldest man he seemed that ever wore grey hairs. . . .
> His body was bent double, feet and head
> Coming together in life's pilgrimage. . . .
> At length, himself unsettling, he the pond

> Stirred with his staff, and fixedly did look
> Upon the muddy water, which he conned,
> As if he had been reading in a book. . . .

(55–81)

Keats's description (drafted in September 1817, when he was visiting Bailey and reading Wordsworth at Oxford) similarly stresses the "unawares" character of the encounter and includes among other details the bodily feebleness of the old man, his gray/white hair, the presence of a staff/wand, and the conning of a hypothetical/real book:

> He [Endymion] saw . . .
> An old man sitting calm and peacefully.
> Upon a weeded rock this old man sat,
> And his white hair was awful, and a mat
> Of weeds were cold beneath his cold thin feet;
> And, ample as the largest winding-sheet,
> A cloak of blue wrapp'd up his aged bones. . . .
> Beside this old man lay a pearly wand,
> And in his lap a book, the which he conn'd
> So stedfastly, that the new denizen
> Had time to keep him in amazed ken,
> To mark these shadowings, and stand in awe.

(3.191–217)

Ode to a Nightingale has several Wordsworthian echoes in wording, image, tone, and cadence: for example, "The weariness, the fever, and the fret" (compare *Tintern Abbey,* lines 52–53: "the fretful stir / Unprofitable, and the fever of the world"); "Where youth grows pale, and spectre-thin, and dies" and "No hungry generations tread thee down" (compare *The Excursion,* 4.760–62: "While man grows old, and dwindles, and decays; / And countless generations of mankind / Depart; and leave no vestige where they trod"); "plaintive anthem" (compare *The Solitary Reaper,* line 18: "plaintive numbers"; Wordsworth's poem has a nightingale in the preceding stanza, and the solitary maiden working in the field is of course relatable to Keats's "sad heart of Ruth . . . amid the alien corn").

Individual connections and relations of this sort are easily displayed. Much more difficult, and impossible to document precisely, is Wordsworth's effect over the whole extent of Keats's art and thought: the subjects and themes that Keats chose to write about, the forms and techniques that he used, and his most serious ideas about poetry and human life. Influence study is by its very nature tentative, and it becomes more complicated when the two writers concerned are contemporaries—so many shared peculiarities can turn out to be the common product of an influence still earlier or elements of what William Hazlitt called "the spirit of the age." Nevertheless, the traces of Wordsworth's presence are perceptible throughout Keats's work. In what follows, I speculate about four areas in which Wordsworth's influence might be considered of first importance to the younger poet's career.

The *Lyrical Ballads* and *Isabella*

Keats's first complete narrative poem, *Endymion,* drafted during April–November 1817, tells the story of a shepherd prince who falls in love with a dream goddess, travels high and deep in search of her, and finally, after many speeches and complications of plot, is reunited with her, the two "vanish[ing] far away" into an eternity of bliss. It is a poem about love, dreaming, and the conflicting claims of human and immortal realms of existence. His next narrative poem, *Isabella,* drafted during February–April 1818, tells the story of a young woman whose lover is murdered by her brothers and who, when she learns of his fate, digs up his body, severs the head, carries it home to plant in a pot of basil, and goes mad and dies. This too is a poem about love but also about betrayal, murder, madness, and death. It is not irrelevant to this difference that the interval between the two poems includes the several weeks in December–February during which Keats met Wordsworth and had the older poet's works and achievement as a modern writer frequently in mind.

Scholars have long recognized, just as Keats did at the time, that the winter of 1817–18 was a period of rapid growth and maturing for the young poet. Even before he finished the first draft of *Endymion,* he was becoming weary of it, and his dissatisfaction grew as he revised and recopied the poem in January–March of the new year. One of the focuses of this dissatisfaction was the idea of "romance" (*Endymion* was subtitled "A Poetic Romance"), and a repeated motif in both his letters and his short poems of the time is the opposition between romance and visionary thinking, "skyey Knight errantry," on the one hand, and human suffering, evil, and "disagreeables" in the real world, on the other. Serious conversations with his friend Bailey at Oxford along with deeper reading and thinking on his own after he returned to Hampstead combined to produce what he described in a letter to his brothers on 23 January: "I think a little change has taken place in my intellect lately" (*KL,* 1:214). The consequent thematic maturity in his short poems that winter and early spring is noteworthy: there is a new focus on problems of human mortality (*In drear nighted December* and the sonnets *When I have fears* and *Four seasons fill the measure of the year*); the banishing of romance as "a barren dream" (the sonnet *On Sitting Down to Read "King Lear" Once Again*); differences between the complications of his own modern times and the simpler circumstances of the poets of old (*Lines on the Mermaid Tavern, Robin Hood,* the sonnet beginning "Spenser, a jealous honorer of thine"); and the contrarieties of life (*Welcome joy, and welcome sorrow*).

One of the best of these short lyrics, *In drear nighted December,* composed in the month in which Keats became personally acquainted with Wordsworth, is quintessentially Wordsworthian in its emphasis on the difference between nature's unconsciousness of change and death and human consciousness of these same unhappy phenomena:

> In drear nighted December,
>   Too happy, happy tree,
> Thy branches ne'er remember
>   Their green felicity—
> The north cannot undo them
> With a sleety whistle through them,
> Nor frozen thawings glue them
>   From budding at the prime.
>
> In drear nighted December,
>   Too happy, happy brook,
> Thy bubblings ne'er remember
>   Apollo's summer look;
> But with a sweet forgetting
> They stay their crystal fretting,
> Never, never petting
>   About the frozen time.
>
> Ah! would 'twere so with many
>   A gentle girl and boy—
> But were there ever any
>   Writh'd not of passed joy?
> The feel of not to feel it,
> When there is none to heal it,

Nor numbed sense to steel it,
    Was never said in rhyme.

Keats's verse epistle beginning "Dear Reynolds, as last night I lay in bed," written some three months later, on 25 March 1818, treats a related Wordsworthian concern, the functioning and nonfunctioning of imagination. In combining images of a painting, a ship, and a castle (23 ff.) and concluding with a vision of cruelty in nature (86 ff.), the epistle has elements in common with Wordsworth's *Elegiac Stanzas Suggested by a Picture of Peele Castle.* It breaks off with an allusion to one of Wordsworth's section headings ("Moods of My Own Mind") in his 1807 *Poems, in Two Volumes:* "Away ye horrid moods, / Moods of one's mind!" (105–6).

These details are part of the recoverable context in which Keats composed his new romance that ends, not in an eternity of bliss, but in madness and death. *Isabella* is a retelling in verse of a story in Boccaccio's *Decameron* (fifth "novel," fourth day), originally undertaken for a volume of verse narratives based on Boccaccio that Keats and Reynolds had planned to publish together. The project was abandoned after completion of this first story—by Reynolds probably because he knew he could not produce poems that would hold their own alongside Keats's (Reynolds was in any case mainly occupied in study of the law), and by Keats probably because he had already, in the single effort, accomplished most of what interested him in the project.

In recent decades, criticism of *Isabella* has focused on its realistic descriptions and the narrator's antiromantic stance as "modern" reteller of an old story whose simplicity and naïveté ("the gentleness of old Romance, / The simple plaining of a minstrel's song" [387–88]) are no longer appropriate. Scholars comparing Keats's version with his source, the fifth edition (1684) of an English translation of 1620, have noted many changes by Keats that emphasize the gruesome aspects of the story—for example, the crude physical efforts involved in the exhumation of the dead lover Lorenzo (Isabella and her nurse "digged not far" in the original, but "Three hours they labour'd," clawing with knife and bare hands, in Keats's modernization); the rotting of the body (miraculously uncorrupted in the original); the suggestion of prolonged sawing or clumsy hacking in the removal of Lorenzo's head (neatly severed with "a keen Razor" in the original); the bizarre details of Isabella's care for the head (repeated kissing, combing its hair, pointing its eyelashes); and her mental deterioration and separation from nature and reality. Scholars have also remarked on the narrator's self-presentation as modern reteller, including apologies both to Boccaccio and to the "Fair reader" for his grisly depiction of "wormy circumstance." The poem is generally viewed as

transitional in Keats's career, anticipating further antiromantic develop-
ments in the narratives and lyrics of the following year, beginning with *The
Eve of St. Agnes.*

The abundance of Wordsworthian elements in the poem, especially elements of the *Lyrical Ballads* and other poems that Wordsworth produced
about the same time, suggests that Wordsworth may have played a significant
role in the transition. Keats's basic story came from Boccaccio, of course, but
Wordsworth wrote several narratives involving abandoned women, betrayal,
and psychological deterioration, and Keats's elaboration of his given materials is certainly more Wordsworthian than Boccaccian. His characterizations
of his principals are like Wordsworth's in (for example) *The Thorn, Michael,*
and the story of Margaret in *The Ruined Cottage* (a poem of 1797–98 that
Keats read in its revised form in book 1 of *The Excursion*). The combination
of romantic pathos and exaggerated realism is another Wordsworthian feature, and Keats's "wormy circumstance" is relatable to the characteristic of
Wordsworth's poetry that Coleridge had recently (in chapter 22 of *Biographia
Literaria,* published in July 1817) called "matter-of-factness." Above all, there is
the Wordsworthian interest in psychology ("the primary laws of our nature,"
as Wordsworth wrote in the preface to *Lyrical Ballads,* "chiefly, as far as
regards the manner in which we associate ideas in a state of excitement") that
is the main concern in the second half of Keats's poem.

Isabella's "burthen" at the end—"O cruelty, / To steal my basil-pot away
from me!"—is vaguely reminiscent of Martha Ray's refrain in *The Thorn:*
"Oh misery! oh misery! / Oh woe is me! oh misery!" ("O misery!" itself
occurs in line 235 of *Isabella.*) There are closer parallels (in imagery, tone,
and general situation) between Keats's description of her alienation from
the objective world—

> And she forgot the stars, the moon, and sun,
>   And she forgot the blue above the trees,
> And she forgot the dells where waters run,
>   And she forgot the chilly autumn breeze;
> She had no knowledge when the day was done,
>   And the new morn she saw not: but in peace
> Hung over her sweet basil evermore,
> And moisten'd it with tears unto the core
>
> (417–24)

—and Martha Ray's similarly intense adherence to a special object (her
thorn is Isabella's basil) in a natural setting of cosmic dimensions:

And she is known to every star,
And every wind that blows;
And there, beside the Thorn, she sits
When the blue daylight's in the skies,
And when the whirlwind's on the hill,
Or frosty air is keen and still. . . .
(*The Thorn*, 69–74)

Isabella's wretched situation in the penultimate stanza of the poem, after her brothers steal away her basil pot—

Piteous she look'd on dead and senseless things,
  Asking for her lost basil amorously;
And with melodious chuckle in the strings
  Of her lorn voice, she oftentimes would cry
After the pilgim in his wanderings,
  To ask him where her basil was . . .
(*Isabella*, 489–94)

—again bears resemblance to some specific lines in Wordsworth, this time the description of Margaret in *The Excursion* when, near the end of her story, she frantically inquires of everyone after her missing husband:

  . . . and [she], in such piteous sort
That any heart had ached to hear her, begged
That, whereso'er I went, I still would ask
For him whom she had lost. . . .
  . . . I have heard, my Friend,
That in yon arbour oftentimes she sate
Alone, through half the vacant sabbath day;
And, if a dog passed by, she still would quit
The shade, and look abroad. On this old bench
For hours she sate; and evermore her eye
Was busy in the distance, shaping things. . . .
  . . . and she with faltering voice
Made many a fond inquiry. . . .
(1.865–92)

Such connections, supported by details of the biographical background, may be thought to constitute fairly impressive circumstantial evidence of Wordsworth's influence at an important turning point in Keats's career.

"Wordsworthian or Egotistical Sublime" and Negative Capability

"Negative Capability," the best known among the aesthetic and literary ideas in Keats's letters, may also be considered a development of the winter of 1817–18, though the concept is discernible in his poetry earlier in 1817 (even if Keats himself was not fully conscious of it theoretically) and continues to be an explicit or hovering component of his critical thinking for the rest of his brief career. It first surfaces prominently in a handful of sentences in part of a letter written on 27 or 28 December 1817 in which he tells his brothers that a night or two earlier, when he went to the theater with his friends Charles Brown and Charles Wentworth Dilke,

> I had not a dispute but a disquisition with Dilke, on various subjects; several things dovetailed in my mind, & at once it struck me, what quality went to form a Man of Achievement especially in Literature & which Shakespeare posessed so enormously—I mean *Negative Capability*, that is when man is capable of being in uncertainties, Mysteries, doubts, without any irritable reaching after fact & reason—Coleridge, for instance, would let go by a fine isolated verisimilitude caught from the Penetralium of mystery, from being incapable of remaining content with half knowledge. This pursued through Volumes would perhaps take us no further than this, that with a great poet the sense of Beauty overcomes every other consideration, or rather obliterates all consideration. (*KL*, 1:193–94)

This passage is frequently related to Keats's remarks to his friend Richard Woodhouse ten months later (27 October 1818) on "the poetical Character":

> As to the poetical Character itself, (I mean that sort of which, if I am any thing, I am a Member; that sort distinguished from the wordsworthian or egotistical sublime; which is a thing per se and stands alone) it is not itself— it has no self—it is every thing and nothing—It has no character—it enjoys light and shade; it lives in gusto, be it foul or fair, high or low, rich or poor, mean or elevated—It has as much delight in conceiving an Iago as an Imo- gen. What shocks the virtuous philosop[h]er, delights the camelion Poet. It does no harm from its relish of the dark side of things any more than from its taste for the bright one; because they both end in speculation. A Poet is the most unpoetical of any thing in existence; because he has no Identity— he is continually . . . filling some other Body. (*KL*, 1:386–87)

Shakespeare, specifically named in the first passage and alluded to (as the conceiver of Iago and Imogen) in the second, is the prime exemplar of this power of sympathetic imagination, the poet's ability, as Woodhouse explained in a comment on the second passage, "to throw his own soul into any object he sees or imagines, so as to . . . speak out of that object—so that his own self will . . . be 'annihilated'" (*KL*, 1:389). The opposite tendency, in which the writer's ego is central and all contraries must be resolved, is represented by Coleridge in the first passage (the Coleridge of *Biographia Literaria* rather than of *The Ancient Mariner, Kubla Khan,* and *Christabel*) and by Wordsworth ("the wordsworthian . . . sublime") in the second.

Scholars have long been interested in the source or sources of this basic idea. Hazlitt is the most frequently mentioned, especially for some remarks about Shakespeare that he delivered in a lecture of 27 January 1818 (a lecture that Keats probably attended and in any case certainly knew about):

> The striking peculiarity of Shakspeare's mind was its generic quality, its power of communication with all other minds—so that it contained a universe of thought and feeling within itself, and had no one peculiar bias, or exclusive excellence more than another. He was just like any other man, but that he was like all other men. He was the least of an egotist that it was possible to be. He was nothing in himself; but he was all that others were, or that they could become. . . . He had only to think of any thing in order to become that thing, with all the circumstances belonging to it. When he conceived of a character, whether real or imaginary, he not only entered into all its thoughts and feelings, but seemed instantly, and as if by touching a secret spring, to be surrounded with all the same objects . . . the same local, outward, and unforeseen accidents which would occur in reality. (Hazlitt 1930, 5:47–48)

In a later lecture in the same series, on 3 March (the evening before Keats left Hampstead to go to Teignmouth), Hazlitt launched into a severe attack on the generalized type of the Wordsworth school, the Lake Poet:

> A thorough adept in this school of poetry and philanthropy is jealous of all excellence but his own. He does not even like to share his reputation with his subject; for he would have it all proceed from his own power and originality of mind. Such a one is slow to admire any thing that is admirable; feels no interest in what is most interesting to others, no grandeur in any thing grand, no beauty in any thing beautiful. He tolerates only what he himself creates. . . . He sees nothing but himself and the universe. . . . His egotism is in some respects a madness. (Hazlitt 1930, 5:163)

Certainly these passages, implicitly contrasting Shakespeare and Wordsworth, have a bearing on Keats's "camelion Poet" letter to Woodhouse, though they postdate the December 1817 statement on Negative Capability.

A passage in Haydon's diary for 22 December 1817 also compares Wordsworth and Shakespeare: "Wordsworth's great power is an intense perception of human feelings regarding the mystery of things by analyzing his own, Shakespeare's an intense power of laying open the heart & mind of man by analyzing the feelings of others acting on themselves. . . . Shakespeare has no moral code, and only leaves it at the option of all how to act by shewing the consequence of such & such conduct in acting" (Haydon 1960, 2:171). Since Keats and Haydon were frequently together around this time, it seems likely that Haydon's conversation was also among the immediate influences. There has to have been some contribution by Dilke, of course, the friend with whom a "disquisition" provoked the "dovetailing" that led to Negative Capability in the letter. And there was also, much more generally and elusively, some nonegotistic element in Keats's own personality acting as an influence. In the December 1817 letter, Keats writes that "*at once* it struck me," but he had dramatically portrayed Negative Capability in the speeches and actions of *Endymion* during the preceding several months—in the "fellowship with essence" passage of 1.777 ff. ("blending pleasurable" in the original manuscript text), in various later comments in the poem about identity and freeing oneself from "self-passion," and even in much of the incidental language (for example, in verbs such as "commune," "melt into," "blend," "mingle," "interknit," "commingle").

My point for the present occasion is simply that Wordsworth has to be considered a prominent element in the development of Negative Capability. Keats had firsthand evidence of Wordsworth's personal (as opposed to poetic) egotism from his meetings with the older poet in the winter of 1817–18. Clarke's comment on the "pretty piece of Paganism" incident years afterward, in *Recollections of Writers* (149), sounds authoritative: "From Keats's description of his mentor's [Wordsworth's] manner, as well as behaviour that evening, it would seem to have been one of [his] usual ebullitions of egoism." And obviously there were complaints from others. "I am sorry," Keats writes to his brothers on 21 February 1818, "that Wordsworth has left a bad impression where-ever he visited in Town—by his egotism, Vanity and bigotry" (*KL*, 1:237). Keats could set aside the personal egotism ("yet he is a great Poet," he adds in the letter just quoted), but *poetic* egotism was a more serious matter. Keats uses "Wordsworth &c" to exemplify the self-regarding stance of contemporary poetry in the important letter to Reynolds of 3 February 1818. "Poetry should be great & unobtrusive," Keats says there, "a thing which enters into one's soul, and does not startle it or amaze it with itself but with its subject." But Wordsworth is the leader among the egotists who "brood and peacock": "Old Matthew spoke to [Wordsworth] some years ago on some nothing, & because he happens in an Evening Walk to imagine the figure of the old man—he must stamp it down in black & white, and it is henceforth sacred" (*KL*, 1:223–24). By October 1818, in the letter to Woodhouse, the antithesis of "camelion" poetry had become "wordsworthian or egotistical sublime," and Woodhouse saw in the letter "the distinction [Keats] draws between himself & those of the Wordsworth School" (*KL*, 1:388). Wordsworth is on the bad side in this opposition but plainly is a significant presence as Shakespeare's contrary. Both poets were essential to the formation of Keats's most famous critical idea.

Wordsworth's "Philosophy" and the Grand March of Keats's Intellect

Wordsworth is also a presence in several other important philosophical passages in Keats's letters. In the often-cited letter to Bailey on "the authenticity of the Imagination," 22 November 1817 (*KL*, 1:184–86), at least half of the significant sentences embody Wordsworthian notions about the mind, feelings, association of ideas, perceiving, creating, remembering—the substance especially of *Tintern Abbey*. Keats's phrase "the holiness of the Heart's affections," for example (in his affirmation of certainty concerning that and "the truth of Imagination"), contains three of Wordsworth's favorite words. Both his idea in the letter that "our Passions . . . [are] creative of essential Beauty" and the "little song" in *Endymion* that he refers to by way of illustration, the Indian maiden's "O Sorrow" in 4.146–81, reflect the basic Wordsworthian doctrine of creative sensibility (Wordsworth's "strong creative power/Of human passion" in *The Excursion*, 1.480–81, epitomizes a main interest throughout his work). The opposition expressed in Keats's "O for a Life of Sensations rather than of Thoughts" pointedly echoes the same opposition running through both *Tintern Abbey* and the Intimations ode. When, in the process of winding up his topic, Keats makes a distinction between "the simple imaginative Mind" that he has been describing and "a complex Mind—one that is imaginative and at the same time careful of its fruits—who would exist partly on sensation partly on thought—to whom it is necessary that years should bring the philosophic Mind," the concluding allusion to the Intimations ode (line 186, "years that bring the philosophic mind") makes clear that Wordsworth is the model he is thinking of.

Wordsworth is central to the "Mansion of Many Apartments" letter of 3 May 1818 to Reynolds, in which the main question is the extent to which Wordsworth, Milton, and Keats himself have seen into the human heart and the mystery of human life (*KL*, 1:278–82). "My Branchings out," Keats tells Reynolds, "have been numerous: one of them is the consideration of Wordsworth's genius and as a help . . . how he differs from Milton." Keats goes on to construct an elaborate simile of human life as "a large Mansion of Many Apartments, two of which I can only describe, the doors of the rest being as yet shut upon me." The first is "the infant or thoughtless Chamber, in which we remain as long as we do not think." "The awakening of the thinking principle" impels one on to the second, the "Chamber of Maiden-Thought," where among its effects is

> that tremendous one of sharpening one's vision into the heart and nature of Man—of convincing ones nerves that the World is full of Misery and Heart-break, Pain, Sickness and oppression—whereby This Chamber of Maiden Thought becomes gradually darken'd and at the same time on all sides of it many doors are set open—but all dark—all leading to dark passages—We see not the ballance of good and evil. We are in a Mist—*We* are now in that state—We feel the "burden of the Mystery," To this point was Wordsworth come, as far as I can conceive when he wrote "Tintern Abbey" and it seems to me that his Genius is explorative of those dark Passages. Now if we live, and go on thinking, we too shall explore them.

The fact that Wordsworth in this scheme advanced further than Milton (whose "Philosophy, human and divine, may be tolerably understood by one not much advanced in years") Keats takes as proof that "there is really a grand march of intellect." He himself, it is clear, intends to progress beyond Wordsworth by the same means. The whole (which has references to both *Tintern Abbey* and *The Excursion*) is presented to Reynolds "to show you how tall I stand by the giant." It is an impressive assessment of the giant Wordsworth's genius and further testimony to the rapidity of Keats's own maturing.

The third of the best-known philosophical passages, several pages on the world as a "vale of Soul-making" in a late April section of Keats's longest journal letter to his brother and sister-in-law in America, 14 February–early May 1819 (*KL*, 2:101–3), again involves Wordsworthian progression:

> The common cognomen of this world among the misguided and superstitious is "a vale of tears" from which we are to be redeemed by a certain arbitrary interposition of God and taken to Heaven—What a little circumscribe[d] straightened notion! Call the world if you Please "The vale of Soul-making." . . . I say "*Soul making*" Soul as distinguished from an Intelligence—There may be intelligences or sparks of the divinity in millions—but they are not Souls till they acquire identities, till each one is personally itself. . . . I will call the *world* a School instituted for the purpose of

teaching little children to read—I will call the *human heart* the *horn Book* used in that School—and I will call the *Child able to read, the Soul* made from that *school* and its *hornbook*. Do you not see how necessary a World of Pains and troubles is to school an Intelligence and make it a soul? . . . As various as the Lives of Men are—so various become their souls, and thus does God make individual beings, Souls, Identical Souls of the sparks of his own essence—This appears to me a faint sketch of a system of Salvation which does not affront our reason and humanity—I am convinced that many difficulties which christians labour under would vanish before it.

Wordsworth is not mentioned (or quoted or even verbally echoed) in the passage; yet commentators on it have referred to Wordsworth, especially to the ideas and images concerning the origin, development, and schooling of the human soul in the Intimations ode. At the time, Keats had recently completed *The Eve of St. Agnes,* some 880 lines of *Hyperion,* and *La Belle Dame sans Merci* (among other works) and was about to begin writing his own great odes.

Peter Bell and the Genesis of Keats's Odes

A final speculation concerning the relationship of Wordsworth and Keats, this time an entirely novel one, is based on the unlikely juxtaposition of *Peter Bell,* Wordsworth's much-ridiculed tale of a lawless potter redeemed by an awakening of imagination, and Keats's great odes, the poems that, above all others, have secured him a place (along with Wordsworth) "among the English Poets." *Peter Bell* was first drafted in 1798, perhaps as a companion piece or counterpart to Coleridge's *The Ancient Mariner,* but it was revised several times in the next decade or so and remained in manuscript until 1819, when it was published on or about 22 April. Just before its appearance, Keats mentions it twice in the spring 1819 journal letter to his brother and sister-in-law, first on 15 April—

> Wordsworth is going to publish a Poem called Peter Bell—what a perverse fellow it is! Why wilt he talk about Peter Bells—I was told not to tell—but to you it will not be tellings—Reynolds hearing that said Peter Bell was coming out, took it into his head to write a skit upon it call'd Peter Bell. He did it as soon as thought on it is to be published this morning, and comes out before the real Peter Bell, with this admirable motto from the "Bold stroke for a Wife" "I am the real Simon Pure" (*KL,* 2:83–84)

—and then six days later, on the twenty-first, when he drafts (in the letter *KL*, 2:93–94) a short review of Reynolds's work that he has agreed to do for Leigh Hunt's *Examiner* (where it appeared on the twenty-fifth). It was a clever project, and Reynolds's *Peter Bell*, published a week before Wordsworth's and causing a great deal of confusion in the press and at the booksellers, is in some parts (most notably the preface and the notes) a brilliant parody. Obviously, having gone to such lengths to make a good joke, Reynolds and Keats would be among the earliest readers of the real *Peter Bell* when it came out. It was only about a week afterward that Keats wrote what we take to be the first of his great odes, the *Ode to Psyche*.

Peter Bell begins with a prologue intended (as Wordsworth makes clear in an accompanying dedicatory epistle to Robert Southey) to establish several ideas about the proper subject matter of poetry, the proper sphere of imagination, and the role of the supernatural. The narrator flies away from earth in a "little Boat" (4), enjoys prying among the stars and planets for awhile, but soon becomes lost and homesick: "Then back to Earth, the dear green Earth . . . I've left my heart at home" (51–55).[4] The boat (a talking boat, modeled on Chaucer's talking eagle in *The House of Fame*), who views the narrator's retreat with scorn, offers to take him to some equally remote places among the "nether precincts"—"Siberian snows," "a land / Where human foot did never stray . . . burning Africa," "the realm of Faery" (91, 96–106)—but these too are rejected by the narrator in a speech packed with significant Wordsworthian doctrine:

> Temptation lurks among your words;
> But, while these pleasures you're pursuing
> Without impediment or let,
> My radiant Pinnace, you forget
> What on the earth is doing.
>
> There was a time when all mankind
> Did listen with a faith sincere
> To tuneful tongues in mystery vers'd;
> *Then* Poets fearlessly rehears'd
> The wonders of a wild career.
>
> Go—but the world's a sleepy world
> And 'tis, I fear, an age too late;
> Take with you some ambitious Youth,
> For I myself, in very truth,
> Am all unfit to be your mate.

Long have I lov'd what I behold,
The night that calms, the day that cheers:
The common growth of mother earth
Suffices me—her tears, her mirth,
Her humblest mirth and tears.

The dragon's wing, the magic ring,
I shall not covet for my dower,
If I along that lowly way
With sympathetic heart may stray
And with a soul of power.

These given, what more need I desire,
To stir—to soothe—or elevate?
What nobler marvels than the mind
May in life's daily prospect find,
May find or there create? . . .

But grant my wishes,—let us now
Descend from this ethereal height. . . .

(121–57)

The first point of interest relative to Keats is the modernist stance of Wordsworth's narrator. Keats had already, partly with Wordsworth's help, been self-consciously "modern" for a year or more (for example, in the view of Boccaccio's "old prose" taken in *Isabella*). There is nevertheless a fresh fervency about the situation in *Ode to Psyche:*

O brightest! though too late for antique vows,
    Too, too late for the fond believing lyre,
When holy were the haunted forest boughs,
    Holy the air, the water, and the fire;
Yet even in these days so far retir'd
    From happy pieties. . . .

(36–41)

Keats's lines echo both the idea and some of the language of the passage just quoted from *Peter Bell* ("There was a time . . . faith sincere . . . an age too late").

My second point has to do with Wordsworth's emphasis on the supreme importance of the human mind ("What nobler marvels than the mind"). The central subject of *Peter Bell* is what the narrator later invokes as "Spirits of the Mind" (833), the working imagination of Peter's own mind. The obvious Keats connection here is the last stanza of *Ode to Psyche,* where the speaker offers his own mind as recompense for Psyche's lack of shrine, grove, oracle, and prophet: "a fane / In some untrodden region of my mind . . . branched thoughts . . . the wreath'd trellis of a working brain . . . shadowy thought" (50–65).

My third point derives from the excursion-return structure of Wordsworth's prologue ("Up goes my Boat between the stars. . . . Then back to Earth . . . let us now / Descend from this ethereal height," 31, 51, 156–57). Such a structure appears only vestigially in *Ode to Psyche* (imaginative exploration of what Psyche does *not* have, followed by imaginative present remedy in the speaker's mind instead) but is central in two of the others, *Ode to a Nightingale* and *Ode on a Grecian Urn* (in each case an imaginative excursion to an ideal realm—the forest of the invisible bird, the art world of the urn—followed by a return to earthly reality), and is represented in what are usually taken to be the final two, *Ode on Melancholy* and *To Autumn,* by negative injunctions ("go not to Lethe," "Think not of them [the songs of spring]").

All five of Keats's great odes symbolize the working imagination. They are modern in stance and earthly (as opposed to ideal) in orientation, and they successively explore, and find impossible or unsatisfactory, such hypothetical alternatives to reality as religious ritual, mythology, fairy-tale romance, the past, the supernatural, the artificial. Rhetorically *Peter Bell* is nearly as unlike a Keats ode as is possible for a poem to be, but its story and ideas could have helped point Keats in the direction he took in the famous series that he began so soon after its appearance.

*   *   *

There are biographical connections between Wordsworth and Keats. There are a great many Wordsworthian echoes in Keats's poetry and letters. There are general likenesses (as well as differences) between the two writers in subject matter, themes, attitudes, and basic structures of thinking. Wordsworth was not the only influence on Keats's career, but he was undeniably an important one. It is probably only a coincidence that Haydon's *Christ's Entry into Jerusalem,* the painting displayed at his "immortal dinner" in late December 1817, has the portraits of Keats and Wordsworth, among the spectators, actually touching one another, Keats's head (in a two-dimensional view) just resting on the top of Wordsworth's. But perhaps Haydon was unconsciously prefiguring how tall Keats would "stand by the giant"—and at the same time showing Wordsworth as one of the bases that would help him stand so tall.

3
Keats and Coleridge

Argument

How the Speaker yearned to fly to the forest to join the Nightingale; and how, having arrived there, he found himself in a less advantageous situation than he previously had fancied; and how, upon full recognition that a mortal Man is not the same as an immortal Bird, he returned to his sole self and discovered himself once again in his own Country.

Since Walter Jackson Bate is the author of standard biographies of both Keats and Coleridge, it is surely appropriate that at least one of the contributions to a volume honoring him should consider the personal and literary relationships of these two Romantic writers. Bate has also given us the standard biography of Samuel Johnson, and one could, without too much ingenuity, propose a meeting ground for Keats and Coleridge in the vast works of that wisest of eighteenth-century literary figures. There is a direct connection between Johnson's description of metaphysical wit as "a kind of *discordia concors;* a combination of dissimilar images, or discovery of occult resemblances in things apparently unlike" ("Abraham Cowley") and Coleridge's equally famous statement, so influential on the New Critics a century later, that the imagination "reveals itself in the balance or reconciliation of opposite or discordant qualities" (*Biographia Literaria,* chap. 14). Johnson's phrase in the title of chapter 44 of *Rasselas,* "The Dangerous Prevalence of Imagination," could serve as a capsule thematization of Keats's major poems from *The Eve of St. Agnes* through *Lamia.*

Let us, however, confine our investigation to the two near-contemporaries. Oddly enough, though scholars have proposed Coleridge as the source of a substantial array of specific echoes and borrowings in Keats's poetry and letters, almost nothing has been written on the more speculative but far more important topic of Coleridge's general effect on Keats's thinking and writing. I would propose that, among living contemporaries, Coleridge was second only to Wordsworth as an important and pervasive influence behind Keats's best accomplishments.[1]

Biographical Background

Keats met Coleridge just once, on the morning of 11 April 1819. Keats, then twenty-three years old, was a third of the way through his "living year"—the first nine months of 1819, during which he wrote nearly all the poems that put him "among the English Poets"—and Coleridge, at forty-six, was decidedly over the hill as poet, critic, and philosopher but was becoming increasingly famous as a talker. Keats described the meeting four days afterward in his longest journal letter to his brother and sister-in-law in America:

> Last Sunday I took a Walk towards highgate and in the lane that winds by the side of Lord Mansfield's park I met Mr Green our Demonstrator at Guy's in conversation with Coleridge—I joined them, after enquiring by a look whether it would be agreeable—I walked with him a[t] his alderman-after dinner pace for near two miles I suppose[.] In those two Miles he broached a thousand things—let me see if I can give you a list—Nightingales, Poetry—on Poetical sensation—Metaphysics—Different genera and species of Dreams—Nightmare—a dream accompanied by a sense of touch—single and double touch—A dream related—First and second consciousness—the difference explained between will and Volition—so m[an]y metaphysicians from a want of smoking the second consciousness—Monsters—the Kraken—Mermaids—southey believes in them—southeys belief too much diluted—A Ghost story—Good morning—I heard his voice as he came towards me—I heard it as he moved away—I had heard it all the interval—if it may be called so. He was civil enough to ask me to call on him at Highgate. (*KL*, 2:88–89)

Coleridge made no record at the time but recalled the event eleven years later in a conversation with John Frere, a recent graduate of Cambridge whose family (including his uncle John Hookham Frere) Coleridge had known for more than a decade. Here is Coleridge's account, as young Frere wrote it down in the form of a dialogue:

> F[*rere*]. You have not read much of Keats, Sir, I think.
>
> C[*oleridge*]. No, I have not. I have seen two Sonnets which I think showed marks of a great genius had he lived. I have also read a poem with a classical name—I forget what. Poor Keats, I saw him once. Mr. Green, whom you have heard me mention, and I were walking out in these parts, and we were overtaken by a young man of a very striking countenance whom Mr. Green recognised and shook hands with, mentioning my name; I wish Mr. Green had introduced me, for I did not know who it was. He passed on, but in a few moments sprung back and said, "Mr. Coleridge, allow me the honour of shaking your hand."
>
> I was struck by the energy of his manner, and gave him my hand.
>
> He passed on and we stood still looking after him, when Mr. Green said, "Do you know who that is? That is Keats, the poet."
>
> "Heavens!" said I, "when I shook him by the hand there was death!" This was about two years before he died.
>
> F[*rere*]. But what was it?
>
> C[*oleridge*]. I cannot describe it. There was a heat and a dampness in the hand. To say that his death was caused by the Review is absurd, but at the same time it is impossible adequately to conceive the effect which it must have had on his mind.
>
> It is very well for those who have a place in the world and are independent to talk of these things, they can bear such a blow, so can those who have a strong religious principle; but all men are not born Philosophers, and all men have not those advantages of birth and education.
>
> Poor Keats had not, and it is impossible I say to conceive the effect which such a Review must have had upon him, knowing as he did that he had his way to make in the world by his own exertions, and conscious of the genius within him. (Green 1917, 405–6)[2]

It is interesting that both Keats's and Coleridge's accounts are focused on the same subject: S. T. Coleridge—as nonstop talker on a bizarre variety of topics (in Keats's letter) and as Great Man, prognosticator of death, and moralizer on the hardships suffered by those lacking independence and religion (in Coleridge's conversation). One of these stances is clearly more consistent with Negative Capability than the other.

Scholars have always been particularly interested in Keats's version of the encounter and the effects it may have had on his poetry. The meeting took place just two weeks before Keats drafted *La Belle Dame sans Merci*, which

involves dreaming, a nightmare, problems of "will and Volition," the supernatural, and a fairy creature having some of the standard traits associated
with mermaids. Only a few days or weeks after that (sometime in May),
Keats wrote *Ode to a Nightingale,* which is even more readily relatable to
Coleridge's topics: "Nightingales, Poetry . . . Poetical sensation—Metaphysics—Different genera and species of Dreams." H. W. Garrod, in one of
the earliest extended discussions of Coleridge's influence on Keats, argues
that the event produced a complex of stimuli leading to the Nightingale
ode: not just the subjects of Coleridge's conversation but additional effects
from other works that the meeting would have caused Keats to recall—for
example, Coleridge's *The Nightingale: A Conversation Poem,* first published
in *Lyrical Ballads;* the chapters on poetic language in *Biographia Literaria;*
and Wordsworth's preface to *Lyrical Ballads* (Garrod 1926, 118–37). Mary
Rebecca Thayer speculates that Keats immediately read or reread Coleridge's
Love (another poem from *Lyrical Ballads*), whose cruel lady, distracted
knight, cave, autumnal setting, and *abcb* ballad stanza with a short fourth
line all have their counterparts in Keats's *La Belle Dame* (Thayer 1945,
270–72). John Beer proposes a significantly more general influence: "it is
distinctly possible that [Coleridge's] conversation left Keats thinking in a
new way about his own experiences, contemplating, for example, the contrast between the warm sensuous moments in which it is hard for human
beings to believe in death and the bleak contemplation of frozen forms
which reminds them inexorably of death's inevitable intervention. And so,
we may reason, Keats was set on the path which would lead him, not long
after, to compose an ode to a nightingale in which that riddling contrast
would be a central theme" (Beer 1977, 281).[3]

But these connections ignore the facts of Keats chronology. Keats had been
writing about dreams, poetry, the supernatural, fairy creatures, knights,
caves, nightingales, and the rest—and, in his letters, even about Coleridge's
poetry and philosophy—for two years or more before the meeting of mid-
April 1819. Beer's description of "the contrast between . . . warm sensuous
moments . . . and the bleak contemplation of frozen forms" is much more
appropriate to *The Eve of St. Agnes,* drafted two or three months earlier. And
nobody's conversation, at any time in his career, was needed to remind Keats
of the inexorability of death. Possibly the chief interest of Keats's account of
the meeting lies in its testimony to the younger writer's steadiness of character, his lack of "anxiety of influence" in the presence of a great literary precursor. The tone of his description in the letter is amusement rather than
awe. It is Coleridge who, self-aggrandizingly, supplies the awe.

What *is* biographically important, on the other hand, is the effect of some of Coleridge's major works published in 1816 and 1817, at an early stage of Keats's development as a poet and thinker. Though Coleridge belongs to the earlier generation of Romantics, his most significant writings (apart from *The Rime of the Ancient Mariner*) were first made widely available in the midst of the activities of the later generation of Romantics. *Christabel* (written mainly in 1798–1800), *Kubla Khan* (1797–98), and *The Pains of Sleep* (1803) were first published in May 1816 in a pamphlet titled *Christabel; Kubla Khan, A Vision; The Pains of Sleep.* The work was much anticipated and widely noticed—by Keats's acquaintances John Hamilton Reynolds, William Hazlitt, and George Felton Mathew, among others—and it was reissued in two subsequent editions before the year was out. *Biographia Literaria* was published in July 1817. *Sibylline Leaves: A Collection of Poems* was also published in July 1817 and contained, among other works, *The Rime of the Ancient Mariner, The Eolian Harp, This Lime-Tree Bower My Prison, To a Gentleman* (Wordsworth), *The Nightingale, Frost at Midnight,* and *Dejection: An Ode.* Most of the poems just named were composed during 1795–1802. For several of them, *Sibylline Leaves* represents the first publication in book form, if not the first publication ever.

Keats mentions Coleridge half a dozen times in his extant letters. On 30 October 1817, commenting on Benjamin Bailey's voraciousness in reading ("I should not like to be Pages in your way when in a tolerable hungry mood—you have no Mercy—your teeth are the Rock tarpeian down which you capsise Epic Poems like Mad"), Keats refers to Coleridge's *Lay Sermons* published in December 1816 and March 1817: "I would not for 40 shillings be Coleridge's Lays in your way" (*KL*, 1:175). Keats had just spent September and the first week of October with Bailey at Oxford, and obviously Coleridge had come up, no doubt frequently, in their conversation. In a note written probably on the first or second Wednesday of November 1817, Keats asks his friends the Dilkes to send him a copy of *Sibylline Leaves* (1:183). In the famous letter to his brothers of late December 1817, Keats uses Coleridge, in contrast to Shakespeare, to epitomize lack of Negative Capability (1:193–94; see the last section of the present chapter). Since there is no preamble or further explanation accompanying the example—"Coleridge, for instance, would let go by a fine isolated verisimilitude caught from the Penetralium of mystery, from being incapable of remaining content with half knowledge"— we may assume that Keats's brothers were also familiar with at least some of Coleridge's writings. In a later letter to his brothers, around the second week of February 1818, Keats reports casually that "Mr [Henry Crabb] Robinson a great friend of Coleridges called on me" (1:227). Writing to Reynolds from Scotland on 13 July 1818, Keats describes the proprietor of the whisky shop in Burns's cottage as downing drinks at the rate of "five for the Quarter and twelve for the hour"—a little joke based on their shared familiarity with the tenth line of *Christabel* (1:324).[4] The latest mention of Coleridge occurs in the passage quoted above describing the meeting of 11 April 1819.

Three further references in Keats circle papers connect Keats and Coleridge. Bailey, writing to Keats's publisher John Taylor on 22 February 1818, mentions that he sent Coleridge a copy of his recently published sermon (*A Discourse Inscribed to the Memory of the Princess Charlotte Augusta*) and received back "a most eccentric letter . . . the oddest thing I ever read." Keats's friend Woodhouse, in a memorandum of 1820, reports the poet's explanation of how he happened to write a certain phrase in book 3 of *Hyperion:* "It seemed," Keats is represented as saying, "to come by chance or magic—to be as it were something given to him." The last seven words echo the same phrasing in Coleridge's prefatory note to *Kubla Khan:* "the Author has frequently purposed to finish for himself what had been originally, as it were, given to him." And, finally, "Coleridge Lamb & Lloyd" appears in Charles Brown's "List of Mʳ John Keats' Books" distributed after his death— a reference to Coleridge's *Poems . . . Second Edition. To Which Are Now Added Poems by Charles Lamb, and Charles Lloyd* (1797), a volume that includes an early version of *The Eolian Harp* (*KC,* 1:10, 129, 256).[5]

In her comprehensive study of Keats's literary relationships with his contemporaries, Beth Lau has collected some 150 echoes, borrowings, and other evidences of Coleridgean influence that scholars over the years have detected in Keats's writings (Lau 1991, 69–114). These range from isolated verbal and narrative details to extended likenesses in theme, character, and plot. At the simple end of the spectrum there are phrases such as "The surgy murmurs of the lonely sea" in *Endymion* 1.121 (seeming to echo "The stilly murmur of the distant Sea" in *The Eolian Harp* 11); "And there she wept, and sigh'd full sore" in *La Belle Dame* 30 (cf. "And how she wept, and clasped his knees" in *Love* 57); Cynthia's "feet, / More bluely vein'd" in *Endymion* 1.624–25 (cf. Geraldine's "blue-veined feet" in *Christabel* 63); and the cluster of "manna-dew/honey-dew" images in *Endymion* 1.766, 2.7 and *La Belle Dame* 26 (all relatable to "honey-dew" in *Kubla Khan* 53).[6] Several scholars have remarked on the numerous likenesses between images of *Endymion* 2.593–636—"caves," "dome," "wild magnificence," "Enormous chasms," "foam and roar," "Streams subterranean," "thousand fountains," "spouting columns," "vines," "trees," "high fantastic roof"—and the dome, measureless caverns, underground river, and fountain in *Kubla Khan. Dejection: An Ode* has been linked thematically with Keats's odes, especially *Ode to a Nightingale,* and with such particulars as "The feel of not to feel it" in Keats's *In drear nighted December* 21 and the combination of beauty and alien coldness in *On Visiting the Tomb of Burns* (cf. Coleridge's "I see, not feel, how beautiful they are" and "For not to think of what I needs must feel" in *Dejection* 38, 87). The influence of *Christabel* on the themes, plots, characters, and descriptions of *The Eve of St. Agnes* and *Lamia* is pervasive.

Obviously some of these connections are more interesting than others. It is hardly surprising, for example, that Keats's *Ode to a Nightingale* contains several dozen terms and images that also appear in Coleridge's *The Nightingale.* Words and phrases such as "no . . . light," "mossy," "murmuring/murmurous," "soft," "verdure/verdurous," "balmy/embalmed," "stars," "sorrow," "music," "grass," "moon," and "breeze" will naturally occur in speech addressed in the evening to a nightingale. There are, however, areas of relationship and influence that seem of genuine importance, among which I single out three— Coleridge's influence on Keats's Gothicism, the relationship of Coleridge's Conversation poems to Keats's odes, and the possible role of *Biographia Literaria* as a stimulus to Keats's thinking about the imagination.

Christabel and Keats's Gothicism

Coleridge and Keats are the two best-known Gothic writers in English poetry. There are plenty of other candidates, including the rest of the principal Romantic poets, but none of these produced Gothic works as major and central in their canons as *The Rime of the Ancient Mariner* and *Christabel* among Coleridge's poems and *The Eve of St. Agnes, La Belle Dame,* and *Lamia* among Keats's. What I would stress on the present occasion is the abundance of remarkable similarities between Coleridge's Gothic writings, especially *Christabel,* and Keats's, especially *The Eve of St. Agnes.* Ernest de Selincourt long ago commented that *St. Agnes* "bears slight traces of the influence of *Christabel*" (Keats 1926, 526),[7] but the evidence, taken all together, amounts to much more than just traces. Thomas McFarland, using Harold Bloom's terminology, calls *Christabel* a "strong precursor" of *The Eve of St. Agnes,* "so insistently . . . that one is led to suspect that Keats had Coleridge's poem open before him as he wrote" (1985, 143). James Twitchell even suggests that *The Eve of St. Agnes* "is a conscious retelling" of *Christabel* (1978, 59).[8] Clearly, since it is a biographical certainty that Keats knew *Christabel* when he came to write his own poem, Coleridge's work has to be numbered among Keats's sources. Both poems, to be sure, are products of the medievalizing tendency that increasingly affected literature, architecture, and landscape painting in the latter half of the eighteenth century and continued long into the nineteenth. But in addition to this general influence, Keats's poem is to an extent specifically the product of Coleridge's. Let us examine some of the details.[9]

In both *Christabel* and *The Eve of St. Agnes,* the most important action takes place in and just outside of a medieval castle or manor house, in the middle of the night, in chilly weather. Owls and dogs (Coleridge's "mastiff bitch," Keats's "wakeful bloodhound") are part of the setting, as is the frequently mentioned moonlight. The protagonists, Christabel and Madeline, are innocent maidens. The seducer-antagonists, Geraldine and Porphyro, while different in gender, are alike depicted in terms of witchcraft and magic enchantment. Christabel's hostile father, Sir Leoline, has for counterpart Madeline's hostile kinsmen, Hildebrand and Lord Maurice. There are beadsmen associated with death in both poems (Coleridge's sacristan tells beads between strokes of the heavy bell, 338–42), as well as ineffectively protective females—the hovering spirit of Christabel's mother and Madeline's nurse Angela, both of whom have occasion to refer to the ritual tolling of bells.

The plots are not so easily compared, because Coleridge's, after the initial establishment of half a dozen unrelated oppositions and concerns (Geraldine versus Christabel, Geraldine versus the spirit of Christabel's mother, Sir Leoline's unspecified problems connected with the death of Christabel's mother, Leoline versus Geraldine's supposed kinsman Lord Roland, Bracy's vision of evil, and Geraldine's character as a lamia), is left incomplete. But there are some basic likenesses of incident: the heroines' dreams of their betrothed lovers (associated in both poems with sighing and not speaking); descriptions of the heroines undressing, praying, and getting into bed; entrancement of the heroines; their seeming complicity in the violation of their own innocence; the setting of a star (in *Christabel*) and the moon (in *St. Agnes*) in conjunction with their downfall.

Shared motifs, in addition to those already mentioned, include superstitious omens, prefiguring dreams, and concern with family honor. The many similarities in specific detail include the heroines' blue eyes (215, 290/296), "ringlets" (46/148) bound up in gems or pearls (65/227), and "rich" attire (67/230);[10] association of the heroines with doves (531 ff./198, 333); references to shields and heraldry (162, 435/214, 216); religious oaths ("Jesu, Maria" and "Mary mother" in *Christabel* 54, 69; "Mercy, Jesu" and "O Christ" in the draft of *St. Agnes*) and the likening of characters to religious figures (Christabel is a youthful hermitess, 320, while Porphyro calls himself a pilgrim, 339); moving in stealth (120/244–51—"creep in stealth" in the 1816 text of *Christabel*); the opening of a door with a key (124/369); the unclasping of upper garments and baring of bosom in the descriptions of undressing (248–52/226–30); and a great many references to chambers, ingeniously devised carvings of angels and other figures, and chain-suspended lamps that flicker (178–84/32, 34, 209, 357). For verbal echoes there are Keats's "high disdain" in line 61 (the same phrase occurs in *Christabel* 416 but also is in *Paradise Lost* 1.98); "Never on such a night have lovers met" in line 170 (cf. Coleridge's "Never till now she uttered yell," 150); "hands, together prest" in line 220 and "Clasp'd like a missal" in line 241 (cf. Coleridge's "palms together prest," 286); "Noiseless as fear in a wide wilderness" in line 250 (cf. Coleridge's "Beauteous in a wilderness," 321); and "woe is mine" and "dove forlorn" in lines 328 and 333 (cf. Coleridge's "maiden most forlorn . . . Woe is me," 195–96).

There is a special concentration of words and images relatable to Keats in Coleridge's "Conclusion" to part 1 of *Christabel* (279 ff.)—for example, "palms together prest," "breast," "Fearfully dreaming," "A star hath set," "hermitess," "wilderness," "vision sweet," "saints." Coleridge's summary description of Christabel praying emphasizes (with "sight" in the first line) the pictorial qualities of the lines:

> It was a lovely sight to see
> The lady Christabel, when she
> Was praying at the old oak tree.
>   Amid the jagged shadows
>   Of mossy leafless boughs,
>   Kneeling in the moonlight,
>   To make her gentle vows;
> Her slender palms together prest,
> Heaving sometimes on her breast;
> Her face resigned to bliss or bale—
> Her face, oh call it fair not pale,
> And both blue eyes more bright than clear,
> Each about to have a tear.
>   (279–91)

This is obviously akin, as Charles Lamb noticed,[11] to the same kind of scene-painting in *The Eve of St. Agnes*, as when Madeline kneels to pray in her moonlit bedchamber:

Rose-bloom fell on her hands, together prest,
And on her silver cross soft amethyst,
And on her hair a glory, like a saint:
She seem'd a splendid angel, newly drest,
Save wings, for heaven. . . .

(220–24)

And the lines continuing the description of Christabel quoted above—
"With open eyes . . . Asleep, and dreaming fearfully" (292–93)—not only
have a close counterpart in Keats's description of Madeline's beginning to
awaken from her dream ("Her blue affrayed eyes wide open shone: . . . Her
eyes were open, but she still beheld, / Now wide awake, the vision of her
sleep," 296, 298–99) but may, by constituting both a source and another
example, be critically useful in helping to clear up a problem that has frequently worried interpreters: how Madeline can be "wide awake" and still
dreaming at the same time.

The similarities between *Christabel* and *Lamia*, to establish briefly
one further set of connections,[12] are not so numerous but are significant nonetheless. In *Lamia* the willing or participating victim, counterpart to Christabel, is Lycius, and the counterpart to the lamia-like enchantress Geraldine has become a real lamia enchantress, the eponymous
heroine. Both Geraldine and Lamia are surrounded by ambiguity. Clearly
depicted as evil creatures at the outset (witch and serpent-woman), they
turn increasingly into victims rather than victimizers, gradually gaining
our sympathy accordingly. Keats's Apollonius parallels Coleridge's bard
Bracy as a character who professes to see the reality of the disguised
enchantress.

We are first shown Geraldine and Lamia in a forest, in a state of distress.
Both characters as lamias are associated with brilliant colors (551/1.46–51).
Christabel and Lycius are put in trances (589, 607/1.296–97). Geraldine and
Apollonius have evil eyes (583–85/2.245–48, 277–90, 295–96). Lycius's "ever
thinking [Lamia] / Not mortal, but of heavenly progeny" (2.86–87) echoes
Coleridge's "Yet he, who saw this Geraldine, / Had deemed her sure a thing
divine" (475–76). Perhaps just coincidentally, both *Christabel* and *Lamia* are
formally divided into "Part I" and "Part II" (though again, Keats's poem is
completed and Coleridge's is not). The most obvious relationship between
the poems lies in their snake motifs and imagery. There are only two
famous lamias in English literature: Geraldine and Keats's Lamia.

These particulars, taken by themselves, are only of minor significance. Borrowed phrases or descriptive details or even a character here and there cannot be said to constitute serious indebtedness. But Keats's Gothic poems do repeat certain atmospheric effects of *Christabel:* the archaizing (whether medieval in *St. Agnes* or classical Greek in *Lamia*), the pictorialism, the various supernatural elements, and what Keats, in describing *Lamia* to his brother and sister-in-law, called "that sort of fire . . . which must take hold of people in some way—give them either pleasant or unpleasant sensation. What they want is a sensation of some sort" (*KL*, 2:189). The enumeration of particulars simply serves as evidence that these more general resemblances did not come about by accident—that Keats did read and was influenced by Coleridge's poem.

As I have said more than once elsewhere, however, Keats in his attitude toward the influences helping to shape his career was one of the least anxious writers on record, and his originality is all the more remarkable when viewed in the context of his relationships with earlier writers. This is exactly the point made by McFarland in his consideration of Keats's "dependence" (in *St. Agnes*) on *Christabel:* "this radical dependence was the matrix of a matchlessly original poem . . . the relation of the two poems, in truth, is a choice illustration of the originality paradox." McFarland goes on, in his comparison of the two poets, to locate Keats's independence above all in his practice of creating a "present" reality—in Coleridge's words in a passage from one of the notebooks, "making every thing present to the Imagination"—by means of words and images appealing strongly to all the senses (McFarland 1985, 143–45). It is unclear, however, why Coleridge is not given credit for achieving the same kind of "presentness" in *Christabel.* Indeed, one could argue that, in frequency and variety of appeals to the senses, *Christabel* is the most Keatsian poem in the Coleridge canon.

I should prefer to locate Keats's "radical" difference from his strong precursor in the more down-to-earth human concerns that he emphasizes. In the interactions between evil enchantress (Geraldine) and her innocent mortal victims (first Christabel and then, prospectively, Leoline and perhaps others), Coleridge seems primarily interested, just as his modern interpreters have been, in the enchantress and the concept of evil that she represents. That is to say, his concerns are abstract, metaphysical, theological. *Christabel* for all its pictures may be a fragment not of a narrative but of a philosophical treatise. Keats, on the other hand, in all of his poems cited so far, seems much more interested in the human problems that arise out of the interactions between mortals and nonmortals—problems centered in the basic character of human life (mutability, mortality, the pleasure-pain complexity) and human nature (illusion, delusion, the cheating by the fancy). As the readiest and most impressive example of Gothic narrative poetry at hand for him, *Christabel* unquestionably helped provide Keats with plot devices, descriptive techniques, and a variety of specific details. What Keats did with these, besides merely improving on them (and completing his stories), is create a kind of humanized, domesticated Gothicism. Our lasting impression of these poems associates them with the realm of the human and the real, rather than the magical and ideal—which is probably why Gothicism is so seldom mentioned in Keats criticism.

The Conversation Poems and Keats's Odes

My "argument" printed as epigraph at the beginning of this essay will already have hinted at a connection between a Coleridge poem and one of Keats's odes. In the preceding chapter in this collection, I suggested that the excursion-return structure of Wordsworth's prologue to *Peter Bell,* published around 22 April 1819, just a week before Keats wrote what we usually take to be the first in the series, *Ode to Psyche,* had something to do with the centrality of the same structure in his great odes, especially in *Ode to a Nightingale* and *Ode on a Grecian Urn. The Rime of the Ancient Mariner,* available all along to Keats in *Lyrical Ballads* but republished in the *Sibylline Leaves* collection of 1817, also obviously has this structure and therefore is another possible general influence on the odes.[13] Coleridge's Latin epigraph, first printed with *The Ancient Mariner* in the text of 1817, contrasts "invisible" with "visible things in the universe," connects the invisible with "a greater and better world," and mentions the problem of "attaining knowledge" of such a world. Keats may have read the poem itself as showing how knowledge of a strange world, resulting from an act of imagination, leads to a change in attitude toward the visible world to which the protagonist returns. This, as it happens, is not unlike the basic plot of Keats's most admired odes.

Much more important, however, is the influence of the best of Coleridge's Conversation poems—*The Eolian Harp, This Lime-Tree Bower My Prison, Frost at Midnight,* and *Dejection: An Ode,* four of the principal works published in *Sibylline Leaves.*[14] These can be linked generically with Keats's major odes, all of which were produced in 1819, two years after the publication of *Sibylline Leaves,* in the category that M. H. Abrams has called "the greater Romantic lyric." Abrams characterizes the group as follows:

> They present a determinate speaker in a particularized, and usually a localized, outdoor setting, whom we overhear as he carries on, in a fluent vernacular which rises easily to a more formal speech, a sustained colloquy, sometimes with himself or with the outer scene, but more frequently with a silent human auditor, present or absent. The speaker begins with a description of the landscape; an aspect or change of aspect in the landscape evokes a varied but integral process of memory, thought, anticipation, and feeling which remains closely intervolved with the outer scene. In the course of this meditation the lyric speaker achieves an insight, faces up to a tragic loss, comes to a moral decision, or resolves an emotional problem. Often the poem rounds upon itself to end where it began, at the outer scene, but with an altered mood and deepened understanding which is the result of the intervening meditation.[15] (Abrams 1965, 527–28)

Along with works by Coleridge and Keats, Abrams also includes Wordsworth's *Tintern Abbey* and *Ode: Intimations of Immortality* among his examples (and Shelley's *Ode to the West Wind*), but it is worth noting that *The Eolian Harp, This Lime-Tree Bower,* and *Frost at Midnight* were all written earlier than *Tintern Abbey,* and *Dejection* was written two years before the completion of the Intimations ode. Coleridge thus has priority over Wordsworth as well as Keats in the genre. Indeed, although (as Abrams has shown) there were forerunners of certain elements in the eighteenth-century local poems and in the combination of description and lyric meditation characteristic of the sonnets of Charlotte Smith and William Lisle Bowles, it is not too much to say that Coleridge single-handedly invented the type. But even were Wordsworth the earliest, rather than Coleridge, still the Coleridgean example would be important. Especially in their formal features, Keats's odes are much more clearly descendants of the Conversation poems than they are of *Tintern Abbey* and the Intimations ode.

It is of course naive to write literary history solely on the basis of major authors and titles, as if the contents of the *Norton Anthology* were the only works ever composed. My main point in this brief section may hold up nevertheless: when we look around for antecedents of the form, style, structure, and general character of Keats's odes, not only the readiest but practically the only works that present themselves are Coleridge's Conversation poems. Let us again look at some of the details.

There are several verbal echoes of *Dejection* in *Ode to a Nightingale* (e.g., Coleridge's description of the moon and stars, dull pain, drowsy grief, groans, and the ideas of sending the soul abroad and connecting "Fancy" with "dreams of happiness") and another set of likenesses between the final paragraph of *Frost at Midnight* and *To Autumn* (e.g., Coleridge's "seasons," "redbreast," "mossy apple-tree," "thatch," "sun-thaw," and "eavedrops").[16] More significant similarities lie in some of the elements specified or implied in Abrams's paradigm of the greater Romantic lyric: the dramatic situation of a first-person speaker addressing auditors or recipients who, even if they are not present, or not human, are imagined to be capable of hearing the speaker's words; the structure resulting from representation of the actual processes of thinking, the movement of the speaker's mind now in one direction of thought, now in another; and the familiar pattern of excursion and return (discernible in some degree in all the poems under consideration but especially prominent in *The Eolian Harp, This Lime-Tree Bower,* and the Nightingale and Grecian Urn odes). As to shared subjects and themes, the most obvious are depression resulting from a sense of alienation from the modern world (*Dejection,* the early stanzas of *Ode to a Nightingale*), the corresponding opposite feeling of reconciliation to nature and the world of process (*This Lime-Tree Bower, To Autumn,* the later stanzas of *Nightingale*), and a prolonged concern with psychology, especially the imaginative workings of the mind (central to all the poems at hand).

There are no clear counterparts to Psyche, the Grecian Urn, and the personified goddess Melancholy in Coleridge's Conversation poems, and no frowning wife, sleeping infant, or absent friends in Keats's odes. A more significant difference, however, resides in the presence of time, change, and death as additional complications in Keats's poems and the relative scarcity of these concerns in Coleridge's. Possibly because he was more theologically minded, Coleridge overall gives little space to considerations of mortality, while Keats, in part possibly because he was a medical student (or simply because he was more realistic), is constantly aware of pain and death as inevitable components not just of his speakers' situations but of human life in general. Thus again, just as in my comparison of his Gothic narratives with *Christabel,* Keats may appear to be the more profoundly human-centered poet. This takes nothing away, however, from the fact that his considerable achievement in the ode uses the form, structure, and some other principal features of a type that Coleridge initiated and that he was very much aware of the older poet's work just when he was about to produce his own best contributions to the genre.

Biographia Literaria and Keats's Ideas of Imagination

One of Keats's most frequently cited letters—to Bailey, 22 November 1817—affirms his belief in "the authenticity of the Imagination," compares the imagination to Adam's dream in *Paradise Lost* ("he awoke and found it truth"), and calls "for a Life of Sensations rather than of Thoughts." Here is the familiar central passage:

> O I wish I was as certain of the end of all your troubles as that of your momentary start about the authenticity of the Imagination. I am certain of nothing but of the holiness of the Heart's affections and the truth of Imagination—What the imagination seizes as Beauty must be truth—whether it existed before or not—for I have the same Idea of all our Passions as of Love they are all in their sublime, creative of essential Beauty. . . . The Imagination may be compared to Adam's dream—he awoke and found it truth. I am the more zealous in this affair, because I have never yet been able to perceive how any thing can be known for truth by consequitive reasoning—and yet it must be—Can it be that even the greatest Philosopher ever arrived at his goal without putting aside numerous objections—However it may be, O for a Life of Sensations rather than of Thoughts!

Keats goes on to speculate on the possibility of "enjoy[ing] ourselves here after by having what we called happiness on Earth repeated in a finer tone" and on the identity of "Imagination and its empyreal reflection" with "human Life and its spiritual repetition," and he gives an example of the role of sensation in this "spiritual repetition" (an association of ideas and images from the past stimulated by the hearing of an old melody). The letter also contains, among other notable passages, Keats's remark about happiness of the moment and his taking part in the life of a sparrow pecking about the gravel: "I look not for [happiness] if it be not in the present hour—nothing startles me beyond the Moment. The setting sun will always set me to rights—or if a Sparrow come before my Window I take part in its existence and pick about the Gravel" (*KL*, 1:184–86).

Keats wrote this letter four months after the publication of *Biographia Literaria* (July 1817), two months after spending several weeks with Bailey at Oxford (September and the first week of October), and probably not much more than a week or so after asking the Dilkes to send him *Sibylline Leaves*. Coleridge was much on the minds of both Keats and Bailey at this time (the latter was just then writing about Coleridge in his sermon on the Princess Charlotte Augusta), and it is possible, as I have suggested elsewhere (Stillinger

1971, 151–57), to take their shared concern over imagination as a worry pro-voked specifically by Coleridge's statements about the primary and second-ary imagination in *Biographia Literaria*.

"Imagination"—in various and sundry theories full of problems and inconsistencies—was of course a large concern of the day in Wordsworth's prefaces, Hazlitt's lectures and essays, Leigh Hunt's poems, and much other writing. *Biographia Literaria* deserves singling out mainly because it was the most recent impressive work treating (or, as nearly all the reviewers com-plained, not treating) the subject. But there are elements in Coleridge's def-initions that could have given Bailey (and Keats as well) the "momentary start" that Keats refers to in the first sentence of the offset passage quoted above. Coleridge speaks in chapter 13 of the secondary imagination's activ-ity as a process of dissolving, diffusing, and dissipating in order to re-create and in chapter 14 of the imagination as a "synthetic and magical power" revealing itself in "the balance or reconciliation of opposite or discordant qualities"—sameness with difference, the general with the concrete, idea with image, and so on through Coleridge's long list of oppositions (*BL*, 1:304, 2:16–17). Possibly Bailey had observed (with a "momentary start") that both of these descriptions by Coleridge involve the distribution and recombination of thoughts, images, and sensations already existing in the mind and that these relatively mechanical processes do not allow for the creation of new thoughts, images, and sensations transcending the associa-tion of ideas—the kind of transcendence suggested by Keats's description of the "seizing" of "Beauty" as authentic "truth—whether it existed before or not" and his use of such terms as "empyreal reflection" and "spiritual rep-etition." Perhaps Keats and Bailey read *Biographia Literaria* as an attempt at "consequitive reasoning." It is not impossible that Coleridge, in the lan-guage of Keats's letter, represented for them the philosopher who could *not* "put aside numerous objections" in order to arrive at his goal.

In any case, Coleridge figures prominently in Keats's definition of Nega-tive Capability five weeks later in a handful of sentences (to his brothers, 27 or 28 December 1817) that in essence repeat the idea just cited of the philosopher putting aside numerous objections. Keats tells of going to the theater with Brown and Dilke and having "not a dispute but a disquisition with Dilke, on various subjects":

> several things dovetailed in my mind, & at once it struck me, what quality went to form a Man of Achievement especially in Literature & which Shake-speare posessed so enormously—I mean *Negative Capability,* that is when

man is capable of being in uncertainties, Mysteries, doubts, without any irritable reaching after fact & reason—Coleridge, for instance, would let go by a fine isolated verisimilitude caught from the Penetralium of mystery, from being incapable of remaining content with half knowledge. This pursued through Volumes would perhaps take us no further than this, that with a great poet the sense of Beauty overcomes every other consideration, or rather obliterates all consideration. (*KL*, 1:193–94)

We would not now choose Coleridge to exemplify the lack of Negative Capability. He was far from being a "consequitive" reasoner and is increasingly (by one camp of Coleridgeans, at least) being described as a thinker who in effect, whether he liked it or not, *had* to remain content with half-knowledge. *Biographia Literaria* is, in some interpretations, the least systematic and least logical work in the standard canon of distinguished critical treatises. But Keats, who was no Coleridge scholar, may have seen him differently and may have been helped in his view by some of the reviews of *Biographia Literaria*—for example, by Hazlitt's comment in the *Edinburgh Review* (August 1817) that Coleridge's "metaphysics have been a dead weight on the wings of his imagination" (Muir 1958, 143) and by John Wilson's trenchant remarks in *Blackwood's* (October 1817) on Coleridge's "inveterate and diseased egotism" and his description of Coleridge as a man "who presumptuously came forward to officiate as High-Priest at mysteries beyond his ken—and who carried himself as if he had been familiarly admitted into the Penetralia of Nature, when in truth he kept perpetually stumbling at the very Threshold."[17]

Interestingly, Coleridge—even while epitomizing lack of the quality "which Shakespeare posessed so enormously" in Keats's letter—nevertheless has to be considered a primary source of Keats's thinking on Negative Capability, especially when we make the customary connection between the letter to his brothers of late December 1817 and Keats's remarks to Woodhouse ten months later (27 October 1818) on "the poetical Character":

> As to the poetical Character itself . . . it is not itself—it has no self—it is every thing and nothing—It has no character—it enjoys light and shade; it lives in gusto, be it foul or fair, high or low, rich or poor, mean or elevated—It has as much delight in conceiving an Iago as an Imogen. What shocks the virtuous philosop[h]er, delights the camelion Poet. . . . A Poet is the most unpoetical of any thing in existence; because he has no Identity—he is continually . . . filling some other Body. . . . (*KL*, 1:386–87)

Hazlitt is frequently cited as a principal influence behind this idea, especially in his remarks about Shakespeare in a lecture of 27 January 1818 ("He was the least of an egotist that it was possible to be. He was nothing in himself. . . . He had only to think of any thing in order to become that thing") and his attack on the egotism of the representative Lake Poet in another lecture of 3 March ("He sees nothing but himself and the universe. . . . His egotism is in some respects a madness"—Hazlitt 1930, 5:47–48, 163).[18] Wordsworth certainly entered into Keats's thinking (Keats uses the phrase "wordsworthian or egotistical sublime" in the letter to Woodhouse). But both the conflict between egotism and the sympathetic imagination and reference to Shakespeare as the best example of the "characterless" poet were commonplace, and Coleridge was ahead of Hazlitt in expressing the idea. Here, for example, just to demonstrate Coleridge's affinity with Keats in the matter, are some passages from Coleridge that Keats could *not* have known firsthand:

> Shakespeare became all things well into w^h he infused himself, while all forms, all things became Milton. . . . (J. Tomalin's report of Coleridge's fourth lecture on Shakespeare and Milton, 28 November 1811, in Coleridge 1987, 1:253)

> The great prerogative of genius (& Shakespeare had felt and availed himself of it) is now to swell itself into the dignity of a god and now to keep dormant some part of that nature, to descend to the lowest characters. . . . (J. P. Collier's report of Coleridge's seventh lecture in the same series, 9 December 1811, in Coleridge 1987, 1:308)

> S[hakespeare] shaped his characters out of the Nature within—but we cannot so safely say, out of *his own* Nature, as an *individual person.* . . . Shakespear in composing had no I but the I representative. (Coleridge's notes for his seventh lecture in the series of 1818, 17 February, in Coleridge 1987, 1:148–49)

> Shakspeare's poetry is characterless; that is, it does not reflect the individual Shakspeare; but John Milton himself is in every line of the Paradise Lost. (*Table-Talk* entry, 12 May 1830, in Coleridge 1865, 71)[19]

Among works that Keats was familiar with (whether or not he actually read or studied them), there is a concentration of such observations in *Biographia Literaria*, especially in chapter 15, on "poetic power" and Shakespeare, which opens with the declaration that "our *myriad-minded* Shakspear" was "the greatest genius, that perhaps human nature has yet produced" (*BL,* 2:19).[20] Speaking generally about indications of the promise of such genius, Coleridge specifies, first, excellence in versification and the musical qualities of poetry, and then, second, "the choice of subjects very remote from the private interests and circumstances of the writer himself" (2:20). In elaborating this second point, using Shakespeare's *Venus and Adonis* as the example, Coleridge describes the poet's consciousness "not only of [his characters'] every outward look and act, but of the flux and reflux of the mind in all its subtlest thoughts and feelings," the poet himself all the while "unparticipating in the passions" and illustrating "the alienation, and . . . the utter *aloofness* of the poet's own feelings, from those of which he is at once the painter and the analyst" (2:21–22). The full description of Shakespeare's power comes at the end of the chapter, in a comparison with Milton much like those quoted above from his lecture of November 1811 and from *Table-Talk:*

> Shakspeare . . . first studied patiently, meditated deeply, understood minutely, till knowledge become habitual and intuitive wedded itself to his habitual feelings, and at length gave birth to that stupendous power, by which he stands alone. . . . [Shakespeare] darts himself forth, and passes into all the forms of human character and passion, the one Proteus of the fire and the flood; . . . [Milton] attracts all forms and things to himself, into the unity of his own ideal. All things and modes of action shape themselves anew in the being of Milton; while Shakspeare becomes all things, yet for ever remaining himself. (2:26–28)

Clarence D. Thorpe says of these passages from chapter 15: "Coleridge is here stating a theory held by other romanticists, by Hazlitt and Keats in particular, which is most happily characterized by Keats as 'negative capability.'" "Keats's idea closely parallels Coleridge's thought when in various utterances Coleridge explains Shakespeare's power of becoming one with his characters to the point of intimate awareness of not only their 'every outward look and act but of the flux and reflux of the mind in all its subtlest thoughts and feelings,' at the same time remaining himself, in self-possessed, aloof abstraction" (Thorpe 1944, 395–96).[21]

Two later passages of *Biographia Literaria* offer possible antecedents for the "negative" part of Keats's Negative Capability—Coleridge's description, in his discussion of Wordsworth's matter-of-factness, of "that *negative* faith, which simply permits the images presented to work by their own force, without either denial or affirmation of their real existence by the judgment" (*BL*, chap. 22, 2:134),[22] and his explanation of what it takes for a reader to accept the wickedness of characters like Don Juan and Milton's Satan: "The poet asks only of the reader, what as a poet he is privileged to ask: viz. that sort of negative faith in the existence of such a being, which we willingly give to productions *professedly ideal*" (chap. 23, 2:214). In his notes to both passages Bate refers back to Coleridge's famous phrase in chapter 14, "that willing suspension of disbelief for the moment, which constitutes poetic faith" (2:6). It is not difficult to relate "willing suspension of disbelief" to the ability to remain "in uncertainties, Mysteries, doubts, without any irritable reaching after fact & reason" in Keats's Negative Capability letter or to relate Coleridge's description of Shakespeare's darting himself forth, passing into all the forms of human character, becoming all things, "the one Proteus of the fire and the flood," to Keats's concept of the "camelion Poet . . . filling some other Body" in the October 1818 letter to Woodhouse. Whether or not we insist on direct connections, the materials of Negative Capability were available to hand, prominent and reiterated, in *Biographia Literaria.*

In addition to Coleridge's possible contributions to the formulation of ideas in Keats's letters, there is, to speak very generally, the example of Keats as a practitioner of Coleridgean primary and secondary imagination. Engell in part 2 of his and Bate's introduction to *Biographia Literaria* quotes Keats's phrase "a greeting of the Spirit" (*KL,* 1:243) to elucidate Coleridge's notion of the "active and productive co-operation of the perceiving (and conceiving) mind with the given data of what is external to us" (*BL,* 1:civ–cv). McFarland uses Keats as a principal exemplar, in *The Eve of St. Agnes, Ode to a Nightingale,* and *To Autumn,* of "the poetic working of secondary imagination" (McFarland 1985, 137–47). It is by now fairly well established that Keats became increasingly doubtful of the "authenticity" of the imagination that he wrote about to Bailey in November 1817, and it can be argued that his skepticism toward the visionary in practically all his major narratives and lyrics of 1819 is tantamount to an acceptance of the naturalized imagination central in the poetry and theories of Coleridge and Wordsworth.[23] The subject is too large and ill-defined for satisfactory treatment in a few paragraphs here, but the mature Keats clearly aligns with the Coleridge-Wordsworthian view of imagination rather than with the more transcendental and visionary schemes of Blake and Shelley.

* * *

Keats has been publicly linked with Coleridge ever since Anthony and William Galignani issued their pirated collection *The Poetical Works of Coleridge, Shelley, and Keats* in Paris at the end of 1829. The Galignani edition was frequently reprinted in the United States, giving at least some readers the impression that the three writers were intimately associated with one another. An 1843 obituary of Isabel Keats in the Louisville *Daily Journal,* for example, mentions that she was "a niece of John Keats, the young English poet, who was the friend and the peer of Coleridge and Shelley" (*KC,* 1:c). As we have seen, there are some interesting biographical connections between Coleridge and Keats, some timely chronological connections (Coleridge's publications in 1816–17 just when Keats was most open to influence and most in need of guidance), a number of significant Coleridgean echoes in Keats's poetry and letters, and general likenesses between the two writers in subject matter, theme, and even basic structures of thinking.

In spite of this evidence of important influence, however, Keats was vastly different from Coleridge in temperament, philosophical tendency, poetic sensibility—in practically every category in which the two men and their works can be compared. Albert Gérard, in an essay written more than half a century ago, makes an interesting contrast based on their theories of knowledge, a contrast obviously drawn to some extent from Keats's own remarks about Coleridge in the Negative Capability letter:

> Coleridge's appeal lies in the fact that he is that phenomenon which has almost completely disappeared from the surface of the earth west of the Elbe: the man who knows all the answers. To be sure, his profuse and successive answers to the ultimate questions about the nature of life and of the universe were many and, as often as not, contradictory—but he held them all with a serene certainty which we cannot but envy. . . . It never occurred to Keats to advertise his conceptions in this way. Coleridge's irritating cocksureness was completely foreign to him. Indeed, he was always careful, in expressing his ideas, to avoid any discussion about their objective value. With his customary frankness and clear-sightedness he generally stresses their personal and subjective character. By so doing, he undoubtedly came nearer than Coleridge to the modern view of belief. (Gérard 1951, 259)

We have learned a great deal more about both Keats and Coleridge in the interim, but Gérard's observations still ring true. Keats was the more human-centered, the more realistic, the more skeptical in his character and writings alike—qualities that have made him one of the heroes of modern literature.

4
Reading Keats's Plots

A MULTITUDE OF CAUSES unknown to former times have combined to produce, in the minds of students, teachers, scholars, and English department administrators, a sharp and theoretically unjustifiable distinction between poetry and other forms of fiction. "Fiction" has come to mean exclusively prose fiction, and journals with titles such as *Modern Fiction Studies* and *Studies in Short Fiction* are universally understood as having to do with novels and short stories. In principle, no one should object to the proposition that *Paradise Lost, Don Juan,* and *The Ring and the Book,* for example, are long fictions or that *The Sick Rose, La Belle Dame sans Merci,* and *Peter Quince at the Clavier* are short fictions. But in practice, as everyone knows, poems are almost always read, taught, and written about in ways markedly different from those used in the study of prose fiction.

In the last two or three decades nearly all the genuine advances in practical criticism—most especially the advances that have increased our appreciation of the *art* of literary art—have been made in connection with the novel and the short story. Thanks to Seymour Chatman and Gérard Genette (to name two extremely helpful contributors to our understanding), readers and critics who study the novel nowadays routinely consider such things as the scope of the subject matter and the scale of detail with which it is treated; the basic structure of the plot and the way events are ordered and emphasized; how many plots the work has and, if there are several, how the plots are related to one another; who the major characters are; who is the protagonist, who is the antagonist, and how the various lesser characters relate to these principals and how they function in other ways in the work; how the characters are presented and characterized; the various kinds of point of view; the presence of a real or an implied narrator; the presence of a real or an implied reader or listener or spectator or "narratee"; the function and importance of the setting of the work; the function and importance of time (or levels of time), along with considerations of tense, duration, and frequency of repetition; and the style or styles of the discourse.

But genre traditions, definitions, and expectations—in other ways so helpful in sharpening our perceptions and appreciation—have tended to set poetry apart from these considerations. Readers and critics of poetry, even at this late date in the history of practical criticism, are still primarily concerned with idea, theme, and "philosophy," seeking in effect to replace the literary work in process (what it *is*, what it *does*) with interpretive conversion, paraphrase, or translation (what it *means*). For much of the poetry of the last two centuries there is a decided mismatch between what the poets themselves thought they were doing and what teachers and critics (and as a consequence readers) have been extracting and describing. Wallace Stevens is just one of many writers who have commented on this kind of critical reductionism: "ideas are not bad in a poem," he says, but when "converted" into prose statement "they are a frightful bore" (1966, 250).

Poems have plots, characters, points of view, settings, and the rest just as regularly as works of prose fiction do. Here, to focus on just the first of these elements, is a short list of the commoner types of plot occurring in narrative and lyric poems of the literature that I know best, British Romantic poetry. There are numerous "binary" oppositions and conflicts, with resolutions involving the triumph of one side, a merging of the two sides, or the introduction of some third term. Many of these oppositions occur in somebody's mind, so that the events are changes of thought or feeling. In the commonest structures of this type, ignorance gives over to knowledge, delusion to awareness, loss to recompense or reconciliation. In more overtly dramatic and narrative poems we have stories of journeys, voyages, and quests. Most frequently the journey takes the form of an excursion and return—excursion into some ideal realm, followed by a changed protagonist's return to reality. There are a great many encounters: the two most common are the encounter between an imagined situation and a matter-of-fact reality (as in Wordsworth's *Resolution and Independence*) and the encounter involving enchantment and unhappy awakening (as in Keats's *La Belle Dame* and *Lamia*). Both kinds produce reversals representing a process of education that may be beneficial but also can sometimes be fatal.

Another type of plot involves violation and its consequence—the violation of a taboo, for example (as in *The Rime of the Ancient Mariner*), or the violation of space. In a sizable number of poems we find competition, crowding, or impingement between spatial divisions. These structures could be collected and studied together as stories of territorial dispute. Other structures depend on layers or divisions of time, most often with an attempt to combine or unify the different layers. There are a great many frame situations in Romantic poems. (Percy Shelley's *Ozymandias,* for example, contains a frame within a frame within a frame. At the core there is King Ozymandias and his vanity. Then there are the ancient sculptor's depiction of Ozymandias's character, the modern traveler who has come upon the remains of the sculptor's monument, and most immediately the first-person narrator who has learned of these things from the traveler. If we add Shelley the creator of the poem to the list, we have four or five levels of narration in a text only fourteen lines long.) Some of the structures are quite elaborate, as in the warp-and-woof complexity of satisfaction and dismay that makes up the texture of Wordsworth's *Tintern Abbey* or the double helical structure of turn and counterturn that has been described in Coleridge's *The Eolian Harp.*[1]

There is considerable usefulness in paying more attention to the plots of poems, the structures that organize the materials of whatever stories we have at hand. One generally workable method of analyzing plot is to identify a beginning state of equilibrium, then a major event or series of events representing disturbance of this initial harmony, and then a progress toward resolution in some way related to the initial state. Another (similarly ancient) approach to plot is one that identifies first of all a protagonist, then some goal or desire associated with the protagonist, then some obstacle that stands in the way of what the protagonist wants, and finally the outcome— what in fact happens—whether comic, tragic, or ironic. When one identifies a protagonist, sees what the protagonist wants, sees what stands in the way, and then follows the events through to a closure, one is, or could be, centrally involved in the dynamics of a literary work. With poetry, as with prose fiction, it is frequently in just such dynamics that the main interest and pleasure reside—not in paraphrasable "meaning" but in story elements as they are shaped and presented in the plot.

As a practical teaching device, there are immediate advantages in the use of both of these simple methods of analysis. Imagine a classroom discussion in which one takes the Wedding-Guest (rather than the Mariner) as the protagonist of *The Rime of the Ancient Mariner*. What does the Wedding-

Guest want? Obviously he wants to get to the wedding. What stands in the way? What stands in the way is a bearded old man who grabs him by the arm, fixes him with a glittering eye, and says, "There was a ship"! This might seem a silly way to begin analyzing so major a work as *The Ancient Mariner,* but it does, for purposes of discussion, immediately call attention to the dramatic frame provided by the encounter and interaction of Wedding-Guest and Mariner, and to the wedding background of the Mariner's tale and, when it is followed out to the end, the artistically significant fact that the Wedding-Guest never does get to the wedding but instead turns "from the bridegroom's door." For another example, try taking Dorothy Wordsworth (rather than her brother William, or the "speaker") as the protagonist of *Tintern Abbey.* What does sister Dorothy want? Perhaps she'd like to say a few words. What stands in the way? In this case it is her brother, who talks nonstop for 159 lines. This example may seem even sillier than the preceding, but again it has the practical result of calling attention to the dramatic situation of the poem, the presence of a silent auditor, and the fact that the speaker does go on at considerable length (a circumstance noted at the time by Keats, Hazlitt, and several thousand other contemporaries).

But these may be considered mainly gimmicks to initiate discussion. I should like to give five examples in which narrative analysis of poetic plots may clarify some disputed matters of interpretation. Sometimes such analysis serves to illuminate what is going on in a work, and sometimes, I should emphasize, it is more useful in showing what is not going on. In this latter situation, narrative analysis may point the way toward relocating the center of interest. The first three of my examples are of this sort, examples in which narrative analysis shows up discrepancies between what actually happens in a text and what the critics typically describe as happening, with the suggestion that we may be going out of our way to overlook the most effective elements of the work we want to understand. The results should apply equally to interpretation and teaching.

The Eve of St. Agnes

Until just a few decades ago, *The Eve of St. Agnes* was mainly read as a romantic love story, a Romeo and Juliet affair with a happy ending. Keats's young lover Porphyro enters a hostile castle, rescues his beloved Madeline, and takes her away to be his bride. More recently, critics have noticed that some of Porphyro's actions do not fit very well with his purported character as romantic hero. Early on in the poem he proposes a "stratagem" (139) that shocks Madeline's old nurse Angela, and then he threatens to rouse Madeline's kinsmen—in effect threatens to get himself killed—if Angela refuses to aid him. Next comes the unfolding of the stratagem: Porphyro has himself taken to a hiding place in Madeline's bedchamber whence he can spy on her as she undresses. Subsequently, after she goes to bed and he determines that she is fast asleep, he climbs into her bed and, while she is still asleep (or in some sort of dreaming state in which she is unaware of what is actually happening), he has his way with her.[2] Madeline, awakening to find a real Porphyro in her bed, is astonished and dismayed. Pretty clearly this is bad behavior on Porphyro's part, and it is connected in the poem with various images of witchcraft, sorcery, Peeping Tomism, seduction, and even rape.

But Madeline is also doing some things that go against the idea of pure romance. She is totally engrossed in pursuing a superstitious ritual known as fasting St. Agnes' Fast, according to which, by following certain practices, she hopes to see her future husband in a dream, make love with him, and awaken still a virgin. The ritual is viewed by Angela as a foolish amusement; Porphyro sees it as the perfect occasion for the working of his stratagem; the narrator takes a scornful attitude, calling the ritual an old wives' tale and a whim and describing Madeline as hoodwinked with faery fancy, metaphorically both blind and dead. We now have a Romeo and Juliet story in which the Romeo character is a Peeping Tom and cowardly seducer and the Juliet character is shown to be renouncing life in favor of a foolish and empty ritual. And this story is framed by a series of images of freezing cold and death: the opening stanzas describe the bitter chill of St. Agnes' Eve and the suffering of animals and humans and even the "sculptur'd dead" (14) in the Beadsman's chapel connected to Madeline's castle. The closing stanzas describe an icy storm, nightmares, and the deaths of both Angela and the Beadsman. At face value, there are many things wrong in this poem, and critics have not been successful in straightening them all out.[3]

In this example, narrative analysis might begin with an attempt to determine who in fact is the protagonist of the story. Madeline is the first major character introduced, as the narration turns "sole-thoughted" to her in the fifth stanza; then Porphyro enters the poem in the ninth stanza with all the fanfare of a stock romantic hero: "Meanwhile, across the moors, / Had come young Porphyro, with heart on fire / For Madeline." One or the other of these principals ought to be the protagonist, but because of some basic resemblances between Keats's poem and the Romeo and Juliet story, readers have sometimes taken the protagonist to be the two characters together, a pair of young lovers facing the oppositions of hostile kinsfolk, an icy storm, and a perilous journey back to Porphyro's home across the moors.

What narrative analysis produces (if I may condense a lengthy account into a few sentences) is a structure of two quests, each with its own protagonist, that through much of the poem are in direct opposition to one another. The initial quest is a spiritual one, Madeline's for her St. Agnes' Eve dream and the idealized (and innocent) union with her future husband. The second, countering quest is a physical one, Porphyro's for sight of and then sexual possession of Madeline's person not in any dream but in physical reality. Both characters desire union, but union in the different worlds of dream and actuality.[4] If we impose values from other poems that Keats wrote about the same time, Porphyro's world of actuality is the one with superior claims. But then Madeline is the more sympathetic character: after the first third of the poem, in which Keats makes much of her self-delusion in pursuing her ritual, the emphasis is increasingly on her role as victim of a stratagem, and at the same time Porphyro's actions are almost irreversibly damaging to his status as romantic hero.

At the end of the poem Porphyro calls Madeline his bride and says that he has a home for her across the moors, and they "glide, like phantoms" (361) out of the castle and disappear into the icy storm. The last lines describing them are: "And they are gone: ay, ages long ago / These lovers fled away into the storm" (370–71). For some (romantically minded) readers, everything is concluded satisfactorily: Porphyro and Madeline are married and live happily ever after. For other readers, these final lines have an ominous ring to them: the lovers "fled away into the storm" and have not been heard from since.

Narrative analysis ultimately shows the inadequacy of any simple reading or interpretation of the poem that is based primarily on the plot. The plot is a messy one, with self-destructive tendencies at almost every turn. Now what, one may ask, is the use of a method of analysis that serves to point up flaws and inconsistencies in the plot? The answer is not too difficult: when we have a poem that (in Horace's and Dr. Johnson's terms) has outlived its century, has attained seemingly permanent status as one of the most often read and admired works in English, *and* has a seriously flawed plot, then we must look elsewhere for the principal causes of our enjoyment. Nowadays, in my own teaching of the poem, I am interested not so much in Porphyro's stratagem and the hoodwinking of Madeline as I am in the numerous distancing elements that *may* make the story romantically acceptable after all. I have my students focus on Keats's style; on the effects achieved by the use of an archaic (and archaizing) metrical form; on the color imagery (which employs mainly shades of red and blue and combinations of the two colors such as purple, rose, and amethyst); on the numerous animals, birds, and insects in the poem; and more generally on the pictorial and painterly qualities of the descriptions. I show photographic slides of medieval tapestries, stained glass, and illuminated manuscripts (all of which are also preponderantly red and blue and are full of animals and birds). Keats himself used the terms "colouring" and "drapery" in the most suggestive of his own critical comments on the poem (*KL*, 2:234). Narrative analysis of his plot might serve to get us more involved in these elements of "colouring" and "drapery," which I have come to think of as the most important sources of the poem's pleasurable effects.

Lamia

A good second example is Keats's last complete narrative poem, *Lamia,* a work of 708 lines based on a brief story in Burton's *Anatomy of Melancholy* about a young man named Lycius who fell in love with what Burton (in a passage always printed at the end of Keats's text) describes as "a phantasm in the habit of a fair gentlewoman." Lycius "tarried with her a while to his great content, and at last married her," but then at the wedding-feast found out that his bride was in reality "a serpent, a lamia," whereupon, as Burton says, "she, plate, house, and all that was in it, vanished in an instant." In Keats's retelling, the shock of this awful discovery and loss is so great that Lycius falls dead on the spot.

Here we have, or appear to have, a story of mortal enchantment followed by abrupt awakening to reality. The poem is frequently read as allegory, and certain passages might seem to support an allegorical interpretation: there are several references to dreaming and to the differences between gods and mortals; we are told that the dreams of gods are "Real," with the implication that the dreams of mortals are, by contrast, false or unreliable (1.126–28); mortal lovers grow pale, while gods who are in love with goddesses do not; there is a significant paragraph about the inseparability of pleasure and pain in human life and about Lycius's mistaken belief that Lamia will separate out the pleasure for him (1.185–96); there is a memorable passage toward the end about "cold philosophy" putting all charms to flight and even destroying a rainbow (2.229–38). But critics have not been able to discover an allegorical interpretation (or any other) that accords with the various elements of story, character, and tone.

What narrative analysis may offer here is an explanation of why the critics have not been successful. When we examine the work to see who is the protagonist—trying out both Lycius and Lamia, the two main characters—we find that there are in fact two different stories in the poem, one of which has to do with the enchantment of Lycius and the other of which has to do with the exposure of Lamia. In the first story, which occupies the last two-thirds of part 1, we are shown Lamia's transformation from serpent to a woman's form and given some clues to her real character: she is associated with demons; she has "elfin blood" running "in madness"; she goes through convulsions and foams at the mouth, and the foam causes the grass to wither and die; her permanent state is an abstraction of "pain and ugliness" (1.146–64). The story then proceeds with the first encounter between Lycius and Lamia in her womanly form. Lycius is instantly smitten, and they withdraw from the world to live together in "a place unknown" (1.388). There are various hints that Lycius is acting under a magic spell: he is "shut up in mysteries" and his mind is "wrapp'd like his mantle" when he first meets Lamia; he falls into a swoon, and when Lamia arouses him with a kiss he is described as wakening "from one trance . . . Into another"; his life is said to be "tangled in her mesh" (1.241–42, 295–97). Lycius is clearly the protagonist of this first story, and Lamia—as evil and deceitful enchantress—is here the antagonist.

In part 2, however, we have quite a different story. Lycius's human nature comes to the fore, and as an expression of both arrogance and vanity he insists on showing off his bride at a wedding-feast. The feast is held, and among the many guests comes, uninvited, Lycius's old tutor, the clear-eyed realist Apollonius. Apollonius exposes Lamia as a serpent, Lamia vanishes, and Lycius dies. In this second story it is primarily Lamia, now a beautiful woman become tragic figure, who has our sympathy. She is the protagonist, while first Lycius and then Apollonius are the antagonists.

I think it is this shift in the center of protagonism—as victim and victimizer exchange roles in the two parts—that has caused critics trouble in their attempts to interpret the poem as a whole. As a matter of biographical fact, there was a six-week interval between the time that Keats completed part 1 and the time that he began part 2, during which he wrote four acts of *Otho the Great* and parts of *The Fall of Hyperion* and *King Stephen*. Possibly he lost track of his narrative intentions, or changed them, during this interruption in the composition. Possibly he became confused about his narrative point of view. This is a once-upon-a-time story in which a discernible narrator gets increasingly excited by the story he is telling—to the point where, toward the end, he berates Lycius as a madman, hands out "spear-grass and the spiteful thistle" to Apollonius, and utters some extravagant and unconvincing statements about the bad effects of "cold philosophy" (2.228–38). Perhaps Keats was experimenting with a new kind of narrative voice, and the experiment did not work.

In any case, he wrote the poem initially as an attempt to gain popularity and make money, and he hoped to do this by arousing his readers' senses. "I am certain," he says in a letter to his brother and sister-in-law, "there is that sort of fire in [*Lamia*] which must take hold of people in some way—give them either pleasant or unpleasant sensation. What they want is a sensation of some sort" (*KL*, 2:189). In this, it turns out (at least in the long run), he pretty well succeeded. The critics continue to have trouble in interpreting, but the readers continue to get "sensation"—for example, in this short passage near the end, when Lamia is rendered powerless by Apollonius's steady gaze, Lycius cries out in anguish, and the noise of the wedding-feast dies down to silence:

> "Lamia!" he cried—and no soft-toned reply.
> The many heard, and the loud revelry
> Grew hush; the stately music no more breathes;
> The myrtle sicken'd in a thousand wreaths.
> By faint degrees, voice, lute, and pleasure ceased;
> A deadly silence step by step increased,
> Until it seem'd a horrid presence there,
> And not a man but felt the terror in his hair.
>
> (2.261–68)

La Belle Dame sans Merci

In *The Eve of St. Agnes* and *Lamia,* regardless of our problems with meaning, we at least know what the characters are saying and doing. The antecedent details of the two stories are cloudy, and the surviving characters' futures are entirely speculative (Do Madeline and Porphyro even survive? Where does Lamia vanish to?), but the unfolding action of the stories is fairly clear. In *La Belle Dame sans Merci*, by contrast, there is little clarity about anything. The characters and events are undoubtedly symbolic, much more so than in the two longer narratives, and the symbolism has always seemed to demand interpretation. But we never learn for sure what ails the knight. His own explanation at the end ("And this is why . . .")

merely intensifies the confusion. In this poem, Keats gets considerable effects from what he leaves out.

One significant element of structure is the questioner, who speaks the first three stanzas and then presumably stays around to hear the knight's reply, which fills the remaining nine stanzas. Ostensibly the questioner's purpose is to ask, "what can ail thee?" But along with his questions, he gives us details of the knight's condition ("alone," "loitering," "haggard," "woe-begone," with a deathly complexion pictured in terms of a lily, "anguish moist and fever dew," and a withering rose); characterizes the landscape (withered sedge, absence of birds, absence of song); and says something about the time of year, mentioning the squirrel's granary and the completion of the harvest. The questioner also, of course, provides the occasion for the knight to tell what happened to him. Perhaps most important of all, Keats's question-and-answer structure reinforces the effects of the poem's subtitle ("A Ballad"), the balladlike stanza, and the archaizing that begins with "knight at arms" in the first line. This piece announces itself as belonging to a class of poems in which the standard materials are elemental, unexplained, and even supernatural occurrences. Naturally there will be a meeting with a mysterious lady. Naturally there will be singing, strange food, lovemaking, bad dreams, and a calamitous reversal.

The wretched knight is of course the protagonist, and his goal, once he encounters her, is union with the beautiful lady. Some major problems are hinted at: he is a mortal, and she is "a fairy's child"; his "latest dream" is a nightmare warning of thralldom and death; and when he awakens, the lady has disappeared. His dream has the effect, on the knight (in the story) and on us (in reading), of turning his beloved Belle Dame into the antagonist, a merciless enchantress who will add him—perhaps already has added him—to her collection of ruined kings, princes, and warriors. "And *this* is why. . . ." He awakens on the cold hill's side, and the poem comes to an abrupt end.

Old-school biographical critics—the same who interpreted Lycius, Lamia, and Apollonius as Keats, Fanny Brawne, and Keats's housemate Charles Brown, principally because both Brown and Apollonius were bald!—have read *La Belle Dame* as an allegory involving Keats and Fanny Brawne (or, more abstractly, Keats and love), and also Keats and tuberculosis (Keats and death). Later writers have focused on categorical differences between the knight as mortal and La Belle Dame as nonmortal, and between the real world of the cold hill's side and the romance world of the lady's "elfin grot." La Belle Dame has even been taken to be another symbol of visionary imagination and the knight to be another of Keats's hoodwinked dreamers. But the poem itself never explains its symbolism, and every interpretation, even the old-school biographical, has to remain hypothetical. The actions are made logical solely by the poem's genre. They are just the sort of actions that happen in ballads.

The Eve of St. Mark

Oddly, *The Eve of St. Mark,* a 119-line fragment that Keats abandoned before setting his plot in motion (if he ever had one), is full of narrative materials and much more readily interpreted than *La Belle Dame.* As it stands, *St. Mark* is primarily description, and the center of interest is a solitary woman reading by a window. The work begins with an outdoors scene: it is a Sunday in early spring, the church bell is ringing for evening prayers, a procession of townspeople makes its way to the church, and we are given various details of background sights and sounds—the cleanliness of the streets, the presence of springtime flowerings, the whispering of the people as they walk along, the shuffling of their feet on the pavement, the music of the church organ. The second and third paragraphs set the indoors scene, where Keats's protagonist, Bertha, is reading about the life of Saint Mark in an old book that is patched, torn, and decorated with pictures of stars, angels, martyrs, candlesticks, and Saint Mark's winged lion. Bertha has been reading all day long, and although she could see the streets and square outside her window if she looked out, she instead has devoted all her attention to the elaborately decorated book. She is described as having an "aching neck and swimming eyes" and as being "dazed with saintly imageries" (55–56).

Next we are returned briefly to the outdoors scene. It is now nighttime. The town has become silent except for the occasional footstep of somebody returning home, and the jackdaws that earlier were noisy have gone to rest "Pair by pair." Their resting place is the church belfry, where the former ringing of the Sabbath prayer bell is replaced by "music of the drowsy chimes" striking at intervals through the night (63–66). The remainder of the fragment presents further details of the indoors scene. Bertha lights a lamp to continue her reading, and the lamp creates a giant shadow of her body on the ceiling, on the walls, and on various furnishings of the room: chair, parrot's cage, and a fire screen decorated with "many monsters"— Siamese doves, Lima mice, birds of paradise, macaw, Indian songbird, Angora cat. Her shadow fills the room "with wildest forms and shades, / As though some ghostly queen of spades / Had come to mock behind her back" (78–87). Keats adds a short passage of imitation Middle English supposedly quoted from the book Bertha is reading, and then the fragment breaks off in the middle of a line.

There is a clear running contrast between details of the outdoors scene and details indoors. The townspeople outside are a crowd, and they are engaged in a social and communal activity, going to church. They also are associated with home and family life, and even the jackdaws have retired like married couples, in pairs. Bertha by contrast is solitary and remote. The townspeople live in a commonplace actuality where time is mostly in the present. Bertha, set apart from this commonplace world, lives amid exotic surroundings, and instead of the townspeople's present time she is totally engrossed in the past, specifically in the martyrdom of Saint Mark, which happened a very long time ago. The townspeople are a plodding group. They move slowly and demurely, shuffle their feet, and whisper. The contrasting images of the indoors scene include perplexity, aching neck, swimming eyes, dazzling, glowering, wild forms, mockery, a dance of shadows—in short, a great deal of nervous, uncomfortable, and even in places tortured sensation and movement.

It would be easy to make up a story growing out of the situation that Keats has depicted: "Once upon a time there was a maiden named Bertha who lived alone near the church and spent all her time reading an old book about Saint Mark. One day. . . ." But as Keats left it, the fragment simply presents these scenes, with their contrasting atmospheres, tones, sensations, and some not very clear implications about different ways that people spend their time. Keats himself, if we can take a hint from a letter in which he copied the fragment, seems to have been mainly interested in the atmosphere and sensations he was creating. He calls it a work "quite in the spirit of Town quietude. I th[i]nk it will give you the sensation of walking about an old county Town in a coolish evening" (*KL,* 2:201).

The interpreting critics have not hesitated to discover conflicts of opposing sides. In one reading, dating back to 1946, the outdoors scene represents the "humdrum life of a provincial town in nineteenth-century England"; Bertha is a "modern" woman reading medieval legends and longing for the glories of a sainthood no longer possible (Houghton 1946). Another critic, two decades later, sees just the opposite values assigned to the contrasting situations: the townspeople and their activities are presented sympathetically, and Bertha is making a mistake—"by ignoring the life in the village outside her room, [she] is cheating herself of reality" (Stillinger 1968a). A still later writer, perceiving a contrast between "two modes of religious experience," thinks the fragment shows Keats responding "to religious matter by subordinating it to the process of reading about it" (Luke 1970). Each of these interpretations fits a selection of the details, and each, even when in conflict with the others, usefully brings out implications that probably are somewhere in the text and certainly were at one time or another in Keats's mind. The point here, though, is that even with a fragment where there is no story as such, the sorting out of oppositions is fundamentally an exercise of narrative analysis.

Ode on a Grecian Urn

A final consideration is the use of narrative analysis in connection with the greater Romantic lyric.[5] Lyric poems are generally, as one would expect, the least susceptible to narrative analysis—most obviously for the reason that being lyrics, they are not narratives. The protagonist of Keats's *To Autumn* wants to describe and celebrate the season of autumn. What stands in the way? Virtually nothing, so he proceeds forthwith. The speaker of *Ode on Melancholy* assumes the posture of a professor lecturing on the whereabouts and nature of melancholy, but apart from experiencing a little difficulty in getting his thoughts together, this protagonist also meets no obstacle and in the received text completes his lecture in three stanzas.

But in other lyric poems—for example, Coleridge's *Frost at Midnight* and Wordsworth's *Tintern Abbey* and *Ode: Intimations of Immortality*—there are opposing contrasts and tensions and a progress of turns and counter-turns that can be described and schematized in narrative terms. Still other lyrics have a large component of actual story. Outside the Romantic period there is the handy example of Yeats's *Sailing to Byzantium.* Everyone would agree that this is a major lyric poem, and yet it has the form of a sea voyage and in four stanzas tells the story of an old man who leaves his native country and sails to Byzantium, where he enrolls his soul in singing school and makes plans to sing to the emperor and the lords and ladies of the city. Keats's *Ode to a Nightingale* is similarly describable as the story of an excursion, this time with a return to something like the place where the speaker-protagonist started.

The fact that narrative analysis works more successfully with some poems than with others is itself a valuable piece of critical information. It is one way of illustrating the difference between lyrics that are essentially static in character and those that are essentially dynamic.[6] Poems such as *To Autumn* and *Ode on Melancholy* have their minds made up before they begin. They are statements rather than processes, statements of thoughts already arrived at before the speakers begin speaking. Poems such as *Frost at Midnight, Tintern Abbey, Ode: Intimations of Immortality,* and *Ode to a Nightingale* are more complicated. They represent the actual processes of thinking and take their shape from the movement of the protagonist's mind, going now in one direction and now in another. Lyrics in this latter class are at least implied narratives, and often they are, like Yeats's and Keats's excursions, explicit narratives.

Keats's *Ode on a Grecian Urn* is seemingly inexhaustible as a subject of critical interpretation. In this poem, as probably in all lyric poems, we may take the first-person speaker as the principal protagonist. The antagonist here is an abstraction—time (and the attendant mutability, natural process, and death)—and what the speaker wants, as we can tell by his admiring exclamations when he contemplates the situation of the lovers, the piper, and the trees depicted on the Grecian urn, is timelessness (the absence of mutability, process, and death). But, as we learn from the opening lines, the speaker-protagonist is a person interested in history, stories, and legends, and in the course of his musings he attempts his own narrative analysis of the situations represented on the urn. Taking the urn-figures as a collective protagonist, he discovers that *their* antagonist is timelessness (just the opposite of his own), as embodied in the increasingly dismal facts that the youth will never kiss the maiden, the piper will never be able to stop piping, the trees will never lose their leaves because they are confined to a single season of the year, and, worst of all, the townspeople engaged in a procession toward some green altar are stopped forever midway between their destination and the town they have left empty, silent, and desolate behind them. The result is a complete reversal of terms and values, so that what was life before is now seen as a kind of death, what was death before becomes the only mode of life, and the speaker's former enemy—time—now becomes his ally.

The story of the urn-figures and the encompassing story of the speaker-protagonist contemplating them are further encompassed in a frame situation in which the speaker functions as a character who asks a great many questions and for a while gets no answers. "What leaf-fring'd legend haunts about thy shape," he inquires, entering into his narrative analysis. He wants to know whether the urn-figures are men or gods, what they are doing, and where these activities are taking place. There are eight questions in a series in the first stanza, and then three more in the fourth stanza about the people in the procession, the altar that is their destination, and the town whence they have come. And to none of these does the speaker get an answer, the urn remaining silent until, at the very end, something or somebody pronounces the famous answer to all questions, "'Beauty is truth, truth beauty,'—that is all / Ye know on earth, and all ye need to know." It has never been definitively decided who is supposed to be speaking these lines and to whom. But in structural terms, as a massive, all-purpose answer following a series of unanswered questions, it *sounds* like a satisfactory resolution of everything hitherto left unsettled in the poem, even if we don't in fact know exactly what the resolution is. It was not until seventy-six years after Keats's death that a critic first called attention to the absence of literal meaning in the equation of beauty and truth.[7]

* * *

Narrative analysis of this sort can assist the teaching and understanding of poems of other periods besides the Romantic and other literatures besides English. It can serve perhaps most usefully to counter our tendency to convert art into statement. All of us—critics, teachers, and students alike—enter too quickly and too directly into interpretation, searching for hidden meanings without sufficiently taking in what is available on the surface. Interpretation might well be redefined as *improvement of reading,* with a more unashamed focus on surface meaning, which is, after all, where the art primarily resides.[8] Narrative analysis does have practical advantages toward this end. Unlike some other methods, it does not reduce or oversimplify the works it is used to describe. Instead, it shows up the complexity of works that are genuinely complex and in many cases serves to clarify the causes or sources of complexity. It does seem an efficient method of seeing things as they are, which is a good way at least to begin an understanding of what one is studying. As M. H. Abrams points out at the end of an essay on five ways of reading *Lycidas,* a "necessary . . . condition for a competent reader of poetry remains what it has always been—a keen eye for the obvious" (1961, 231).

5

Keats's Extempore Effusions and the Question of Intentionality

KEATS'S ORIGINAL DRAFT of his account of Madeline undressing, in the twenty-sixth stanza of *The Eve of St. Agnes,* shows the poet's creativity momentarily bogging down near the climax of his sensational narrative. Madeline's (soon-to-be) lover, Porphyro, is hiding in a closet, eagerly waiting to watch her prepare for bed, and Keats sets the scene with the celebrated stanzas 24–25 describing the triple-arched casement and the moonlight shining through to fall on Madeline at her prayers. Stanza 25 concludes in the draft, "[Porphyro] grew faint / She knelt too pure a thing, too free from mo[r]tal taint."[1]

Now, after a line space in the manuscript, Keats launches into stanza 26: "But soon his heart revives—her prayers said / She lays aside her necl"— then cancels the last four words, rewrites the second line as "She strips her hair of all its wreathed pearl" (subsequently changing the last two words to "pearled wreathes"), sets down four more words of continuation in a third line ("Unclasps her bosom jewels"), but deletes this for a new third line, this time a full pentameter: "And twist[s] it in one knot upon her head." At this point he has an acceptable *a* rhyme for the first and third lines ("said/head") but alternative *b* rhymes in the second line (first "pearl," then "wreathes") that would, to meet the demands of the Spenserian stanza (*ababbcbcc*), require three more rhymes with the same sound in the fourth, fifth, and seventh lines. The prospects in either case do not seem promising. For rhymes with "pearl," in the first instance, "girl" would not qualify—Madeline is not Fanny Brawne, *pace* the biographical interpreters—and while "curl" or "uncurl" could be used in connection with Madeline's hair (and "churl" in connection with Porphyro's behavior!), none of the other obvious possibilities ("hurl," "swirl," "twirl," "whirl") accords with the nearly still-life character of the painterly description. For rhymes with "wreathes" Keats would have been pretty much restricted to "breathes," "seethes," and, if the "th" is read as unvoiced, "heaths" and "sheaths," of which only the first ("breathes") relates to anything else mentioned so far in the poem.

Canceling, therefore, all of the preceding, Keats begins again with stanza 26: "But soon his heart revives—her prayers done" (subsequently changing the last three words to "her prayers soon done" and then "her praying done") and continues: "Of all her [immediately revised to "its"] wreathed pearl she strips her hair / Unclasps her warmed jewels one by one / Loosens the boddice from her"—this last a line that has to rhyme with "hair" and seems destined to lead, sooner or later, to "bare." A flurry of divestings now takes place as Keats tries to imagine, and then cancels, one incomplete version after another of what Madeline is loosening: "her bursting," "her Boddice lace string," "her Boddice; and her bosom bar[e]," "her" (all these at the bottom of a page), and, beginning the line anew at the top of the next page, "Loosens her fragrant boddice and doth bare / Her"—at which point Keats again comes to a halt, deletes all that he has written of the stanza, and starts over.

The opening of the next attempt, this time headed with a stanza number (one of only three such numbers in the entire draft), repeats much of the preceding text just canceled: "But soon [subsequently revised to "Anon"] his heart revives—her praying done, / Of all its wreathe'd pearl her hair she strips / Unclasps her warmed jewels one by one / Loosens her fragrant boddice; and down slips / Her sweet attire." But now two more *b* rhymes are needed in the stanza to go with "strips" and "slips" in the second and fourth lines. Keats solves the problem by changing "strips" to "frees," rewriting "and down slips" successively as "to her knees" and "by degrees," and then completing the fifth line with "knees": "by degrees / Her sweet attire creeps rusteling to her knees" (the last five words following two earlier attempts to describe the descent of the fabric: "falls light" and "creeps down by"). The remainder of the stanza takes shape somewhat more readily. Keats writes "Half hidden like a Syren of the Sea / And more melodious," then cancels the last three words, changes "Syren" to "Mermaid" and "of the Sea" to "in sea weed," and continues: "She stands awhile in thought [changed, for the sake of the pentameter, to "dreaming thought"]; and sees / In fancy fair Saint Agnes in [changed to "on"] her bed / But dares not look behind or all the charm is dead" (the last word a replacement for "fl"—the beginning of "fled").

The final text of the stanza in Keats's original draft is as follows:

26

Anon his heart revives—her praying done,
   Of all its wreathe'd pearl her hair she frees:
Unclasps her warmed jewels one by one
   Loosens her fragrant boddice; by degrees
Her sweet attire creeps rusteling to her knees
Half hidden like a Mermaid in sea weed
She stands awhile in dreaming thought; and sees
In fancy fair Saint Agnes on her bed
But dares not look behind or all the charm is dead

Keats has written some twenty-five or more complete or partial lines to arrive at these nine, and the final wording here is very close to the text that we read in modern standard editions (there are five single-word alterations in later texts—"vespers" for "praying" in the first line, "pearls" for "pearl" in the second, "rich" for "sweet" in the fifth, "in" for "on" in the eighth, "fled" for "dead" in the ninth—and one lengthier change: "Pensive awhile she dreams awake" in the seventh line).

But this is not, in general, how Keats composed his poems. What is most interesting about this momentary failure of creativity—a fumbling with *b* rhymes, I suggest, rather than with lingerie—is its rarity. Keats almost never took so many lines to arrive at near-final text, even in the most difficult of the formal schemes that he used: the Spenserian stanza (as here), ottava rima (in *Isabella*), the sonnet, and the sonnetlike stanzas of his major odes. Manuscript after manuscript shows him getting *most* of the words right the first time. And for all the textual and biographical materials at our disposal, we really don't have the slightest idea how he managed to do this.

Those materials—which include Keats's own holographs, transcripts by relatives and close associates, the early printings of the poems, and Keats's and his friends' comments in letters, journals, and biographical and textual annotations, as well as the critical observations of modern scholars[2]—do allow some generalizations about the occasions and at least the mechanical procedures by which Keats's poems came into existence. I shall single out three points for discussion here.

In the first place, there is a remarkable degree of *spontaneity*—composition on the spur of the moment ("extempore effusion" in the title of this essay)—all through Keats's poems, from the very early *Stay, ruby breasted warbler stay,* which Richard Woodhouse noted "was written off in a few

Minutes" when "some young ladies . . . desired fresh words" for an old tune they were singing,[3] to the very late ode *To Autumn*, which Keats drafted shortly after an acutely pleasurable experience of the season's air and landscape while walking around Winchester: "this struck me so much in my sunday's walk that I composed upon it" (*KL*, 2:167). The Chapman's Homer sonnet was drafted and delivered to Charles Cowden Clarke the next morning after Keats stayed up all night reading Homer with Clarke. The "Great spirits" sonnet (*Addressed to the Same*) is another next-morning product, composed after an evening with the painter Benjamin Robert Haydon that Keats says "wrought me up" (*KL*, 1:117). According to a note by his brother Tom, the Vulgar Superstitions sonnet was "Written in 15 Minutes," very likely in the same circumstances that produced *On the Grasshopper and Cricket, To the Nile,* and probably also *On Receiving a Laurel Crown:* sonnet-writing competitions with Leigh Hunt (and on one occasion with Percy Shelley as well) in which the allotted time was a quarter of an hour. In the first instance (*Grasshopper*), Keats "won as to time"; in the second (*To the Nile*), both Keats and Shelley finished "within the time" while "Leigh Hunt remained up till 2 oClock in the Morning before his was finished"; in the posited third instance (*Laurel Crown*), Keats appears to be making a sonnet out of the predicament of *not* being able to write a sonnet: "Minutes are flying swiftly; and as yet / Nothing unearthly has enticed my brain / Into a delphic labyrinth. . . . Still time is fleeting, and no dream arises."

Keats wrote the dedicatory sonnet printed at the beginning of his *Poems* of 1817 (*To Leigh Hunt, Esq.*) in circumstances that C. C. Clarke uses to exemplify "his facility in composition": "he was surrounded by several of his friends when the last proof-sheet of his little book was brought in; and he was requested to send the dedication, if he intended one. He went to a side-table, and in a few minutes, while all had been talking, he returned and read the Dedicatory Sonnet." *God of the golden bow* was produced "shortly after" an incident in which Keats felt he had acted foolishly in company at Hunt's; the Elgin Marbles sonnets were an immediate response to seeing the fragments at the British Museum; *On a Leander* was in effect a thank-you note for a gift from a friend. *Lines on Seeing a Lock of Milton's Hair* was written on the instant, when Hunt "surprised me with a real authenticated Lock of *Milton's Hair*. . . . This I did at Hunt's at his request—perhaps I should have done something better alone and at home"; the first page of Keats's draft (at Harvard) is on a leaf in one of Hunt's notebooks. Keats wrote his *King Lear* sonnet when he "sat down to read King Lear . . . and felt the greatness of the thing up to the writing of a Sonnet preparatory thereto" (*KL*,

1:210–12). A lesser reader might pour a coffee or a glass of wine in such a situation. Keats wrote one of his better-known sonnets.

Hence burgundy is one of many instances of Keats spontaneously shifting into verse in his letters: "I cannot write in prose," he tells John Hamilton Reynolds; "It is a sun-shiny day and I cannot so here goes," followed by a flow of anapestic trimeters (*KL,* 1:220). Virtually all of Keats's poems from his walking tour in the summer of 1818 are occasional pieces, composed on the spot, often in letters to Tom or Fanny Keats: *On Visiting the Tomb of Burns, Old Meg, Ah! ken ye what I met the day, To Ailsa Rock,* and so on. One sonnet (*This mortal body*) he wrote in the cottage in which Burns was born—"for the mere sake of writing some lines under the roof," he explains (1:324)—and another (*Read me a lesson, Muse*) on the top of Ben Nevis, while he was perched (as his friend Charles Brown describes the situation) "a few feet from the edge of that fearful precipice, fifteen hundred feet perpendicular from the valley below." He drafted several poems in the course of writing his longest journal letter, in the spring of 1819, including *Character of C. B., La Belle Dame sans Merci, Song of Four Fairies,* and the second sonnet *On Fame.* And we have Brown's account of the circumstances in which Keats is supposed to have written *Ode to a Nightingale* (a poem that Brown classes with "fugitive pieces") in "two or three hours" while sitting in a "grass-plot under a plum-tree" (*KC,* 2:65).[4]

These are just some of the better-known or more obvious examples of Keats's facility in drafting upon, or for, an occasion. Remarkably, there is practically no evidence that he wrote his longer or more ambitious poems in any other way.[5] The extant holographs of documented spontaneity—the enthusiastic responses, the entries in sonnet competitions, the drafts in the letters—are no different in appearance from the extant drafts of the best odes and narratives. (The long narratives were not, of course, written at single sittings, but they can easily be viewed as aggregations of shorter units: fifty- or sixty-line daily stints in *Endymion* and the other works in couplets and blank verse, and a page or two of stanzas at a time in *Isabella* and the other narratives in stanzas.) Regardless of category, the drafts are more or less messy according to the demands of the poetic form—messier in sonnets, odes, and Spenserian stanzas and, just as one would expect, cleaner in couplets (as in *The Eve of St. Mark* and *Lamia*) and blank verse (*Hyperion* and *Otho the Great*).

Keats theorizes about such naturalness in one of his axioms in poetry formulated in a letter of 27 February 1818 to his publisher John Taylor: "if Poetry comes not as naturally as the Leaves to a tree it had better not come at all" (*KL*, 1:238–39). Woodhouse refers to this axiom near the beginning of the single most valuable comment we have on Keats's "mode of writing":

> [Keats] has repeatedly said in conversation that he never sits down to write unless he is full of ideas—and then thoughts come about him in troops, as though soliciting to be accepted, and he selects. One of his maxims is that if Poetry does not come naturally, it had better not come at all. The moment he feels any dearth he discontinues writing and waits for a happier moment. He is generally more troubled by a redundancy than by a poverty of images, and he culls what appears to him at the time the best. He never corrects, unless perhaps a word here or there should occur to him as preferable to an expression he has already used. He is impatient of correcting, and says he would rather burn the piece in question and write another [on] something else. "My judgment" (he says) "is as active while I am actually writing as my imagination. In fact all my faculties are strongly excited, and in their full play. And shall I afterwards, when my imagination is idle, and the heat in which I wrote has gone off, sit down coldly to criticise when in possession of only one faculty, what I have written when almost inspired?" This fact explains the reason of the perfectness, fullness, richness and completion of most that comes from him. He has said that he has often not been aware of the beauty of some thought or expression until after he has composed and written it down. It has then struck him with astonishment—and seemed rather the production of another person than his own. He has wondered how he came to hit upon it. This was the case with the description of Apollo in the third book of *Hyperion*. . . . Such Keats said was his sensation of aston-ishment and pleasure when he had produced the lines [specifically 3.81–82]. . . . It seemed to come by chance or magic—to be as it were some-thing given to him. (*KC*, 1:128–29)[6]

As a matter of fact, the extant drafts do frequently show "correcting," and the scholarly recovery of what Keats wrote in the first place has sometimes been extremely useful in critical interpretation ("The real grass" in both the draft and the fair copy of *Endymion* 4.622, for example, and "Was it a vision real" in the draft of *Ode to a Nightingale* 79). But typically these revisions are confined to single words and phrases (in Woodhouse's description just quoted, "a word here or there . . . preferable to an expression he has already used") and are concerned primarily with stylistic matters: logic and accu-racy, sound effects, and the requirements of meter. The revisions within the drafts, then, are of interest mainly negatively: they have so *little* to do with the creative process. Either some trial-and-error activity of initial composi-tion took place in Keats's mind before he ever put pen to paper, or else we must believe what Woodhouse reported from conversations with Keats: there was never any significant amount of trial-and-error activity at all in the process—a large share of Keats's lines came "by chance or magic."

My second general point, which can be made much more quickly, is that Keats's revisions in fair copies and other manuscripts subsequent to the original drafts are similarly unrevealing concerning processes of poetic creativity. For works that he took seriously, Keats characteristically wrote two manuscripts, a draft and a fair copy. For many poems we either have both the draft and the fair copy or can reconstruct the text of one, or the other, and sometimes both, from transcripts and notes by Woodhouse, Brown, and others close to the poet.

With a single exception, the long narrative and dramatic works beginning in 1817—*Endymion, Isabella, The Eve of St. Agnes, Hyperion, Lamia, The Jealousies,* and the co-authored tragedy *Otho the Great*—show no significant changes in plot, character, theme, or narrative method in the revisions that Keats made when he recopied the drafts in second or revised manuscripts. A clarifying stanza was added (and then, at his publishers' insistence, was dropped) near the beginning of *The Eve of St. Agnes;* an eighteen-line description of flowers, food, and rowdy behavior at the wedding-feast was cut from the middle of part 2 of *Lamia;* the first scene of *Otho* was entirely rewritten. But for the most part, Keats's revisions in the second manuscripts of these works are again confined to single words and phrases, with the main concerns pretty much the same as those of the reviewers of the day: style and expression. (The one exception is of course *Hyperion,* which in revision, as *The Fall of Hyperion,* was changed so drastically as to become an entirely new work. In some technical sense, one of these Hyperion poems is a variant of the other, but nobody has ever suggested printing only one in an edition of Keats's works and relegating the distinctive readings of the other to a textual apparatus.)

The same generalization holds for Keats's second or subsequent manuscripts of his shorter poems, where the revisions almost always represent tinkering, polishing, and fine-tuning rather than a second session of genuine creativity. (The addition and then cancellation of a stanza in *Ode on Melancholy* and a possible rearrangement of stanzas in *La Belle Dame* are the most extensive among the recoverable alterations.) So also is the case with the handful of poems that appeared in magazines before they were published in one of Keats's books—three sonnets in the *Examiner* (*O Solitude, Chapman's Homer,* and *To Kosciusko*) and two odes in *Annals of the Fine Arts* (*Nightingale* and *Grecian Urn*), where the variants between the earlier and later printed texts are again mainly isolated words and matters of expression.

Thus the Keats canon, *texturally* as well as textually, is vastly different from the canons of poets such as Wordsworth and Coleridge who repeatedly rewrote their poems during careers spanning many decades. Wordsworth's "obsessive" revising has been a point of critical controversy surrounding the ongoing Cornell University Press edition of his works, and there continues to be debate over *which* of the four or five principal versions—1798–99, 1804, 1805, circa 1819, or 1850—is the "real" *Prelude.* Coleridge's successive revisions of *The Rime of the Ancient Mariner* (from old spelling with "Argument" to modern spelling with "Argument," modern spelling without "Argument," poetic text alone, text with Latin epigraph and marginal glosses) are well known, as are the significant structural and philosophical changes, along with stylistic revisions, that he made in *The Eolian Harp, Frost at Midnight,* and *Dejection: An Ode.* The texts and apparatus of E. H. Coleridge's Oxford English Texts edition of 1912 reveal (or perhaps conceal) at least ten separate versions of *Monody on the Death of Chatterton* produced over a period of forty-four years. J. C. C. Mays, who has edited the poems for the Collected Coleridge, has surely discovered several additional ones among the manuscripts (though it will take a while longer to uncover them in Mays's elaborate variorum apparatuses).

Keats's entire poetic career was less than four years long, and he died at age twenty-five, little more than a year after writing his best poems. Obviously, he never had the chance to revise over a span of decades, or a succession of editions, in the way Wordsworth and Coleridge did. From his practice while alive, however, and the statement quoted by Woodhouse in the comment given above on Keats's "mode of writing" ("And shall I afterwards . . . sit down coldly to criticise . . . what I have written when almost inspired?"), it may seem rather unlikely that Keats, had he lived, would ever have produced radically altered versions of *The Eve of St. Agnes, La Belle Dame,* the major odes, or *Lamia.* Keats was a fundamentally different sort of poet from Wordsworth and Coleridge, and it should be plain that one of the many differences lies in his attitude toward revision.

My third general observation based on the textual and biographical materials is that others besides Keats had a hand in the revision of his poems.[7] *Isabella* is a useful example, because we have an extraordinary amount of information about it in letters, extant holographs of the poem, and transcripts (including the copy used by the printer of the first published text, in Keats's volume of 1820, *Lamia, Isabella, The Eve of St. Agnes, and Other Poems*). J. H. Reynolds proposed an alteration when he read Keats's fair copy. Woodhouse began tinkering with the text, pointing to faulty rhymes and meter and suggesting improvements, when he made a shorthand transcript of the fair copy, and he introduced further changes in two successive longhand transcripts based on the shorthand. The publisher Taylor also made changes in the final transcript (the setting copy). And Keats, responding to queries and suggestions in the transcript, also introduced new readings at the last minute. Keats of course remains the nominal author of *Isabella* (as well as the actual author of a high proportion of the words), but Woodhouse and Taylor between them are responsible for the title (Keats's own heading was "The Pot of Basil," which became the printed text's subtitle), for most of the punctuation and other "accidentals" throughout, and for some of the wording of about 60 of the 504 lines— roughly 1 line out of every 8 in the poem.

Earlier Taylor had made significant revisions in both pencil and ink while editing Keats's fair copy of *Endymion* for the printer, marking vaguenesses and inaccuracies in wording, faulty rhymes, and passages of physical and rhetorical extravagance (an awkward reference to "Leda's bosom," for example, too much physical intimacy between Endymion and his sister, and phrases such as "maddest Kisses" and "hot eyeballs . . . burnt and sear'd"). Later both Woodhouse and Taylor, dismayed by the sexual explicitness of some of Keats's revisions in *The Eve of St. Agnes*, worked over the poem in Woodhouse's transcripts and produced a composite version (still our standard text) of readings of Keats's draft, readings of his revised fair copy, and new readings that do not appear in any manuscript and, as a consequence, are more likely to be inventions of the well-meaning editors than of Keats himself. Woodhouse and Taylor also had a hand in printer's copy alterations and proof changes in *Lamia*. And all along, with shorter and longer poems alike, Keats routinely handed his manuscripts over to Woodhouse and Charles Brown for transcribing, punctuating, and correction of the spelling and other details. There is abundant evidence that he considered their transcripts (rather than the holographs from which they were taken) the principal finished versions of the poems before publication. Indeed, for some of the pieces Keats had *only* Woodhouse's and Brown's transcripts available when he gathered his poems for the volume of 1820.

The known facts of the revising, editing, and printing of these poems give us a rather attractive overall picture of Keats, Woodhouse, Taylor, Reynolds, and Brown all pulling together to make Keats's lines presentable to the public. And for the most part, though not always, Keats welcomed his friends' help, indeed regularly depended on it, and was gratefully aware that his poems were the better for it. But the attractive picture does entail some theoretical problems relating to diffusion of authority in the texts. Practical critics, and frequently theorists as well, tend to rely on single authorship to validate their interpretations ("this is what *the author* meant"), and editors of the Greg-Bowers-Tanselle persuasion[8] take single authorship, "final" or otherwise, as an inviolable standard ("this is what *the author* intended us to read"). In both realms—interpretation and editing—Keats scholars are having to adjust to the fact that Woodhouse, Taylor, and others are responsible for small and occasionally larger effects all through some of Keats's best-known poetry.

On the present occasion, however, I wish to call attention to an even more basic problem concerning intentionality in Keats's poetry, a problem that goes back to the way Keats drafted his pieces in the first place and to Keats's and Woodhouse's remarks about naturalness, "chance," and "magic" in the process of composition. The heart of the problem is whether Keats, characteristically writing even his greatest poems in the manner of extempore effusions, can be said to have had any specific intentions *at all* in the sense in which scholars interpret and edit according to the standard of authorial intention.

There is an enormous body of books and essays on the subject of intentionality in art and literature, especially on the place of authorial intention in literary criticism and interpretation. W. K. Wimsatt and Monroe Beardsley's essay "The Intentional Fallacy" (1946) was an early landmark, provoking considerable debate at the time and repeated citation and discussion in the first four decades after it initially appeared. E. D. Hirsch's *Validity in Interpretation* (1967) was another landmark, twenty years later, that continued for some time to be at the center of the controversy. And still later Steven Knapp and Walter Benn Michaels's "Against Theory" (1982) set off another extended flurry of special issues and symposia.[9] The point of contention (stated in the simplest possible terms) is whether or not the "meaning" of a text is the same as the author's intended meaning. Wimsatt and Beardsley said, or thought they intended to say, that the question was beside the point, while Hirsch as well as Knapp and Michaels argued, in different ways, that the meaning of a text *has* to be the author's intended meaning. Significantly (for present purposes), all principal sides in this controversy routinely assume that authors do in fact have intended meanings.

A better view is that some poets have such intentions in drafting their works while others do not and that Keats in general belongs in the latter class. Perhaps the distinction should be made between a poetry of themes and ideas, on the one hand, and what might be called a poetry of subject matter, on the other. Wordsworth and Coleridge frequently appear to be centrally concerned with ideas as ideas. Wordsworth especially, in prefaces and notes to his poems, makes a point of explaining just what the ideas are, and Coleridge too, in prefaces and notes, evinces a similar emphasis by, in effect, apologizing for his poems' lack of serious thematic intention. Both writers' prefaces and notes (like their revisions of the texts themselves) come after the initial drafting, of course, and can be seen as their own critical interpretations as they become readers of what they created. But such interpretations do impart an air of high intellectual and moral purpose to the works.

Keats, by contrast, seems to operate more like the artist depicted by R. G. Collingwood in *The Principles of Art* (1958, 29): "the artist has no idea what the experience is which demands expression until he has expressed it. What he wants to say is not present to him as an end towards which means have to be devised; it becomes clear to him only as the poem takes shape in his mind."[10] *Endymion,* as Keats described it before he had gotten very far into it, is a perfect example of Collingwood's artistry without prior intention: the poem was to be "a test, a trial of my Powers of Imagination and chiefly of my invention . . . by which I must make 4000 Lines of one bare circumstance and fill them with Poetry" (*KL,* 1:169–70). *Isabella* and *Lamia* can be seen as similar tests of invention in the retelling of stories in Boccaccio and Burton. *The Eve of St. Agnes* represents inventions based on "a popular superstition," and a principal effect of *The Eve of St. Mark* was to "give [the reader] the sensation of walking about an old county Town in a coolish evening" (*KL,* 2:139, 201). *Ode to Psyche* was written to atone for history's neglect of the goddess, and *To Autumn* was written to celebrate the beauty of the slow-dying season.

I do not advocate reversion to the anti-intellectual position of H. W. Garrod ("I think [Keats] the great poet he is only when the senses capture him, when he finds truth in beauty, that is to say, when he does not trouble to find truth at all," 1926, 63). But we may have gone on too long, in too many books and articles, expounding Keats's intended "meaning" in the symbolism of the nightingale, the Grecian urn's climactic utterance (*if* it is the urn who speaks the quoted lines), and the hoodwinking of Madeline. Keats's thoughts, in Woodhouse's note quoted above, came *while* he was creating— "in troops, as though soliciting to be accepted"—and he culled "what appear[ed] to him at the time the best" from a "redundancy . . . of images." It does not sound as if he made an outline before starting to write.

If denial of prior intention in Keats's spontaneous art undermines the validity of interpretation in certain theoretical schemes, perhaps there will be some compensation in the refocusing of our critical attention on Keats's subject matter, pictorial effects, music, and narrative and dramatic techniques. These were the components that interested him not only in his own poetry but in that of Shakespeare, Spenser, Milton, and the rest of the "laurel'd peers" whom he hoped one day to join. When he wrote, in a marginal annotation in an edition of Shakespeare, "Is *Criticism* a true thing?" he was objecting to Dr. Johnson's faulting Shakespeare for having "lost an opportunity of exhibiting a moral lesson" in *As You Like It* (Keats 1938, 5:276).[11] Seizing on moral lessons was all right for the eighteenth century, as it continued to be in literary interpretation for much of the twentieth century. But Keats was, as he would say, "righter" in his skepticism of its being a "true thing."

6

Multiple Readers, Multiple Texts, Multiple Keats

MY TOPIC IS THE MULTIPLE MEANINGS of Keats's poems, the multiple Keats who created the multiple meanings, and what I think is the real reason for the year-long tribute of admiration and affection that marked the bicentennial of his birth in 1995. My argument involves a notion of comic misfittingness, and I shall begin with three epitomizing examples in the form of a joke; a poem about Byron, Shelley, and Keats as the Three Stooges; and a typically zany passage from one of Keats's letters. Here is the joke:

> Two fishermen are out in the middle of a reservoir in a rented boat, catching fish hand over fist, pulling them in as fast as they can get their lines back in the water.
>
> *First fisherman:* This is a great place to fish. Don't you think we should mark the exact spot?
> *Second fisherman:* Sure, I'll put an X right here on the side of the boat. [*Marks an X on the side of the boat.*]
> *First fisherman:* That's a stupid thing to do. That's dumb. [*Pause.*] What if we don't get the same boat?

This will sound like something from a standup comedian on television, but in fact I have appropriated it from a poem (*The Pirate Map*) by my colleague Mike Madonick that appeared in 1993 in *Cimarron Review*. In Madonick's telling, the fishermen are literary theorists named Jacques and Harold. As their dialogue continues, the two decide that the fish they have caught are not real fish at all, merely linguistic constructs.

I use the joke to introduce the basic idea of incongruity. Everything funny has a central element of incongruity: something does not fit with something else. In Madonick's joke, the first incongruity is the idea of marking the spot with an X on the side of the boat. There is a second incongruity when the other fisherman thinks that putting an X on the boat is dumb for the wrong reason: they might not get the same boat next time. When we add the implied identities of the fishermen—two of the most famous literary theorists of our time—the result is a still more complicated set of incongruities. Why would these two be out fishing together? Why would they say such dumb things?

The poem about Byron, Shelley, and Keats as the Three Stooges is by Charles Webb, who teaches writing at California State University at Long Beach. This was the final poem read at the concluding session of a Keats conference held at the Clark Library in Los Angeles in April 1995. It begins as follows:

> Decide to temper Romantic *Sturm und Drang* with comedy.
>   Keats shaves his head;
>   Shelley frizzes out his hair;
> Byron submits to a bowl cut.
>
>   *My heart aches, and a drowsy numbness pains*
>   *My sense, as though of hemlock I had drunk,*
> Keats sighs, his head stuck in a cannon.
>
>   *Eternal Spirit of the chainless Mind!*
>   *Brightest in dungeons, Liberty!*
> Byron shouts, and lights the fuse.
>
>   *O wild West Wind, thou breath of Autumn's being,*
>   *Thou, from whose unseen presence the leaves dead*
>   *Are driven, like ghosts from an enchanter fleeing,*
> Shelley booms, and drops a cannonball on Byron's toe.

The poem continues with further slapstick intermingled with famous lines from the three poets, until—Webb says—

> Until they die, too young, careening
>   Into immortality covered with flour, squealing,
>   Drainpipes on their heads—which explains why
> For many years, the greatest poems

In English have all ended *Nyuk, nyuk, nyuk,*
    And why, reading *She walks in beauty like the night . . .*
We are as clouds that veil the midnight moon . . .

Season of mists and mellow fruitfulness . . .
    You may feel ghostly pliers tweak your nose,
And ghostly fingers poke the tear ducts in both eyes.

When Webb showed this poem to Beth Lau, his colleague at Long Beach, she referred him to a similarly ludicrous passage about "Tee wang dillo dee" from the last of Keats's journal letters to his brother and sister-in-law in America. In the passage, written on 17 January 1820, Keats is talking about his social life and the people he has seen lately:

I know three people of no wit at all, each distinct in his excellence. A. B, and C. A is the [f]oolishest, B the sulkiest, C is a negative—A makes you yawn, B makes you hate, as for C you never see him though he is six feet high. I bear the first, I forbear the second[.] I am not certain that the third is. The first is gruel, the Second Ditch water, the third is spilt—he ought to be wip'd up. . . . Tee wang dillo dee. . This you must know is the Amen to nonsense. I know many places where Amen should be scratched out . . . and in its place "T wang-dillo-dee," written. This is the word I shall henceforth be tempted to write at the end of most modern Poems—Every American Book ought to have it. It would be a good distinction in Society. My Lords Wellington, Castlereagh and Canning and many more would do well to wear T wang-dillo-dee written on their Backs instead of wearing ribbands in their Button holes—How many people would go sideways along walls and quickset hedges to keep their T wang dillo dee out of sight, or wear large pigtails to hide it. . . . Thieves and murderers would gain rank in the world—for would any one of them have the poorness of Spirit to condescend to be a T wang dillo dee—"I have robb'd in many a dwelling house, I have kill'd many a fowl many a goose and many a Man," (would such a gentleman say) "but thank heaven I was never yet a T wang dillo dee"—Some philosophers in the Moon who spy at our Globe as we do at theirs say that T wang dillo dee is written in large Letters on our Globe of Earth—They say the beginning of the T is just on the spot where London stands. London being built within the Flourish— *wan* reach[es] downward and slant[s] as far a[s] Tumbutoo in africa, the tail of the G. goes slap across the Atlantic into the Rio della Plata—the remainder of the Letters wrap round new holland and the last e terminates on land we have not yet discoverd. However I must be silent, these are dangerous times to libel a man in, much more a world. (*KL,* 2:245–47)

At the conference in Los Angeles, Webb read this passage from Keats's letter and then recited his poem about the Three Stooges, adding "Tee wang dillo dee" at the end:

> You may feel ghostly pliers tweak your nose,
> And ghostly fingers poke the tear ducts in both eyes.
> Tee wang dillo dee.

Thus the celebration of Keats in Los Angeles concluded with a tweaking of the nose, tears in the eyes, and Tee wang dillo dee. Everyone was delighted.

Just why was everyone delighted? What is it about such fundamental incongruities as the portrayal of the young Romantics as the Three Stooges and Keats's ridiculous excursus on Tee wang dillo dee that gives people so much pleasure? At the same Los Angeles conference the day before, I had delivered a paper on multiple interpretations of *The Eve of St. Agnes*. When I heard Webb's poem in connection with the passage from Keats's letter, I thought I understood better than I had before just why there are so many different and contradictory meanings in Keats's good poems and why these differences and contradictions are received as attractive rather than disturbing or displeasing. I wish to relate this comic misfittingness to some of the incongruities present in Keats's best-liked poems. There are many general names for the phenomenon: *difference, division, disjunction, disharmony, contrariness,* and so on. Whatever name we give it, it is the extreme opposite of the concept of unity that used to be central in our critical activity.

While literary art involves both unity and disunity, literary criticism until just a few decades ago placed much more emphasis on the former and much less on the latter. We have been constructing unity in works, in groups of works, in single authors, in groups of authors, in whole periods and whole centuries and making much of these unities, as if we had found them instead of constructed them. Throughout much of its history, the critical enterprise has depended on several kinds of oneness: a single author for each work; a single text of each work; a (hypothetical) single reader for the work, usually each critic individually positing him- or herself as an ideal reader; and, what obviously follows from the concept of a single reader, a single interpretation of the work, which of course was the critic's own reading.

In more recent thinking, each of these onenesses has been supplanted by a plural. We now have multiple authors rather than single solitary geniuses. We now acknowledge the existence of multiple versions of important works rather than just one text per work.[1] Instead of a single real or ideal reader, we have multiple readers all over the place—classrooms full of individual readers in our college and high school literature courses, journals and books full of readers in our academic libraries, and auditoriums full of readers at our conferences. All these readers are constructing interpretations as fast as they read. As one might imagine, when it is a complex work that is being read, the interpretations differ from one another as much as the readers do. It is not possible that only one of the interpretations is correct and all the others are wrong.

I am interested in what happens when each of the principal elements of the literary transaction—author, text, and reader—is viewed as a complex of multiples. My aim is to explain, first, why there are so many different ideas of what a Keats poem means, and, second, why we think Keats was a great poet and therefore why we expended so much energy in the celebration of his two hundredth birthday.

Multiple Texts

Keats is not one of the famous revisers of English poetry. Coleridge and Wordsworth, in contrast, were obsessive revisers all their lives. Some eighteen separate versions of *The Rime of the Ancient Mariner* have been identified, all of them authored by Coleridge, and there are twenty or more separate texts of *The Prelude.* Keats never had the chance to revise over a span of decades or a succession of editions the way Coleridge and Wordsworth did. But his practice during his brief life and his comments emphasizing the importance of spontaneity in writing make it seem unlikely that he would have produced radically altered versions of his major poems even if he had lived as long as the older poets.

Nevertheless, virtually all of Keats's poems do exist in multiple texts. For *Endymion,* there are three principal authorial versions: the text of the original draft, the text of the revised fair copy that Keats wrote out for the printer, and the first printed text, representing the words of the fair copy plus subsequent changes made by the publisher and the printer (as well as still further changes made by Keats in response). For each of the other complete long narratives—*Isabella, The Eve of St. Agnes,* and *Lamia*—there is the same array of draft, fair copy, and first printed text. For *La Belle Dame sans Merci,* we have two principal versions in manuscripts by Keats and his friends and the first printing of the poem in Leigh Hunt's *Indicator.* For *Ode to a Nightingale* and *Ode on a Grecian Urn,* there are the first published versions in a magazine, the next published versions in Keats's *Lamia* volume of

1820, and still other versions that differ from these in authoritative manuscripts. For the one hundred poems and fragments that were first published posthumously, there are almost always variant versions in the surviving sources—for example, two quite different endings of the *Bright star* sonnet, one with the speaker living on forever and the other with the speaker dying.

Thus, even though Keats was not an obsessive reviser, still he—sometimes with the help of others—created multiple texts of his poems. We are becoming increasingly sophisticated about these texts. We have long known about the two main versions of *La Belle Dame,* and Elizabeth Cook in her Oxford Authors *John Keats* (1990) printed an alternative text of *The Eve of St. Agnes* in an appendix. Nicholas Roe in his Everyman *Selected Poems* of Keats (1995) is well aware of the existence of competing versions and makes some interesting departures from what has hitherto been the standard.

This multiplicity of versions bears on the constitution of the Keats canon: How many *Eves of St. Agnes* did Keats actually write, for example? It also has ramifications for the ontological identity—sometimes called the "mode of existence"—of any specific work in the canon: Is *The Eve of St. Agnes* a single version of the work or all the versions taken together? If it is all the versions taken together, is the work constituted by the process of its revisions, one after another, or by all the versions considered as existing simultaneously? In addition, multiplicity of versions raises practical questions about the editorial treatment of the poems, the most obvious one being which version to choose for reprinting in a standard edition or an anthology when we are allowed only one version per title. It certainly complicates the business of interpretation, as when critics expound composite rather than discrete versions of a work or cite one version to help interpret another (e.g., an earlier text to explain a later one). Finally, multiplicity of texts enters into matters of basic communication, as when critics argue about significant details in a work but in fact are using different versions of the work and therefore may be considered to be referring to different works.

But this is enough about multiple texts for present purposes. I wish to turn to a more problematic element of the transaction.

Multiple Readers and Their Multiple Readings

There have been a great many readers of Keats's poems—many hundreds of thousands—over the past 180 years. What makes multiple reading a professional problem is that each reader has an experience of the poems that is different in some respects from the experiences of all the other readers, and this produces many different personal readings. When the readings are publicly described—for example, in classroom discussions, lectures, conference papers, journal articles, and book chapters—many different interpretations are being launched into the air.

This situation has been widely acknowledged only recently. In the golden age of literary criticism, by which I mean the last couple of decades of the nineteenth century and the first sixty or seventy years of the twentieth century, virtually everybody's professional work was based on a simple notion of a single perfect text and a single ideal reader. The interaction of a single reader with a single text produced a single (most nearly correct) interpretation. As criticism progressed in its treatment of any particular work, the first ideal reader was supplanted by a second ideal reader, the first having been found to be wrong (or less nearly correct than the second), and then the second was supplanted by a third, and so on. The result, historically, has been that readers succeeded readers, one after another, but still there was always just one text and one reader.

I shall give some examples from criticism of *The Eve of St. Agnes*. For the first 130 years after it was published, readers viewed the poem mainly as a series of pretty pictures—a rich Romantic tapestry, as it was called by some critics, beginning with Leigh Hunt in Keats's own time.[2] The pretty pictures were the Beadsman praying in his chapel, Porphyro entering the castle, Porphyro and Angela sitting by the fireplace, Madeline and Angela meeting on the stairs, Madeline undressing in her bedchamber, Madeline praying before she gets into bed, Porphyro setting out the banquet, Porphyro and Madeline tiptoeing out of the castle.

Then in 1953 there appeared Earl Wasserman's brilliant and provocative reading of the poem as a metaphysical allegory based on two passages in Keats's letters.[3] In the first passage, Keats compares the imagination to Adam's dream of the creation of Eve in *Paradise Lost:* Adam "awoke and found it truth." This is a type of dreaming, or visionary, imagination, and for Keats it prefigures an earthly happiness repeated spiritually in a finer tone somewhere else. In Wasserman's application to the poem, Madeline is having just such a prefigurative dream when she practices her St. Agnes' Eve ritual: she dreams of the lover she will marry, and then she awakens to find he is there in truth. The other passage that Wasserman uses from the letters is the famous simile comparing human life to a "Mansion of Many Apartments." In Wasserman's interpretation, Madeline's castle represents human life, and Porphyro, passing upward to a closet adjoining her bedchamber and thence into the bedchamber itself, is progressing from apartment to apartment in the mansion of life on a spiritual journey to join Madeline in some kind of higher (transcendental) reality.

There seemed at the time to be a number of things wrong with Wasserman's interpretation, and I launched my own career as a Keats critic by pointing them out in an essay first published in 1961 titled "The Hoodwinking of Madeline." Madeline, when she awakens, is not happy to find a real Porphyro in her bed. Porphyro has been sneaking around the castle like a Peeping Tom. Rather than experiencing spiritual repetition in a finer tone, leading to a higher reality, the two principals seem to be having sex, with only one of them conscious of what is going on. The story is full of echoes of bad happenings in earlier works: the rape of Philomel, Satan seducing Eve, Lovelace raping the unconscious Clarissa Harlowe, and others. I went on in considerable detail, and my essay was well known for a while as the dirty-minded reading of *The Eve of St. Agnes.* When I republished the essay as a chapter in a book, a reviewer (R. H. Fogle) commented in verse in the Phi Beta Kappa *Key Reporter:*

> Alack for Madeline, poor hoodwink'd maid—
> By Porphyro then, now Stillinger betrayed. (Fogle 1972, 5)

A decade after "The Hoodwinking of Madeline" first appeared, Stuart Sperry (1971) published his fine essay titled "Romance as Wish-Fulfillment" in which he established Wasserman and me as two extremes of critical opinion on the poem. He charged Wasserman with being too romantically metaphysical and me with being too antiromantically realistic, and he skillfully steered a middle course between our interpretations. Thus for the next two decades the standard opening for an essay on *The Eve of St. Agnes* was to recite a kind of Goldilocks and the Three Bears litany in which Wasserman was too high-flying, I was too down-to-earth, and Sperry was "just right." This was, of course, always followed by a "but": Sperry was just right in his way, *but* all previous critics, including Sperry, had overlooked such-and-such—which then led into yet another new reading.

The notable thing about this activity is that each successive interpretation of the poem was intended to supersede all the previous interpretations—Wasserman making obsolete the idea that the poem is merely a rich Romantic tapestry; I making quite clear that Wasserman's reading was wrong in all the major particulars; Sperry showing how both Wasserman and I were oversimplifying the important points; and each subsequent critic again putting down an ever-growing body of predecessors. This was the era of single-meaning interpretation, which to some extent continues to the present day.

Since Sperry, there have been a great many readings of the poem. I identified some of these in my lecture in Los Angeles, in a handout titled "Fifty-nine Ways of Looking at *The Eve of St. Agnes*" (see the appendix printed at the end of this chapter). I did not have time then, and of course do not have space here, to describe each reading individually.[4] The readings are grouped into nine thematic categories, each of which contains contradictory versions. Older readings of the poem appear in all nine of the categories. The more recent ones having a basis in Deconstructionist, Marxist, and feminist theory appear mainly in the last two sections.

I shall comment on just the final item, "politics of interpretation," as an example of the sort of complication that the list represents. Interpretation is not (primarily) political in the Marxist or feminist sense, but it is political in the more general sense of having to do with power—who gets to say what is going on in the poem. Take the storm that comes up just after Madeline loses her virginity. There are several different opinions about this storm. Madeline seems afraid of it; she thinks Porphyro will abandon her. Porphyro describes it as an "elfin-storm from faery land"—a timely "boon" to help hide their escape from the castle. The narrator says it is a real storm, calling attention to the wind, the sleet, and the icy cold. Then Madeline and Porphyro go out into the storm and have not been heard from since. At this point, the critics take over. One group thinks that Madeline and Porphyro perish in the storm. Another large group believes that they live happily ever after in Porphyro's home across the moors. Another group argues that Madeline and Porphyro enter Dante's second circle of hell and are perpetually orbiting the world with other famous lovers who sinned carnally. Still other critics think it does not matter: Madeline and Porphyro would be dead now in any case, because this all happened "ages long ago." And so on.[5]

"Fifty-nine Ways of Looking at *The Eve of St. Agnes*" is just a token array of possible interpretations of the poem. Colleagues to whom I have shown the list and people in my lecture audiences have proposed still others. One freshman said at the end of a lecture that he had always thought the two secondary characters, Angela and the Beadsman, were having a sexual affair. There is nothing in the text to support such an idea, but I told him that it could be number sixty in my list, and later I thought of some reasons why it is not a totally worthless suggestion.

Now I shall try to explain why there have been so many different readings of *The Eve of St. Agnes*. In general, the explanation lies in the nature of the transaction between a complex work and a complex readership. On one hand, we have *The Eve of St. Agnes,* sending out many thousands of impulses of meaning in every direction, so many that the reader cannot possibly take in all of them and therefore has to make a selection. On the other hand, we have a readership that consists of, first, any individual reader (along with the complexity represented by the sum of that reader's personal knowledge and experience at the time of reading) and, second, the combination of all the readers who have ever read the poem taken together simultaneously. Each individual reader will be creative rather than passive while engaged in the activity of reading and will be creative in a way different from all the other readers. That is, each individual reader will assemble a unique combination of selected and emphasized meanings, adding and suppressing according to his or her own creative activity.[6]

So we already have two conditions producing multiplicity of meaning: a large number of readers over a long period of time and an excess of textual meaning. I shall use the opening stanza to illustrate this excess of meaning and what happens in the process of reading.

> St. Agnes' Eve—Ah, bitter chill it was!
> The owl, for all his feathers, was a-cold;
> The hare limp'd trembling through the frozen grass,
> And silent was the flock in woolly fold:
> Numb were the Beadsman's fingers, while he told
> His rosary, and while his frosted breath,
> Like pious incense from a censer old,
> Seem'd taking flight for heaven, without a death,
> Past the sweet Virgin's picture, while his prayer he saith.

Twenty or more ideas and images are evoked by just the first four lines of this stanza. "St. Agnes" carries at least the ideas of saintliness, martyrdom, and virginity. There is "eve" in the sense of evening and nighttime, as well as the more specific sense of the night before a saint's day, and then come bitterness, chill, owl, feathers, cold, hare, limping, trembling, frozenness, grass, silence, flock, woolliness, and fold (this last both a farm structure and a social concept). The next four lines of the stanza contain fourteen more images: numbness, beadsman, fingers, telling (or counting), rosary, frostedness, breath, piety, incense, censer, oldness, flight, heaven, and death. The last line of the stanza has at least three more: Virgin, picture, and praying. Altogether, I count thirty-seven images, each with almost innumerable possible shades of meaning, in just the first nine lines of the poem.

An individual reader cannot possibly absorb and respond to all thirty-seven of these separate stimuli. So the reader selects some; overlooks, ignores, or suppresses others; and creates his or her peculiar version of the content of the nine lines. Readers cannot help selecting and creating in this way. It is the main way that people read. And because each reader will put his or her spin on the images thus selected, when the work is complex in the manner of *The Eve of St. Agnes,* each reader-constructed version necessarily differs from every other reader-constructed version. Mathematically, the possibilities for variation are astronomical. And so we have significant differences in the readings and, if the readers write them up, a considerable accumulation of different readings in the critical literature.

With Keats's poems, there is still another condition in addition to large numbers of readers and the text's excess of meaning, and this is the characteristically Keatsian frequency of ambiguous and contradictory details in the texts. The opening description of the Beadsman can serve as an example. Certain details in the first two stanzas emphasize the Beadsman's piety, patience, and sympathy for the dead who lie about the chapel where he is praying. A reader might get the idea that the Beadsman is to be admired. Other details, which tend to make him pitiable rather than admirable, stress the Beadsman's joyless self-denial and harsh penance. The fact that he is barefoot is an especially painful detail, given the emphasis on bitter cold in the opening stanzas. The different kinds of detail produce conflicting perceptions of the Beadsman, which in turn have a bearing on the reader's view of important matters that come up later in the poem, because the ritualistic, self-denying Beadsman prefigures the ritualistic, self-denying Madeline in the main narrative. What one thinks of the Beadsman to an extent carries over into what one thinks of Madeline.

For more complicated examples of contradictory detail in the poem, consider these statements about the two main characters:

Porphyro is Prince Charming, on a mission to rescue an imprisoned maiden.
He is a confederate of sorcerers, a worker of evil magic.
He is a Peeping Tom.
He is an ardent lover.
He is a rapist.
He is Madeline's future husband.

Madeline is beautiful and desirable, the belle of the ball.
She is hoodwinked with faery fancy, shutting herself off from the real world.

> She is a pious Christian.
> She is a victim of self-deception.
> She is a victim of Porphyro's stratagem.
> She is Porphyro's happy bride.

About half of these statements are not congruent with the other half, yet each statement is true in the sense that there is support for it in the text and agreement about it among some of the readers and critics. Oppositions of this sort are central to the plot, characterizations, speeches, and descriptions. No wonder different readers have different ideas of what is going on in the poem.

In my lecture in Los Angeles I went on at some length concerning the reading process; how Coleridge's concept of unity underlies the activity; how Keats's various statements about reading support the idea of multiple interpretation; and how, despite the fact that we always expect new readings from students and critics, much of our current teaching and writing about literature continues to endorse the traditional goal of single-meaning interpretation. I set forth a practical theory of multiple interpretation and discussed the principal objection that arises whenever one favors a reader-response system of meaning and value—namely, the problem of the validity, or truth, of an interpretation. On what grounds does one decide what is correct and what is not correct? On what grounds does a teacher tell a student that the student's interpretation is wrong? How can literature be a field of knowledge when anybody and everybody can be a player? There are several defenses against this general objection, and I brought in all the ones I knew of, including one I invented myself—the concept of no-fault reading, whereby even the freshman who thinks that Angela and the Beadsman are having an affair is not really doing any damage and actually, if the discussion were focusing too exclusively on Madeline and Porphyro, could be making a positive contribution by shifting the focus to the minor characters and raising questions about what they are doing in the poem.

Multiple Keats

The remaining element of the transaction is the multiple of authorship, and here I shall be focusing on the responsibility for the excess of textual meaning and abundance of contradictory details illustrated in the preceding section.

Everybody is familiar with the poet's variety and versatility and therefore with the idea of multiple Keatses. There were several Keatses on view in connection with the poet's bicentennial in 1995, at the Houghton Library at Harvard, the Grolier Club in New York, the Dove Cottage Museum in Grasmere, and elsewhere: the Keats of the poetry drafts (produced as if by magic, he told his friend Richard Woodhouse, *KC*, 1:129); the Keats of the boldly inscribed fair copies; the Keats first known to the public in the magazines and the three original volumes; the posthumous Keats, creator of the one hundred poems first published after his death; the personal Keats seen in the privacy of his surviving letters; the Keats who was the beloved friend at the center of what we now call the Keats Circle; the Keats of the various portraits; and the Keats who served as artistic collaborator, providing materials for subsequent nineteenth- and twentieth-century book designers, printers, and binders who created so many beautiful printings of his poems.[7]

These are just the most obvious types represented by the manuscripts, books, and memorabilia in the bicentennial exhibitions. To them we can add many more Keatses both from traditional criticism and scholarship over the years and from poststructuralist theory more recently. These include aesthetic Keats, the champion of art for art's sake; sensuous Keats, who burst Joy's grape, with or without cayenne pepper on his tongue, and created some of the most palpable imagery in all of British poetry; philosophical Keats, who described "the vale of Soul-making" and thought of life as a "Mansion of Many Apartments"; theoretical Keats, the formulator of "Negative Capability" and "camelion poetry"; topographical Keats, the well-traveled tourist who wrote a sonnet while dangling his legs from a precipice at the top of Ben Nevis; and theatrical Keats, the theater reviewer and unproduced playwright. There are also intertextual Keatses, including Spenserian Keats, Leigh Huntian Keats, Shakespearean Keats, Miltonic Keats, Dantesque Keats—the list goes on almost indefinitely. Other Keatses include political Keats, especially in his early poems and letters, but through the rest of his career as well; radical Keats, a more sharply focused political Keats; vulgar Keats, the only canonical male Romantic poet besides Blake who did not attend a university and the one with the lowliest upbringing; Cockney Keats, a more specific tag deriving from his supposed lowly upbringing plus the "Cockney School" articles in *Blackwood's* and, 180 years later, the investigations of Nicholas Roe (1997) and Jeffrey Cox (1998); suburban Keats, a variant of the preceding produced by the research of Elizabeth Jones (1995, 1996); effeminate Keats, identified first by reviewers who were his contemporaries and in present-day criticism by Susan Wolfson (1990, 1995b), Marjorie Levinson (1988), and others; masculine (even macho) Keats; and consumptive Keats, the one who dies movingly and heroically every time we read a biography or make our way to the end of the letters.

The list could go on and on. Still, these multiple Keatses are a random sampling of single Keatses—now one, now another, according to the approach, the method, the occasion, and the texts at hand. I am interested in something a little more complicated.

The phrase "Multiple Keats" in my chapter title is meant to stand for an internal complexity in Keats that is constituted primarily by self-division—an unresolved imaginative dividedness between the serious and the humorous, the straight and the ironic, the fanciful and the real, the high-flying and the down-to-earth, the sentimental and the satiric, the puffed up and the deflated. It manifests itself in many places, both in biographical anecdote and in Keats's writings—and in the writings, both in the letters and in the poetry, and in the poetry, both in the frivolous pieces tossed off for immediate amusement and in the most serious efforts that Keats hoped would earn him a place among the English poets. One way of representing this self-division is by referring to various kinds of comedy: the antic, the zany, the farcical, the ridiculous—for example, the illustrations of comic incongruity with which I began this essay.

Somebody in the NASSR (North American Society for the Study of Romanticism) user group raised the question of whether Keats had a sense of humor, and responses poured in to such an extent that one got the idea there were hardly any letters and poems in which Keats was *not* in some way being funny. Hundreds of passages in the letters contain puns, practical jokes, self-mockery, and comic description. Everyone has his or her favorite examples. One of mine appears in the last of the letters that Keats wrote during his walking tour in the summer of 1818. The letter is to Georgiana Keats's mother, Mrs. James Wylie, on 6 August:

> Tom tells me that you called on Mr Haslam with a Newspaper giving an account of a Gentleman in a Fur cap, falling over a precipice in Kirkud-brightshire. . . . As for Fur caps I do not remember one beside my own, except at Carlisle—this was a very good Fur cap, I met in the High Street, & I daresay was the unfortunate one.

At this point, Keats invokes a bit of classical mythology to explain the newspaper account he has invented. The Three Fates, seeing two fur caps in the North, threw dice to eliminate one of them, and so the other fur cap, the one at Carlisle, went over the precipice and was drowned. Then Keats imagines that it would not have been so bad if he himself had been the loser, provided he had been only half drowned:

[B]eing half drowned by falling from a precipice is a very romantic affair. . . . How glorious to be introduced in a drawing room to a Lady who reads Novels, with . . . "Miss so & so, this is Mr so & so. who fell off a precipice, & was half drowned." Now I refer it to you whether I should loose so fine an opportunity of making my fortune—No romance lady could resist me—None—Being run under a Waggon; side lamed at a playhouse; Apoplectic, through Brandy; & a thousand other tolerably decent things for badness would be nothing; but being tumbled over a precipice into the sea—Oh it would make my fortune—especially if you could continue to hint . . . that I was not upset on my own account, but that I dashed into the waves after Jessy of Dumblane—& pulled her out by the hair.

Six weeks before Keats wrote this, Georgiana had left London to settle in America with her new husband, Keats's brother George. Emigration in those days was a serious disruption of family relationships—in most cases, the family members who stayed behind never again saw the ones who left—and Keats in this letter offers condolences to Georgiana's mother as if her daughter had died: "I should like to have remained near you, were it but for an atom of consolation, after parting with so dear a daughter. . . . I wish above all things, to say a word of Comfort to you, but I know not how. It is impossible to prove that black is white, It is impossible to make out, that sorrow is joy or joy is sorrow" (*KL,* 1:358–60). It is at this point in the letter that, without any transition whatsoever, Keats launches into his account of the gentleman in the fur cap falling over a precipice in Kirkcudbrightshire.

This oscillation between seriousness and hilarity, which we find throughout the letters, is one of their chief attractions to readers. Even in his last known letter, written from Rome two and a half months before he died, when he was already leading what he called a "posthumous existence," Keats mentions punning: "I ride the little horse—and, at my worst, even in Quarantine, summoned up more puns, in a sort of desperation, in one week than in any year of my life." He ends this letter with a poignantly comic gesture: "I can scarcely bid you good bye even in a letter. I always made an awkward bow" (*KL,* 2:359–60).

There are numerous poems and passages that are openly funny—the early lines about Keats's trinity of women, wine, and snuff; the sonnet celebrating the grand climacteric of Mrs. Reynolds's cat; the whimsical self-description beginning "There was a naughty boy"; the lines about the cursed gadfly; the lines about the cursed bagpipe; the silly dialogue between Mrs. Cameron and Ben Nevis; the Spenserian stanzas making fun of his friend Charles Brown; and the extended self-parody in *The Jealousies,* to name just a few. The comedy in these pieces regularly depends on some kind of incongruous juxtaposition, as in the overthrow of expectation with a punchline. It is characteristically Keatsian to put together things that do not themselves go together.[8]

Keats wrote about this juxtaposing of contraries in the well-known lines that begin "Welcome joy, and welcome sorrow" and are sometimes printed under the title *A Song of Opposites:*

> Welcome joy, and welcome sorrow,
>   Lethe's weed, and Hermes' feather,
> Come to-day, and come to-morrow,
>   I do love you both together!
>   I love to mark sad faces in fair weather,
> And hear a merry laugh amid the thunder;
>   Fair and foul I love together. . . .
>
>   (1–7)

There are many such comic juxtapositions in poems that are not primarily funny. The opening of the fragmentary *Calidore*—"Young Calidore is paddling o'er the lake"—could be an early smokable (as Keats would say) example, if we remember that Keats almost always took an ironic view of chivalric trappings. This was the time of the early poetry-writing contests, and it is easy to imagine a situation in which Keats was challenged to write a length of rhymed couplets following from the opening "Young Calidore is paddling o'er the lake." In fact, he wrote 162 lines before coming to a halt, still plotless.

Take the phrase "O bliss! / A naked waist" toward the end of the second book of *Endymion*. This is sometimes cited to illustrate Keats's vulgarity or bad judgment. Endymion has been wandering from cave to cave underground until he arrives at a bower and finds

> The smoothest mossy bed and deepest, where
> He threw himself, and just into the air
> Stretching his indolent arms, he took, O bliss!
> A naked waist: "Fair Cupid, whence is this?" [Endymion asks]
> A well-known voice sigh'd, "Sweetest, here am I!"
> At which soft ravishment, with doating cry
> They trembled to each other.
>
>   (2.710–16)

That "Sweetest, here am I!" is pure Chaucer, like something lifted from *Troilus and Criseyde*. Keats is recounting a passionate episode in the poem, with detailed physical description. But even though the narrator gets extremely worked up over what he is describing—he has to stop to invoke Helicon and the Muses—there is no question about the intentionally comic mixture of irony and literary allusion in "O bliss! / A naked waist. . . . 'Sweetest, here am I!'"

Another example from the same poem comes in the middle of book 4, when Endymion is in bed with his newly beloved Indian maiden and his heavenly love Phoebe rises and glares down on the couple:

> O state perplexing! On the pinion bed,
> Too well awake, he feels the panting side
> Of his delicious lady. He who died
> For soaring too audacious in the sun,
> When that same treacherous wax began to run,
> Felt not more tongue-tied than Endymion. . . .
> Ah, what perplexity! . . .
>
> (4.439–47)

There are the grotesque images of the dream or nightmare at the beginning of the verse epistle to John Hamilton Reynolds:

> Things all disjointed come from north and south,
> Two witch's eyes above a cherub's mouth,
> Voltaire with casque and shield and habergeon,
> And Alexander with his night-cap on—
> Old Socrates a tying his cravat;
> And Hazlitt playing with Miss Edgeworth's cat.
>
> (5–10)

This ridiculous set of allusions leads into one of Keats's most serious considerations of the dangers of overinvesting in visionary imagination. In *The Eve of St. Mark,* another serious poem exploring the pros and cons of imaginative investment, similarly grotesque images adorn both the ancient volume that Bertha reads and the fire screen across the room. The earlier description ends anticlimactically with angels and mice. The latter passage has, among its "many monsters," not only mice again but several kinds of bird and, at the end of the list, the traditional enemy of both mice and birds, a fat cat.

Less central images that are not in accord with their surroundings but probably are there for the value of the incongruity include Porphyro's Pink Panther-like tiptoeing across Madeline's bedroom to check whether she is asleep and the redness of Hermes's blushing ears when, in the first paragraph of *Lamia,* he thinks of the beautiful nymph he is pursuing. (An early writer on the humor in *Lamia* remarks, "There are many other parts of the body which can be described as turning red when the tone is serious—the cheeks, the forehead, the throat, all these can burn with dignity. But not the ears. Red ears are funny" [Dunbar 1959, 19]). In *The Fall of Hyperion,* Keats describes himself and the goddess Moneta, standing side by side, as "a stunt bramble by a solemn pine" (1.293).

It does not require a major leap of criticism to go from local incongruities of the sort I have just exemplified to more serious mismatches that are central to our experience of the most important poems. I have already mentioned some that pervade the goings-on in *The Eve of St. Agnes:* Porphyro is the hero of the poem, an ardent lover, a Prince Charming to the rescue, and Madeline's future husband. At the same time, he is associated with images of sorcery, voyeurism, cruel seduction, and rape. Madeline is the beautiful heroine, the belle of the ball, Sleeping Beauty, a pious Christian, and Porphyro's bride. She is also a foolish victim of both Porphyro's stratagem and her own self-deception.

There are statements and situations of doubtful compatibility everywhere one turns in Keats's good poems. Consider the speaker's musing about death in the sixth stanza of *Ode to a Nightingale:* "Now more than ever seems it rich to die, / To cease upon the midnight with no pain, / While thou art pouring forth thy soul abroad / In such an ecstasy!" The richness of this thought is immediately nullified by the realism of mortal extinction: "Still wouldst thou sing, and I have ears in vain— / To thy high requiem become a sod" (55–60). Consider the situation in the fourth stanza of *Ode on a Grecian Urn:* there is a lovingly described procession of townspeople on their way to some green altar—so far so good. Immediately, however, comes the realization that these people will never get to their destination, they will never go back to the town they came from, and their "little town" will be desolate "for evermore." Or take the lines about the happy/frustrated lovers two stanzas earlier in the same poem:

> Bold lover, never, never canst thou kiss,
> Though winning near the goal—yet, do not grieve;
> She cannot fade, though thou hast not thy bliss,
> For ever wilt thou love, and she be fair!
>
> (17–20)

These lines do not have to be paraphrased to make the point. In the ode *To Autumn* we get, first, a series of statements about how beautiful the season is; then the realization that all this beauty is dying; and finally (perhaps), if we put these two contrary notions together, the idea that somehow death is beautiful.

At this point it might seem that I am coming dangerously close to the old New Criticism of fifty and sixty years ago—the "mystic oxymoron" of Kenneth Burke (1943), for example, and "oxymoronic fusion" of Earl Wasserman (1953, 13–62). Well, why not? We all learned to read from the New Critics, and we constantly use New Critical methods in the privacy of our classrooms and personal reading. Maybe "mystic oxymoron" and "oxymoronic fusion" are not such bad terms for the kind of authorial and textual complexity I am trying to describe.

The Idea of Canonical Complexity

For conclusion, I shall just point out the obvious: what happens when the two sides, author and reader, are brought together by the text. On one side we have the Keats of the whimsical incongruities and the more serious disjunctions, contraries, and mystic oxymorons: surely a complex multiple authorship, even if it resides almost entirely in the single historical entity John Keats, born more than two hundred years ago. On the other side we have an incredibly complex readership: all those multiple readers whom I referred to earlier. And we of course have multiple interpretations, the only possible outcome when you combine complex authorship and complex readership.

Physicists in recent years have been writing about complex adaptive and evolving systems.[9] These are not bad terms for the model of reading I am developing. The authorship side of the literary transaction can be considered a complex adaptive system. Authors do read their own works in the process of writing, interpret in the process of reading, and constantly interact with the works they are creating. The text, in the middle of the scheme, is not complexly adaptive. It doesn't do anything—it just sits there (in a manner of speaking) and is done to. But, obviously, it can be considered a complex evolving system, in the sense that it undergoes change every time somebody does something to it. The readership side is an infinitely expanding activity of further complex adaptive systems. Each individual reader is a center of virtually infinite possibilities for imaginative response in the process of reading, and there is an infinite number of individual readers (past, present, and future), each responding differently from all the others.

When we combine these complexities, what we have, to get back to the terminology of English departments, is nothing less than a canonical work and a canonical author. It is the nature of canonical works to have more meanings than any one reader can possibly take in at a reading and therefore to be, for all practical purposes, interpretively inexhaustible. In physics, the complexity of something is defined by the number of words (or propositions or equations) that are required to describe it: the simpler the entity, the shorter the description; the more complex, the longer the description. My "Fifty-nine Ways" is just a tip-of-the-iceberg example of what it would take to describe the meaning of *The Eve of St. Agnes.*

Who is ultimately responsible for this grand complexity of author, text, and reader? I believe the one indispensable element is the author. The reader's interpretive constructions, however infinite and inexhaustible, have to begin with materials already in the text waiting for the reader to come along. It is the author who put them there. I think it is above all because Keats provided so many, and such complicated, details—the starting materials for the fifty-nine (or fifty-nine *hundred*) ways of reading *The Eve of St. Agnes* and the rest of the good poems—that we made so much of him in the celebrations of his two hundredth birthday. It is not a bad achievement for somebody who had to quit writing entirely at the age of twenty-three.

APPENDIX
Fifty-nine Ways of Looking at
The Eve of St. Agnes

Love, Sex, Marriage

1. Human love (a celebration of love overcoming all obstacles)
2. Keats's love life
3. Keats's love specifically for Fanny Brawne
4. Celebration of sexual love
5. Celebration of Christian marriage
6. Erotic love versus religious purity
7. Sexual politics I: Porphyro as the Peeping Tom/rapist, Madeline as the victim
8. Sexual politics II: Madeline as the seducer, Porphyro as the victim (a husband caught at last!)

Magic, Fairy Tale, Myth

9. Romance, enthrallment, enchantment
10. Sleeping Beauty
11. Porphyro as liberator of Madeline
12. Porphyro as vampire
13. The triumph of fairy over Christian religion
14. Initiation and transformation of maiden into mother
15. A version of Joseph Campbell's monomyth
16. The Fortunate Fall
17. Masturbatory ritual

Imagination

18. Authenticity of dreams
19. The visionary imagination succeeding (celebration)
20. The visionary imagination failing miserably (skepticism)
21. Porphyro's creative (seizing, adaptive) imagination
22. Contrast (or conflict) of two kinds of imagination

23. The hoodwinking of *everyone* (Beadsman, Angela, Madeline, Porphyro, the kinsmen and revelers)

Wish Fullfillment (subhead of the preceding)

24. Narrative of desire
25. Fantasy of wish fulfillment
26. Successful merging of romance and reality, or of beauty and truth

Poetry, Art, Creativity

27. Parable (allegory) of literary creativity
28. Antiromance; illustration of the limitations of romance
29. Remake of *Romeo and Juliet* I: imitation
30. Remake of *Romeo and Juliet* II: modernization ("tough-minded 'modern' recasting" as in *Isabella*)
31. Exercise in Gothicism
32. Satire on (parody of) Gothicism
33. Completion of Coleridge's *Christabel*
34. Rich Romantic tapestry
35. Pure aestheticism: art is the only thing that matters

Religion

36. Religion of experience
37. Religion of beauty
38. Love as a religious sacrament
39. Keats's attack on religion
40. Ironic version of the Annunciation
41. Parody of a saint's life
42. Paganism versus religion; the triumph of old religion over Christianity

Human Experience More Generally

43. Mortality and Madeline's fall from innocence
44. Tragedy
45. The inconsequentiality of human life (death takes all)

Epistemology, Ambiguity

46. Uncertainty of the phenomenal world
47. The semiotics of vision (looking, gazing); scopophilia
48. Ambiguousness of idealism and reality
49. Poem of disjunctions, equivocation—open-endedness in the extreme
50. Poem about speech, language, communication (and their unreliability)
51. Poem about the weather, the seasons, day and night, etc. (phenomenological reading)

Politics

52. Family politics (the *Romeo and Juliet* situation, with emphasis on social conflict)
53. The rottenness of aristocratic society (*Hamlet* theme)
54. The crisis of feudalism (feudal decay, mercantile ascendancy, disruption of the class system)
55. Dynastic oppression (Madeline the victim)
56. Patriarchal domination of women (ditto)
57. Keats's disparagement of women (characters and readers alike)
58. Poem about escape—from the castle, from family and/or society, from reality (etc.)
59. Politics of interpretation: who gets to say what things mean (Madeline? Porphyro? the narrator? the critic? the teacher? the reader?)

7

The "Story" of Keats

THE "STORY" OF KEATS—how a young man of no apparent distinction in family or social origins, education, or early accomplishments grew up to become one of the ten or twelve most admired poets in all of English literature—is really several stories, some of them not entirely consistent or compatible with some of the others.[1] I shall focus on two of them in the present chapter. The first is the story of Keats the young genius whose life and career were cut short—some said by the hostility of reviewers—just as he was about to produce the major works that his friends thought him capable of. This is the Keats of Shelley's *Adonais*, of Byron's famous quip in the eleventh canto of *Don Juan* that Keats's "mind, that very fiery particle," was "snuffed out by an article," and of the inscriptions on his gravestone in the Protestant Cemetery in Rome: the broken lyre symbolizing unfulfilled aspirations; the words that the poet himself requested, "Here lies one whose name was writ in water"; and his friends' well-meant embellishments mentioning the poet's "bitterness of . . . heart, at the malicious power of his enemies." The product of this first "story" is the Keats whom the British public thought of, if they remembered him at all, during the first three decades following his death on 23 February 1821.

The second story, which is more a critical construct than imagined facts of biography, tells how Keats rapidly rose to canonicity, beginning in the middle of the nineteenth century, as his poems became increasingly published, read, quoted, and talked and written about. This is a story about readers' changing interests and values, and how Keats, once he got some readers, has appealed to each separate one of those interests and values ever since. The two stories are connected in that the first, along with some noteworthy attempts by the poet's friends to correct its principal details, became the means of providing the audience and the accompanying attention that enabled the second. The first story is, in effect, the history of Keats getting into the canon by way of biographical interest. The second is, in effect, the history of Keats staying in the canon by virtue of the complexity and open-endedness of his writings. Whether or not these stories are true, it is a fact that Keats has been, just as he predicted he would be (*KL,* 1:394), "among the English Poets" for the last 150 years. What was lacking in the thirty years preceding that period—that is, in the 1820s through the 1840s—was a sufficient readership.

* * *

Some of the first story is biographically accurate. Keats did die young, at age twenty-five, and his active writing career amounted to little more than three and a half years, from the earliest sentimental effusions in his first published volume, *Poems* (1817), through the late ode, *To Autumn,* the last attempts at *The Fall of Hyperion* in the fall of 1819, and some private odes and sonnets to Fanny Brawne (1819 or possibly early 1820). Certainly he would have written more had he lived longer, though we have very little idea where his developing interests would have taken him. But it is clearly erroneous to think that the brevity of his life and career prevented him from achieving anything of significance. On the contrary, even if cut off just as he was getting under way, this "poet of promise" left a body of mature work in narrative and lyric forms sufficient to make him a major writer by anybody's standards. The imagined poet of promise was in fact a poet of enormous accomplishments.

The traditional notions of Keats's low origins and patchy education also have required adjustment. His father was head innkeeper, livery stabler, and principal manager at the Swan and Hoop, a prosperous London lodging owned by his father-in-law (Keats's grandfather), John Jennings. Notwithstanding the reports of hostile reviewers and the fables of literary history, the poet's "low" origins were actually soundly middle class, as we reckon these things today. As for education, from 1803 to 1811 Keats attended an excellent boarding school, John Clarke's at Enfield, north of London, and proved an insatiable reader and remarkable learner. He then served a four-year apprenticeship to an apothecary-surgeon (1811–15) followed by a first year of courses as a medical student at Guy's Hospital in London. He passed the apothecaries' exam and received his certificate to practice as apothecary and surgeon in July 1816, at which point he abandoned medicine for a full-time career in poetry. The literary part of his education was as comprehensive as that of many another famous writer, and the scientific (and human) aspects of his medical training were a further enrichment.

What has most needed correcting is the idea that Keats was killed by the reviewers. Of all the elements of the story, this is the most often repeated and perforce the most firmly established, extending even into some of the Shelley scholarship of the twentieth century.[2] The assassins in the tale are the two most notorious pronouncers on Keats's second volume, the long poem *Endymion* (1818)—John Gibson Lockhart, writing in *Blackwood's Edinburgh Magazine* for August 1818, and John Wilson Croker, in the *Quarterly Review* for April 1818 (both reviews actually appeared in September, just after a nagging sore throat had forced Keats's early return from an impressive but physically demanding walking tour of northern England, Ireland, and Scotland with his robust friend Charles Brown). Lockhart, in the fourth of his series of articles on the "Cockney School of Poetry," calls *Endymion* "imperturbable drivelling idiocy"; quotes passages of "very pretty raving" and "loose, nerveless versification, and Cockney rhymes"; and concludes by urging Keats to abandon poetry and return to his apothecary's shop (Matthews 1971, 98, 100, 104, 109–10). Croker, declaring that he could not get past the first book of *Endymion* and could make no sense even of that, goes on at length about faulty diction and versification. He too relegates Keats's poetry to the "Cockney School," characterized by "the most incongruous ideas in the most uncouth language" (111). Both reviewers, denouncing the liberalism implied by Keats's connections with his anti-Tory mentor Leigh Hunt, make clear that their criticism has a political bias.

Keats's admirers—some scores of his acquaintances at the time and many hundreds of thousands of readers subsequently over the past 185 years—have hated Lockhart and Croker for their contemptuous treatment. But the poet himself seems to have been very little affected. With Shakespeare as his "presider," he had higher standards than his assailants did. "Praise or blame," he told his publisher J. A. Hessey on 8 October 1818, "has but a momentary effect on the man whose love of beauty in the abstract makes him a severe critic on his own Works. My own domestic criticism has given me pain without comparison beyond what Blackwood or the Quarterly could possibly inflict" (*KL*, 1:373–74). To his brother and sister-in-law in America, he commented a week later, "This is a mere matter of the moment—I think I shall be among the English Poets after my death. Even as a Matter of present interest the attempt to crush me in the Quarterly has only brought me more into notice" (*KL*, 1:394).

It was consumption—what we now call tuberculosis—that killed Keats. But the sentimental fable of fatally harsh reviews quickly arose during the final stage of his illness and got into print soon after his death. Here is an example from Shelley's (admittedly self-serving) preface to *Adonais* (1821):

> The genius of the lamented person to whose memory I have dedicated these unworthy verses, was not less delicate and fragile than it was beautiful; and where cankerworms abound, what wonder if its young flower was blighted in the bud? The savage criticism on his *Endymion,* which appeared in the *Quarterly Review,* produced the most violent effect on his susceptible mind; the agitation thus originated ended in the rupture of a blood-vessel in the lungs; a rapid consumption ensued, and the succeeding acknowledgements from more candid critics, of the true greatness of his powers, were ineffectual to heal the wound thus wantonly inflicted.

"Delicate," "fragile," "blighted in the bud" set the tone, and Shelley's descriptions of Keats in the poem—for example, as "a pale flower by some sad maiden cherished . . . The bloom, whose petals nipt before they blew / Died on the promise of the fruit" (*Adonais* 48, 52–53)—further emphasize the poet's pitiful weakness.

Shelley did not know Keats very well. Those who did, a group of fiercely loyal surviving friends, almost immediately conceived the idea of writing a memoir to tell the truth about the poet's "beautiful character,"[3] a character that did not include delicacy and fragility. Hessey's publishing partner John Taylor sent announcements to both the *New Times* and the *Morning Chronicle* (29 March, 9 April, and 4 June 1821) to the effect that "speedily will be published, a biographical memoir of the late John Keats" (Brown 1966, 89). Then followed a prolonged squabble among the surviving friends over which of them was best qualified to do the job and who had the rights to his unpublished poems, letters, and other papers. Charles Brown, Keats's housemate during 1819–20 and the friend closest to him while he was writing *The Eve of St. Agnes,* the odes, and the rest of his most important poems, was a frontrunner, but it was more than a decade before he could begin serious work on the project.

The first memoir in print was Leigh Hunt's chapter, "Mr. Keats, with a Criticism on His Writings," in his *Lord Byron and Some of His Contemporaries* (1828), a lively account that opens with a lengthy paragraph on Keats's physical appearance and contains ten pages of excellently chosen quotations (including the whole of the Nightingale ode) to illustrate his descriptive genius as well as most of his letter of 10 May 1817 on his aspiration "to be in the Mouth of Fame" (*KL,* 1:136–40). Hunt draws on and supports elements of the "story" that had been taking shape, with details of the poet's "origin" ("of the humblest description"), his schooling ("the rudiments of a classical education"), and the bad effects of the reviews (a "system of calumny" that injured "a young and sensitive nature"). Hunt presents Keats as a sickly person all his life and concludes with details supplied by Joseph Severn of the poet's final illness and death in Rome (Hunt 1828, 1:407–50).

Hunt's memoir is one of a small cluster of events of the late 1820s marking the beginning of Keats's emergence from obscurity. The first English edition of Shelley's *Adonais* appeared in the following year (1829), a publication sponsored by the so-called Cambridge Apostles—Richard Monckton Milnes, Alfred Tennyson, and Arthur Hallam—and printed from a copy of the original 1821 Pisa edition that Hallam had brought back from Italy. Also in 1829 appeared a pirated *Poetical Works of Coleridge, Shelley, and Keats,* constituting the first collected edition of Keats's poems, with a memoir of Keats based on Hunt's *Lord Byron,* from the Paris publishers Anthony and William Galignani. Because of copyright laws, this Paris edition could not be sold in England, but it was freely available in the United States, where the Keats section was reprinted several times. It was a principal cause of the rapid growth of Keats's reputation among American readers.[4]

Brown thought Hunt's account of Keats, as he told Fanny Brawne on 17 December 1829, "worse than disappointing; I cannot bear it." But in combination with Galignani's edition, just then being printed, it had the effect of spurring Brown to action: "I am resolved to write his life, persuaded that no one, except yourself [Fanny Brawne], knew him better" (Brown 1966, 295). He read through the letters in his possession and wrote to friends seeking information and papers but also entered into a prolonged and increasingly bitter controversy with his old schoolfellow Charles Dilke concerning the honesty of George Keats in his financial dealings with the poet. One result of this last was George's injunction against the printing of any of his brother's unpublished poems in Brown's possession, a considerable obstacle to Brown's plans.

Brown, who had been living in Italy, returned to England and settled at Plymouth in the spring of 1835 and soon afterward became a member and an officer of the Plymouth Institution, a local organization for the promotion of literature, science, and the fine arts. It was for a lecture at the institution, on 29 December 1836, that Brown finally wrote his "Life of John Keats." Though not published until 1937, it is a work of considerable importance in the history of Keats's reputation.[5] After several unsuccessful attempts to get it published on his own, Brown, about to immigrate to New Zealand in the spring of 1841, gave the manuscript along with his copies of Keats's unpublished poems to Richard Monckton Milnes, whom he had met in Italy and considered a good choice as a person who had not known Keats firsthand and therefore could rise above the conflicting interests of the surviving friends. Seven years later, Brown's work became the basis of the first full-scale biography, Milnes's *Life, Letters, and Literary Remains, of John Keats* (1848).

In the history of his reputation, 1848 is the year after which Keats has always been "among the English Poets." With the help of Brown's manuscript "Life" as well as information from several others who had known Keats intimately and contributed their letters and reminiscences, Milnes gave Keats more respectable origins, a richer education, a healthier constitution, and a much fuller and more vital character. He included sixty-six poems (forty of them hitherto unpublished) from Brown's and others' manuscripts as well as some eighty of the poet's letters, most of them published for the first time. In much of the two-volume compilation, Milnes let Keats speak for himself through his letters, and the result—just as readers of the poet's letters have been discovering ever since—is the portrait of an interesting and thoroughly attractive personality, one that at the time was guaranteed to stimulate interest in the poetry. Milnes's work was widely reviewed, and Keats's reputation rose dramatically. Most important among the consequences was the new demand for Keats's works in print. The three lifetime volumes (the print runs no more than five hundred copies) were no longer available, and a cheap collected edition published by William Smith in 1840 had not been a commercial success. But some fifty editions or "quasi editions"—reprints presented as new editions—of the complete poems were published in the four decades between the year of Milnes's work and that of the next two biographies, by Sidney Colvin and William Michael Rossetti (brother of Dante Gabriel and Christina), both published in 1887.[6] With Milnes and fresh biographical interest facilitating the development, Keats at last got the requisite readership, and he has been "with Shakespeare," which is where Matthew Arnold placed him in an introductory essay of 1880, ever since.

*   *   *

In the second story that I am presenting, "poor Keats" (the subject of the first) gives way to smart Keats, accomplished Keats, and lucky Keats—this last, among other reasons, because it was just by chance that Brown, preparing to sail to New Zealand, gave his "Life of John Keats" and the unpublished poems to Milnes. In the first story, Keats is "with" Thomas Chatterton (to whom Keats dedicated *Endymion*), Henry Kirke White, and a few other per-manently young poets famous for dying before they fulfilled their promise. In the second story, Keats is with Shakespeare—and Chaucer, Spenser, Milton, and a handful of others—at the top of all lists of the most esteemed writers in English poetry. Regardless of the critical standards in use at a particular time, Keats regularly comes through with flying colors.

Keats has been likened to Shakespeare for some central stylistic similarities: richness of language, concreteness and particularity of descriptions, and an almost magical dexterity in harmonizing and varying the sounds and rhythms of the lines. For many decades now, while readers have grumbled at Milton's high seriousness, Pope's mechanically constructed couplets, Wordsworth's excessive plainness, Coleridge's shaky theology, Tennyson's wasteful musicality, and so on, commentators on Shakespeare and Keats have unstintingly praised their command of language and technique. Both writers have been the subjects of an immense quantity of critical writing. Along with their art, their lives and times have been exhaustively researched for clues to increased understanding, and their texts have been analyzed and interpreted endlessly, lending themselves to every kind of critical and theoretical approach.

This openness to interpretation shared by the two poets may result from their self-division. Their authorial character (as we infer from their writings) and the works themselves are full of ambiguities and contradictions; or, to put it in terms of Keats's definition of Negative Capability ("which Shakespeare posessed so enormously"), are full of "uncertainties, Mysteries, doubts, without any irritable reaching after fact & reason" (*KL,* 1:193). These two qualities—the durable attractiveness of the works and the kinds of ambiguity that the contradictions produce in those works—are causally related: the writings of Shakespeare and Keats are attractive *because of* the uncertainties, doubts, ambiguities, and contradictions.[7]

One of the wisest and most comprehensive short definitions of canonicity in print is that by the intellectual historian David Harlan:

> Canonical works are those texts that have gradually revealed themselves to be multi-dimensional and omni-significant, those works that have produced a plenitude of meanings and interpretations, only a small percentage of which make themselves available at any single reading. Canonical texts . . . generate new ways of seeing old things and new things we have never seen before. No matter how subtly or radically we change our approach to them, they always respond with something new; no matter how many times we

reinterpret them, they always have something illuminating to tell us. Their very indeterminacy means that they can never be exhausted. . . . Canonical works are multi-dimensional, omni-significant, inexhaustible, perpetually new, and, for all these reasons, "permanently valuable."[8] (Harlan 1989, 598)

This emphasis on multiplicity of meanings, indeterminacy, and interpretive inexhaustibility applies admirably to Keats, both as a person and as a poet.

In 1995, when exhibitions celebrating the bicentennial of Keats's birth were staged at Harvard, the Grolier Club in New York, the Clark Library in Los Angeles, the Dove Cottage Museum in Grasmere, and elsewhere, several Keatses were on display. There were the Keats of some extremely messy poetry drafts; the Keats of the confidently written-out fair copies; Keats as he appeared in the contemporary magazines and the three lifetime volumes; posthumous Keats, in his character as creator of another hundred poems that gradually became known after his death; the personal Keats of the day-to-day thinking and activities of his surviving letters; Keats as the well-loved friend at the center of a group now known as "the Keats Circle"; Keats of the various portraits that were made of him; and Keats the artistic collaborator, providing materials for subsequent nineteenth- and twentieth-century book designers, printers, and binders.

Many more Keatses can be extracted from criticism and scholarship over the years (including the several hundred papers delivered at the bicentennial celebrations): aesthetic Keats, the champion of art for art's sake; sensuous Keats, the creator of some of the most palpable imagery in all of British poetry; philosophical Keats, the describer of the Vale of Soul-making and life as a Mansion of Many Apartments; theoretical Keats, the formulator of Negative Capability and the idea of the "camelion Poet"; topographical Keats, the well-traveled tourist through the Lakes and Scotland; theatrical Keats, the theater reviewer and unproduced playwright; intertextual Keats, including Spenserian Keats, Leigh Huntian Keats, Shakespearean Keats, Miltonic Keats, and many others; political Keats, especially in the early poems and letters; a more sharply focused radical Keats; vulgar Keats, the only canonical male Romantic poet besides Blake who did not attend a university; Cockney Keats, a reference both to the 1818 Cockney School articles in *Blackwood's* and to the poet's supposed "lowly" upbringing, described in the earliest biographical accounts after his death; suburban Keats, referring to Keats's politically tinged connections with Hampstead and Leigh Hunt on the outskirts of London; effeminate Keats, the fainting flower of Shelley's *Adonais;* masculine Keats, his friends' defense against the notion of the fainting flower; heroic Keats, the one who suffers and matures from the trials of existence; and consumptive Keats, the one who dies so movingly every time we make our way to the end of the letters.

These different manifestations of the ever-changing chameleon Keats, selected from a large array of possibilities, are interesting in themselves but do not add up to the more concentrated canonical complexity—which I call Multiple Keats—that I think is at the heart of Keats's widespread and long-standing appeal to readers. Multiple Keats (in a definition already formulated in chapter 6) stands for an internal complexity in the poet constituted primarily by self-division—a sort of unresolved imaginative dividedness between the serious and the humorous, the straight and the ironic, the fanciful and the real, the high-flying and the down-to-earth, the sentimental and the satiric, the puffed up and the deflated. It shows itself in many places, both in biographical anecdote and in Keats's writings—and in the poetry, both in the frivolous pieces tossed off for immediate amusement and in the most serious efforts that Keats hoped would one day earn him a place among the English poets. One way of representing this self-division is by referring to various kinds of comedy: the antic, the zany, the farcical, the ridiculous, all of which have a basis in some form of incongruity or misfittingness. Something doesn't fit with something else.

There are hundreds of passages in Keats's letters involving puns, practical jokes, self-mockery, and comic description—many of them in incongruous juxtaposition with serious matters such as a friend's or his own illness, lack of money, disappointment in love, anxiety about the future, or an unfavorable review. Likewise, a sizable number of Keats's poems and passages in the poems are openly funny: the early lines about his trinity of women, wine, and snuff; the sonnet celebrating the grand climacteric of Mrs. Reynolds's cat; the whimsical self-description beginning "There was a naughty boy"; the lines about the cursed gadfly; the lines about the cursed bagpipe; the silly dialogue between Ben Nevis and Mrs. Cameron; the Spenserian stanzas making fun of his friend Charles Brown; and the extended self-parody in *The Jealousies*. The comedy in these pieces, just as with the jokes in the letters, regularly depends on juxtaposition of incongruities, as in the overthrow of expectations with a punch line.

Keats often puts the comic and the serious together in poems that are not primarily funny. Consider, for a handful of quick examples, Endymion pausing to rest on his extended travels and, when he casually stretches "his indolent arms" into the air, unintentionally clasping "O bliss! / A naked waist" (*Endymion* 2.711–13); Isabella and Lorenzo's myopic lovesickness in the opening stanzas of *Isabella;* the "monstrous" mice, birds, and Angora cat on Bertha's fire screen in *The Eve of St. Mark* (78–82); Porphyro's cartoonlike tip-toeing across Madeline's bedroom to check whether she is asleep in *The Eve of St. Agnes* (244–52); and the redness of Hermes's blushing ears in the first paragraph of *Lamia* (1.22–26). And there are larger, more serious mismatches— comic misfittingness without the comedy, as it were—everywhere one turns in the major poems. Porphyro is the hero of *The Eve of St. Agnes,* an ardent lover, a Prince Charming to the rescue, Madeline's future husband, and at the same time is associated with images of sorcery, Peeping Tomism, cruel seduction, and rape, while Madeline is the beautiful heroine, the belle of the ball, Sleeping Beauty, a pious Christian, Porphyro's bride, and at the same time is a foolish victim of both his stratagem and her own self-deception. In the sixth stanza of *Ode to a Nightingale,* the speaker first thinks it would be "rich to die, / To cease upon the midnight with no pain," and then the richness of his thought is immediately nullified by the realism of mortal extinction: "Still wouldst thou sing, and I have ears in vain— / To thy high requiem become a sod," he laments to the nightingale (55–60). In *To Autumn* we read a series of statements about the season's beauties, then we are made to realize that all this beauty is dying, and finally (perhaps), if we put these two contrary notions together, we understand that death is somehow beautiful.

In *Ode on a Grecian Urn,* which I shall use as a single extended example of the way Keats's characteristic self-dividedness shows up in the juxtaposed opposites of his poetry, the hypothetical romance world of "Tempe or the dales of Arcady" (7) in ancient Greece stands in obvious and pointed contrast to the speaker's own modern world of process and mortality. On the painted surface of one side of the urn (the subject of stanzas 2 and 3), the piper's melodies are imagined to be "unheard" and therefore "sweeter"; the piper never tires; the lovers, pursuing and pursued, never age or lose their beauty ("She cannot fade, though thou hast not thy bliss, / For ever wilt thou love, and she be fair!"); the "happy" trees never shed their leaves (it is eternal "spring"); everything is "far above" the "breathing . . . passion" of living humans, who are subject to "a heart high-sorrowful and cloy'd, / A burning forehead, and a parching tongue." On the other side of the urn (stanza 4), a sacrificial procession of "mysterious priest," lowing heifer, and townspeople is stopped forever on the way to some "green altar"; they will neither reach their destination nor go back to the "little town" that they came from (though the heifer also will never reach the altar, and the people, like the lovers, will not age or die). This too is different from the process of life in the real (the poet's) world.

There is a greater density of opposites in this poem than in perhaps any other of comparable length in all of British literature. The first image of the urn, as a "still unravish'd bride of quietness," immediately evokes the unstated counternotions of violence and sexual fulfillment in "ravished" bride. "Quietness" implies a contrary noisiness. The allied image of the urn as "foster-child of silence and slow time" makes one think of natural child. Pairings of this sort are a principal element of the ode's structure and very shortly are made explicit in the first two stanzas in such phrases as "deities or mortals, or . . . both," "men or gods," "mad pursuit . . . struggle to escape," "Heard melodies . . . those unheard," "sensual . . . spirit," and so on. This pairing of opposites turns, in the ode's final two lines, into a pairing of abstractions brought together in the urn's message: "Beauty is truth, truth beauty. . . ." What is important, for present purposes, is the near balance of pluses and minuses accorded to both sides of these pairs. Throughout the poem, in the phrases I have quoted and in the larger oppositions connected with time and timelessness, the two contrasted sides tend to get the speaker's, and the poem's, approval and disapproval almost equally.

Earlier critics—for example, the American New Humanists of the 1920s—tended to read the poem as unequivocal celebration of the timeless world of art, and they censured Keats for the supposed Romantic escapism that such celebration implied. Then in the close attention of the New Criticism to ironies, ambiguities, and paradoxes, readers began to notice (just as the speaker in the ode, being a clever reader, had noticed all along in perhaps half the lines of the poem) that the art world has its drawbacks as a hypothetical alternative to the human world: the piper cannot stop playing ("thou canst not leave / Thy song"); the lovers can never finally kiss or make love ("never, never canst thou kiss, / Though winning near the goal"); the trees are confined to a single season ("nor ever bid the spring adieu"); the permanent halting of the sacrificial procession leaves an unseen "little town" forever "silent" and "desolate." Some critics took these misgivings, especially the last image (38–40), to signify the poet's rejection of the ideal: the urn in the final stanza, now a "Cold Pastoral," is only a work of art after all, a "tease" just like eternity itself, somehow "a friend to man" but not of much practical help, since the concluding aphorism ("Beauty is truth, truth beauty"), as compelling as its terms are, really makes very little sense.

Both kinds of critical rendering—proideal (therefore escapist) and prore-ality (therefore skeptical of the ideal)—are necessarily one-sided. The poem itself is actually on both sides at once, because the urn, like the ideal that it represents, is both admired and gently pitied throughout the speaker's musings. Readers do not keep returning to the ode to learn that life in the real world is preferable to life on an urn (or vice versa). Rather, they are repeatedly drawn to the spectacle of the speaker's full feeling for uncertainties, mysteries, and doubts in the face of these oppositions. At any point, a resolution could go either way, and they read and reread, I think, to see how the conflict will conclude each time anew.

Ode on a Grecian Urn is an exemplary illustration of Keats's canonical complexity, as the accumulated critical literature on it attests.[9] The poem abounds in multiple and conflicting possibilities for interpretation—in the terms of David Harlan's definition that I quoted above, it is "multidimensional, omni-significant, inexhaustible, perpetually new"—and it also, in very practical terms, gets the highest ratings (for example, in publishers' surveys) from teachers using the Norton and other anthologies in graduate and undergraduate literature classes. It seems to be the nature of canonical works to have, or to provide the basis for, more meanings than any reader can process at a single reading and therefore to be, in a manner of speaking, infinitely readable. In literature courses having a seminar or lecture-discussion format, canonical works elicit more discussion because of their greater density, ambiguity, and self-contradiction. They are, above all, the works that are more interesting to read, teach, and talk about.

*   *   *

My second "story" of Keats, therefore, is quite simply (but also quite remarkably) the story of Keats writing a reckonable number of poems of this sort of complexity—among them, *The Eve of St. Agnes, La Belle Dame sans Merci,* the odes on a Grecian Urn, to a Nightingale, and to Autumn, *Lamia,* the Hyperion fragments, and several sonnets—and of large numbers of readers from the 1850s to the present day finding them interesting, moving, and delightful.

I do not mean to suggest that readers admire indeterminacy and the component qualities—uncertainty, ambiguity, contradiction, and so on—in the abstract. My point is that a poem's indeterminacy, uncertainty, and the rest make every individual reader's reading possible: in effect, the text of a complex poem validates what the reader wants to read in it. Thus for some readers *The Eve of St. Agnes* has been (and still is) a poem about love, even specifically Keats's love for Fanny Brawne, while for others it is a poem about the authenticity of dreams, about stratagems, about wish fulfillment, about artistic creativity, about Gothic literature, about family politics, about the crisis of feudalism, about escape, about critical interpretation, and so on

and on.[10] As one can see even in the briefest sampling of the critical literature, there have been (and presumably will continue to be) many different
explanations of what ails the knight at arms in *La Belle Dame*. There are
multiple possibilities for interpreting each of the odes and the rest of the
poems in the canonical list. The key to understanding the universality of
Keats's appeal is the fact that in every case the text may be seen to support
the interpretation, even when the interpretation stands in direct conflict
with another interpretation based on exactly the same text.

What was absolutely necessary, then, was Keats's attainment of a large
readership to make all this multiple interpreting possible, and he did this
posthumously, chameleon-like, by being all things to all people who sought
out his texts. In the middle of the nineteenth century, when biographical
interest in writers was at an all-time high, Keats's fame got an enormous
boost from the publication of Milnes's *Life, Letters, and Literary Remains*
(1848), in which many readers learned for the first time about the liveliness
of the poet's personality, the heroism of his struggle to achieve something
lasting in literature, the cruelty of the reviewers, and the tragic shortness of
his life. Not long afterward, when first the Pre-Raphaelites and then the art-
for-art's-sake enthusiasts made much of him, Keats represented their ideals
on two counts: he filled poems such as *Isabella* and *The Eve of St. Agnes* with
gorgeous, exquisitely detailed pictures that could be transferred, as it were,
directly onto the painters' canvases, and he seemed to act as a theorist as
well as a practitioner of aestheticism—in the famous exclamation to Benjamin Bailey, "O for a Life of Sensations rather than of Thoughts," for
example, and his numerous affirmations of the importance of beauty over
all other things (*KL*, 1:185, 1:194, 1:266, 1:388, 1:403, 1:404, 2:19, 2:263).

In the early decades of the twentieth century, when the philosophical and
moral ideas of a writer were considered of prime importance (an era marked
in Keats studies by the 1926 publication of Clarence Thorpe's *The Mind of
John Keats*), the poet could again provide what was wanted, this time in the
thematic seriousness of the Hyperion fragments and especially, again, in
statements in his letters concerning such concepts as Negative Capability, life
as a Mansion of Many Apartments, and the world as a Vale of Soul-making.
In the midcentury heyday of New Criticism, Keats supplied poem after poem
for "close readings" in the classrooms and the critical journals. More recently,
evidence of political and social concerns is among the prime critical desider-
ata, and again Keats has come through—in a Modern Language Association
symposium on "Keats and Politics" and in a spate of fresh books and articles
on the topic by Daniel Watkins, Nicholas Roe, and others.[11]

Most important is the fact that all through these decades, as one set of values and emphases succeeded another, Keats has continued to be the author of *The Eve of St. Agnes, Hyperion, La Belle Dame, Lamia,* and the great odes—poems that seem open to every possible interpretation and therefore are eminently adaptable to whatever special interest or approach seeks them out. For biographical matter, there is the spectacle of Keats speaking personally to the Urn or the Nightingale or figuring in love situations in the guise of Porphyro, the knight at arms, or Lycius in *Lamia.* For the art interests of the later nineteenth century, no writer created so many pictures in poetry since Spenser and Shakespeare, and nobody so fervently expressed the love of beauty—beauty was truth itself at the end of the Grecian Urn ode. For Matthew Arnold and all subsequent Arnoldians, the poems have been full of moral situations and therefore moral ideas—especially in the numerous contrasts of human life with some hypothetical alternative. For the New Critics—and for generations of teachers and readers influenced by them—Keats's complexity of language has provoked repeated investigation, analysis, and interpretive response. For the current concern with politics, consider just the tiny example of "peaceful citadel" in one of the emptied towns imagined in the penultimate stanza of *Ode on a Grecian Urn:* the image joins the contrary notions of peace and war (a citadel is a military fortress) and has faint nonpastoral implications both for the religious activity of the townsfolk away on their sacrificial procession and, more generally, for the pastoral tranquillity of Tempe and the dales of Arcady (where, we already have heard, maidens "struggle to escape" the "mad pursuit" of men or gods). "Peaceful" and "citadel" are just two words from the poem, but they could be the starting point for an essay titled, for example, "The Ominous Politics of *Ode on a Grecian Urn.*" This kind of interpretive plenitude—allowing the possibility of a critical essay for every two words of text, as it were—can illustrate what Keats has been for readers since the middle of the nineteenth century: a figure whose life, letters, and poems taken together are rich and varied enough to satisfy every idea of what a poet and poetry should be.

PART II

Wordsworth
and Coleridge

8

Textual Primitivism and the Editing of Wordsworth

STUDENTS OF ROMANTICISM have long been familiar with the spectacle of Wordsworth revising himself. He wrote his poems over and over in a process that with some works went on for decades before publication (e.g., *Peter Bell, Guilt and Sorrow,* and *The Prelude,* first published twenty-one, forty-eight, and forty-five years, respectively, after they were initially completed) and with others continued for decades *after* first publication (e.g., some of the pieces of *Lyrical Ballads* that Wordsworth kept altering for the next forty years). Frequently the interval between original composition and significant revision involved not only temporal but psychological distance, and in such cases the revising poet may be thought of as having a separate identity from the poet who composed in the first place. Wordsworth was keenly aware of temporal and psychological separations, as a condition not so much of poetry writing as of life more generally—for example, in these lines from the opening paragraph of *The Prelude,* book 2:

> . . . so wide appears
> The vacancy between me and those days,
> Which yet have such self-presence in my mind,
> That, musing on them, often do I seem
> Two consciousnesses, conscious of myself
> And of some other Being.[1]
>
> (28–33)

And he made such "vacancies" a moving cause of worry or celebration in some of his best-known poems (*Tintern Abbey, Nutting,* the Intimations ode, and shorter lyrics such as *To a Butterfly* ["Stay near me"], *To the Cuckoo,* and *My heart leaps up*).

In twentieth-century Wordsworth scholarship, however, and with alarming acceleration in the last two decades and on into the twenty-first century, the later Wordsworth is being forced out of the picture, and a kind of textual primitivism has taken hold that in effect is burying, possibly forever, some of Wordsworth's most admired writing. Ironically, this is in large part an unintended result of one of the truly important and valuable editing projects of recent times, the Cornell Wordsworth. The disappearance of the revised Wordsworth can be studied in shorter and longer poems alike, but *The Prelude* offers the richest single example because of its lengthy history and the abundance of extant materials. I shall turn to it first, briefly rehearsing the routine facts of composition and publication and then considering some of the consequences of the way in which twentieth-century scholars have discovered and promoted other versions preliminary to the one that we think Wordsworth wanted us to read. Historically, it is argument over *The Prelude* (How many *Preludes* are there? Which one is the "real" *Prelude?*) that has led to the more general textual and critical predicament I am concerned with.

*   *   *

Wordsworth began drafting the work that ultimately became his masterpiece at Goslar, Germany, during the autumn and winter of 1798–99, resumed composition back in England the following autumn, and by the end of 1799 had produced a two-part fragmentary work of 978 lines.[2] Much of the rest of what we now think of as *The Prelude* was first drafted in 1804–5. Wordsworth seems in the early months of 1804 to have carried the 1799 project forward with a five-book scheme in mind, and then, in mid-March, to have abruptly set that aside in favor of a much grander plan. After little more than a year of amazing productivity, he completed a poem of thirteen books—close to 8,500 lines—in May 1805. He then, intermittently during the next thirty-four years, revised and retouched it, section by section and line by line, altering in one way or another nearly half of those 8,500 lines. The latest revisions of any consequence date from 1839, by which time the original book 10 had been divided into two. The poem was first published, in the fourteen-book version, in July 1850, three months after the poet's death.

For seventy-five years the printed text of 1850 was the only version known outside the Wordsworth family. Then in 1926, in one of the landmark editing feats of the twentieth century—slapdash in detail, as it has turned out, but of the utmost importance as a stimulus to appreciation and understanding of Wordsworth's achievement—Ernest de Selincourt made public the thirteen-book version of 1805, taken from manuscripts A and B (in the hands of the poet's sister and wife), in an edition giving the texts of 1805 and 1850 on facing pages. De Selincourt's edition, revised by Helen Darbishire in 1959, with corrections and additions to both the text and the apparatuses and notes, was the much-admired standard for scholarly and critical use until a spate of new editions appeared in the 1970s. Stephen Gill revised de Selincourt's text of 1805 (which had been separately issued by Oxford University Press) in 1970, and J. C. Maxwell produced *The Prelude: A Parallel Text,* again with facing texts of 1805 and 1850, for Penguin in 1971. The so-called two-part *Prelude* of 1798–99, constructed on the basis of manuscripts V and U (again in the hands of Dorothy Wordsworth and Mary Hutchinson), was published three times between 1974 and 1979—first in a text prepared by Jonathan Wordsworth and Stephen Gill for M. H. Abrams's *Norton Anthology of English Literature,* third edition (1974); then in the Cornell Wordsworth volume devoted solely to the 1798–99 version edited by Stephen Parrish (1977); and finally in the Norton Critical Edition of *The Prelude, 1799, 1805, 1850,* edited by Jonathan Wordsworth, Abrams, and Gill (1979). A five-book version of early 1804 has been constructed and championed by Jonathan Wordsworth (1977). W. J. B. Owen's magisterial reediting of the fourteen-book version, this time from the latest authoritative manuscript rather than the printed text of 1850, appeared in the Cornell Wordsworth series in 1985. And a major reediting of the thirteen-book text and related manuscripts by Mark Reed added two more large *Prelude* volumes to the Cornell series in 1991.

How many of the distinctive versions of *The Prelude,* if any, Wordsworth himself considered finished is a moot question. Scholars nowadays tend to recognize three, four, or five stages but do not agree concerning their completeness and (in general) are careful to guard against excessive claims. The earliest stage, the two-part work of 1798–99, begins in the middle of a line with two pronouns lacking antecedents: "Was it for this . . . ?" It gives us draft versions of some of the most memorable passages of the later texts— boat stealing, ice-skating, the drowned man of Esthwaite, spots of time, "Blest the infant Babe," and so on—but without connecting one with another structurally or thematically. The work is probably best viewed (and probably was so regarded by Wordsworth) as an assemblage of materials for a serious poem to come. It is unquestionably of interest and deserves the attention it has received, but the fact that it exists in fair copies is not enough to persuade even its several editors that it was ever thought of as a finished poem.

The second of the stages, the five-book version of early 1804, has only a hypothetical existence based on Wordsworth's remark in a letter to Francis Wrangham of late January or early February 1804: "At present I am engaged in a Poem on my own earlier life which will take five parts or books to complete, three of which are nearly finished" (Wordsworth 1967, 436). Jonathan Wordsworth has elaborately reconstructed the supposed contents of the five books—or what *would* have been the five books had the poet carried out the project—and praised the result as "in many ways the most impressive of the *Preludes,* bringing together in a densely packed, unique, and formally satisfying unit the great poetry of Wordsworth's original inspiration at Goslar in 1798, and the new magnificent sequences of early 1804." But the work in this stage, as Jonathan Wordsworth himself admits, "does not survive as a whole in fair copy and cannot be printed, as can *1799* and *1805*" (1997, 1)[3]—a condition that seriously stands in the way of its being "impressive" and "satisfying."

The third stage can be printed and read and has been available in successively more accurate texts ever since 1926—the thirteen-book *Prelude* of 1805. This is the earliest version that Mark Reed (1975, 628, 635) thinks Wordsworth considered a complete poem, and I am inclined to agree, at least provisionally. The fourth stage, a relative latecomer in the array, is an intermediate version, circa 1819, falling between 1805 and the "final" text of the late 1830s. Though not fair-copied (and therefore perhaps having a foot in the hypothetical category of the five-book poem earlier), it exists as a distinctive level of revision all through the thirteen books, a revision that, according to its discoverer, Mark Reed (who sets forth details in the last section of his introduction to *The Thirteen-Book "Prelude,"* 1:62 ff.), produces a more lofty and formalized rhetoric than in any of the other stages earlier or later. The fifth stage is of course the version we have had the longest—the latest that Wordsworth had a hand in, the one that, by means of an intermediary copy and the agency of the poet's widow (who gave the poem its title), his nephew Christopher Wordsworth, and several helpers at the press, was posthumously published in 1850.

Of all these versions, the most reckonable, and clearly the ones having the best claim to be considered complete poems, are the thirteen-book text of 1805 and the fourteen-book text of 1850 (the versions of the facing-page editions of the last seventy-five years). The earlier has plenty of historical value as the text that Wordsworth read aloud to Coleridge, recently returned from Malta, on a succession of evenings in December 1806 and January 1807. Wordsworth did not publish it because, at the time and for many years afterward, he continued to have hopes of writing the magnum opus (*The Recluse*) for which *The Prelude* was supposed to be an introduction. The 1850 text has the legitimacy traditionally accorded to the latest authoritative version. Wordsworth himself anticipated textual scholars of the first half of the twentieth century in this principle: "you know," he reminded Alexander Dyce in a letter of mid-April 1830, "what importance I attach to following strictly the last Copy of the text of an Author" (Wordsworth 1979a, part 2, 236). Latest also has an attractive practical advantage: "first," "earliest," and especially "earliest complete" are elusive entities, frequently difficult or even impossible to establish, but we can almost always determine what is latest with a high degree of certainty.

The fact remains, however, that, apart from a handful of short excerpts, Wordsworth never published any version of *The Prelude* (a remarkable fact of literary history in itself), and we are left with two principal texts that are separated by thirty-four years and differ from one another in thousands of substantive and accidental details. Oddly, this plurality of texts has made a great many scholars and critics uncomfortable, as if multiple authorship were undesirable even when all the authors have the same name. Almost from the first publication of the 1805 text, in the 1920s, there has been controversy over which of the *Preludes*, left-hand or right-hand sides of the facing pages, is superior—whether poetically, aesthetically, biographically, psychoanalytically, and even, for some readers, politically, religiously, or philosophically. In recent years the controversy has begun to have some unfortunate consequences on our view of Wordsworth's texts more generally.

*   *   *

When de Selincourt published the 1805 version he was by no means merely producing a variant text and apparatus of antiquarian interest. For several reasons (and surely the normal human desire to aggrandize one's achievements was among them), he presented 1805 as a better, more authentic, more vital creation than the received text of 1850. Critical opinion from Victorian times had thoroughly established the notion of two Wordsworths— the youthful, radical, freethinking, and highly innovative genius of the *Lyrical Ballads* and *Poems, in Two Volumes,* and the pitiful old man (old, in this view, practically before he was forty) who had declined into flat versification, boring subjects (railroads, capital punishment!), and, what was much worse, political conservatism and religious orthodoxy. This latter was the Wordsworth depicted by the thirty-one-year-old Robert Browning as "The Lost Leader," a traitor who "alone sinks to the rear and the slaves." It was natural that the new version of *The Prelude*, in a manuscript text written during the great decade of creativity and dated almost half a century earlier than the text of the first edition, would be looked at eagerly for revelations concerning the political and philosophical ideas of the younger Wordsworth.

De Selincourt played up this interest in his introduction, where, after a thirty-page account of the manuscripts and the known facts concerning composition, he entered into comparison of the early and late texts, first "in point of style" (with sections on "later improvements" and "later deterioration") and then as to "changes of idea." The section on later stylistic improvements begins innocently enough—"No one would doubt that the 1850 version is a better composition than the A [1805] text"—and goes on to praise the stronger phrasings, the more closely knit texture, the greater precision of diction (in short, the craftsmanship) of 1850. The section on later deterioration, seemingly offered in order to strike a judicious balance, counters with examples of abstract language, "pompous phrase-making," loss of the earlier text's "delicate simplicity." Shortly thereafter, rather out of the blue, comes a separate section headed "The ideal text of 'The Prelude'":

> The ideal text of *The Prelude* . . . would follow no single manuscript. It would retain from the earliest version such familiar details as have any autobiographical significance. Of purely stylistic changes from that text, it would accept those only which Wordsworth might have made (and some he would certainly have made), had he prepared the poem for the press in his greatest period, changes designed to remove crudities of expression, and to develop or clarify his original meaning: but it would reject those later excrescences of a manner less pure, at times even meretricious, which are out of key with the spirit in which the poem was first conceived and executed. Most firmly it would reject all modifications of his original thought and attitude to his theme.

The main point of this statement, and especially the last sentence just quoted, becomes clear with the final three sections that follow it, in which de Selincourt depicts only deterioration—changes of idea concerning the poet's life at Cambridge, resulting in "criticisms directed by a man of seventy winters against his own past"; changes in his attitude to the French Revolution, showing "clear signs of his growing conservatism"; and, in the longest section of all, changes in his "Philosophy of life and religion." Wordsworth "felt it incumbent on him to remove from *The Prelude* all that might be interpreted as giving support to . . . heresy"; these "most to be regretted" alterations are "foreign to [the work's] original spirit," and they "cover up the traces of his early pantheism," "disguise his former faith," and "have no rightful place in the poem" (Wordsworth 1959, lvii, lxi, lxiii, lxiv, lxvi, lxviii, lxxi–lxxiv).[4]

The *Times Literary Supplement* reviewer felt that de Selincourt "makes . . . too much of what Wordsworth alters, and too little of what he keeps," and refused to approve the editor's notion of an ideal text (Anon. 1926). Leslie Nathan Broughton, in the *Journal of English and Germanic Philology*, likewise judged that de Selincourt was too severe on Wordsworth's religious changes: "After all what concerns us most is the Wordsworth of the years prior to the writing of the poem, and of him at best we can have only an approximation. As for the rest, whether we have the Wordsworth of 1804 or 1820 matters little; he may be a man of thirty-four or of sixty-nine trying to recall his youth" (Broughton 1927, 431). Generally, however, the reviewers accepted, echoed, and even enlarged on de Selincourt's strictures, beginning with de Selincourt's own student Helen Darbishire, who, writing in *Nineteenth Century and After,* commented that "the changes most to be deplored in [Wordsworth's] later text are those which overlay or obscure that naïve immediate expression [of the inner workings of his mind]. They generally mar the poetry; they always disguise the truth" (Darbishire 1926, 720).[5] G. C. Moore Smith, in *Modern Language Review,* remarking on the "very different spirit [in 1805] from the poem as revised for publication when the poet was an old man" and "the many changes which were for the worse," gave "hearty assent" to de Selincourt's suggestion for an ideal text (Smith 1926, 443–46). Wordsworth's biographer George McLean Harper, in the *Saturday Review of Literature,* similarly approved of the ideal text, describing 1850 as "an incongruous mixture of [Wordsworth's] early convictions with the conservative views of his old age" (Harper 1926). Henry King, in a piece in the *Adelphi* headed "Wordsworth's Decline," had "no hesitation in declaring that I vastly prefer the original version": "for the most part the revisions are a depressing record of growing timidity and impotence"; the poem "is a fascinating study in poetic degeneration" and "makes a unique, but alas! a terribly depressing record, of the decline of a great poet" (King 1926).

This preponderant opinion among the 1926–27 reviewers is the one that, in both modest statements and high flights of rhetoric, has prevailed ever since. Here, for example, is a statement from a standard literary history of the 1930s: "Of all these troubled years the *Prelude* tells the engrossing story; but it should be read in its first impassioned form, written close to the events, though unpublished until 1926, not in the version to which Wordsworth reduced it in old age when he was no longer a great poet" (Osgood 1935, 396). Edith C. Batho, in *The Later Wordsworth* (1933), and Mary E. Burton, in *The One Wordsworth* (1942), the latter work devoted specifically to a defense of the *Prelude* revisions, argued for unity and continuity in Wordsworth's career—one Wordsworth rather than two—and Raymond Dexter Havens's comprehensive study of *The Prelude* published in 1941 aimed throughout at explication of the 1850 text.[6] But these stand out as exceptions. Biographers and critics in large numbers resorted to 1805 for its supposed greater truthfulness, and the earlier version became the standard for routine scholarly quotation and reference.

Subsequently there has been, especially in short and medium-size journal articles, a great deal of highly sophisticated analysis and interpretation based on comparison of earlier and later texts, most often 1805 against 1850 but also 1798–99 (and sometimes 1804) against 1805—and not infrequently earlier texts against both 1805 and 1850.[7] This is much to the good, and the general trend of the studies has been that while Wordsworth may have had different purposes during different periods of his work on the poem, he seems to have known what he was doing all along. But comparative *evaluations* of early and later versions still mechanically favor the earlier, and where de Selincourt had tried to give a balanced view of the two texts' stylistic differences, later critics, wishing to align quality of style with quality of ideas, have declared 1805 preferable not only as biography, politics, and philosophy but also as poetry. We see this in remarks such as Richard Schell's acknowledgment ("of course") that 1805 "is generally superior biographically and aesthetically to the 1850 version of the poem" (Schell 1975, 593) and Jonathan Arac's casual reference to "the piously revised text of 1850" (Arac 1983, 145–46).[8] An extreme statement of the same tendency is Philip Hobsbaum's, in an essay titled "The Essential Wordsworth": "The promulgation of the 1850 text is a matter for keen regret." Using verbs such as "maltreat," "fade out," and "blur" to describe Wordsworth's revisions, Hobsbaum finds 1805 so conspicuously better in artistic and narrative technique that he thinks the Victorian novelists, if they had been able to read the earlier version, would have written long poems instead of novels: "It is . . . not too much to suggest that, had *The Prelude* been published when it was written, in 1805, these successors [George Eliot and other novelists] would not have used prose as the medium for their fictions" (Hobsbaum 1979, 187, 190, 191, 193).

Hobsbaum has no standing as a Wordsworth critic, but another extremist who on occasion employs the same extravagance of rhetoric has considerable reputation: Jonathan Wordsworth. The first sentence of the preface to *The Music of Humanity* (1969) sets forth a theme, and implies a program, of much of Jonathan Wordsworth's scholarship of the 1970s and 1980s: "On the whole poets are known by the best versions of their works: Wordsworth is almost exclusively known by the worst" (J. Wordsworth 1969, xiii).[9] In separate essays, then prominently in the Norton Critical Edition of *The Prelude* (in which he was senior editor principally responsible for, among other parts, the earlier texts and the sections on "Composition and Texts"), and still later in *William Wordsworth: The Borders of Vision* (1982), he has passionately advocated early texts of *The Prelude*—1805 over 1850, 1804 over 1805, 1798–99 over 1804 and/or 1805—and of other poems as well, beginning, of course, with *The Ruined Cottage*. Here, as part of a comparison of the 1805 and 1850 texts of the ascent of Snowdon in the final book of *The Prelude,* is a typical example of his opinion of Wordsworth as reviser:

> Wordsworth does not merely destroy one of his greatest pieces of poetry [in his later alterations], he weakens precisely those aspects which had made it the fitting climax to his poem. To watch him in full retreat is to be reminded of the grandeur of the claims that he no longer dares to make. It is difficult to know whether it is the episode itself, or the gloss, that suffers most in revision. From the moment when the light first falls upon the turf, only half a dozen isolated lines have not been changed for the worse.

The 1850 revision, we are advised, has "nebulous, safe, apologetic lines," "a cosier moon . . . seen in conventional terms," elements that are "intrusive and distracting," "irrelevant," and representative of "dwindling," "self-abasing," and "fudging" (J. Wordsworth 1982, 328–31).[10]

Surely this is strange language to apply to one of the most admired episodes in *The Prelude* of 1850 (as it is in that of 1805). Such judgments are not totally irresponsible, however. Jonathan Wordsworth is the principal discoverer and best expositor of some of the early texts he is promoting, and his gusto is understandable. And when he organizes and chairs a Wordsworth Summer Conference debate (in Grasmere, August 1984) on the "relative merits" of 1805 and 1850, dividing up the proponents into "teams," the result is mainly good fun—an entertaining activity to span the time between hiking excursions and evenings in the pub.[11] But certain aspects of his influence are more worrisome, extending into the Cornell

Wordsworth (of which he has been an advisory editor from the beginning) and the state of the poet's texts more generally.

*   *   *

The Cornell Wordsworth, in some twenty volumes beginning with *The Salisbury Plain Poems,* edited by Stephen Gill (1975), is a work of immense practical usefulness for the study of Wordsworth and one of the most significant editing projects in Romantic literature of the past century. Concerned with presenting full and accurate texts of early versions of Wordsworth's poems, rather than the hitherto customary later or "final" texts, the new series is conspicuous for several praiseworthy features: its spaciousness of treatment (several hundred pages may be given to the materials underlying a poem of only a few hundred lines), generosity of detail (frequently there are *three* separate printings—in photographs of the manuscript, exact transcription, and reading text—of a single version of a poem), and ingenuity of presentation (the editors use several sizes and styles of type, several kinds of brackets, deletion linings, superimposition shadings, and some other devices). Throughout it embodies a concept of "no-fault" editing: the scholarly procedures are clearly explained, all necessary information concerning a text is given in one place or another in the appropriate volume, and special circumstances are plainly noted wherever they occur. One may disagree with a choice of reading text or with a decision to emend (or not to emend), but the alternatives are nearly always available in the apparatuses. One may disagree with some detail in the transcription of Wordsworth's or a copyist's handwriting, but the photographs are there for all to see. The series is universally admired as a model of painstaking editorial work, and the press has done a superb job with the design and production of the volumes. Nevertheless, the Cornell Wordsworth, in its condemnation of "the worst" of Wordsworth[12] and its understandable eagerness to discover, promulgate, and extol early versions to take the place of later ones, is in the process of doing away with the later Wordsworth once and for all. I shall briefly sketch what I see as four problems associated with the project, beginning with two that seem less consequential than the ones that follow.

First, there is the elusiveness of the "earliest complete state" of a work, the expressed goal of some part or another of more than half the volumes in the series. The difficulty of determining what is "earliest" in combination with what is "complete" may show up in isolated details of a text—single lines, phrases, even words—and also in whole versions. Here is an example from the volume entitled *"The Ruined Cottage" and "The Pedlar,"* expertly edited by James Butler (Wordsworth 1979c). In the middle of his introduction (15) Butler quotes the following passage from the Alfoxden Notebook:

> Why is it we feel
> So little for each other but for this
> That we with nature have no sympathy
> Or with such idle objects as have no power to hold
> Articulate language.

Butler says in a footnote that he is quoting "the unrevised base text" of the passage, but the photograph and facing transcription of the notebook's leaf 20v (120–21) show some deletion and revision in the next-to-last line:

>   things
> Or with such ~~idle objects~~ as have no
>   power to hold

Almost surely Wordsworth deleted "idle objects" and inserted "things" *before* continuing with the rest of the line, "as have no power to hold" (the final three words are runover, not interlineation). The "earliest complete" version of the line is the pentameter "Or with such things as have no power to hold," and the longer line quoted as "unrevised base text"—thirteen or fourteen syllables that fit no known metrical pattern—is a scholarly construct that had no existence as a unit in anybody's mind before Butler presented it in the late 1970s.

The fact is that wherever deletions, interlineations, and many other kinds of alteration occur, inevitably there are questions of sequence and chronology, and until one arrives at the *final* text of a version, the possible combinations of revised and unrevised readings (not to mention the complication of several successive alterations in a single passage or even a single line) are, with a work of substantial length, virtually endless. Both *The Ruined Cottage* and *The Pedlar* are poems of substantial length. In earlier and later manuscript texts of both works there are additions and alterations—Wordsworth filling gaps left by a copyist, revisions over erasures (with the erased text sometimes recoverable, sometimes not), "occasional minor corrections of meter, grammar, and internal inconsistencies" (Butler in Wordsworth 1979c, 37). I am confident that Butler has done the best possible job of choosing among original and revised readings in constructing his texts. But the results are editorial constructs, simply approximations to the ideal, and the "earliest completeness" of so complicated a network of particulars has to remain a matter of speculation.

A question may also be raised (but not definitively answered) concerning the completeness of these poems as a whole. *The Ruined Cottage* exists in two distinctly different texts dating from 1798 and 1799, was revised further as part of *The Pedlar* in several more versions of 1802–4, and ultimately was incorporated into book 1 of *The Excursion* and first published in 1814. These prepublication forms are currently considered "lost poems" or "new poems" in the Wordsworth canon, and the manuscript D text of *The Ruined Cottage* in particular, first published by Jonathan Wordsworth in *The Music of Humanity* (1969), has widespread circulation among the Wordsworth selections in *The Norton Anthology of English Literature.* It is doubtful, however, whether the poet himself considered any version complete before the printed text of 1814. As Stephen Gill has pointed out in a thoughtful essay on Wordsworth's texts generally, the manuscript D *Ruined Cottage* is complete mainly because scholars have declared it to be so: "Only those prepared to study all of the evidence in Butler's edition can be expected to realize that the text most readily available is . . . an editorial creation" (Gill 1983, 188).[13] Very likely the same will apply to other so-called lost poems being discovered by the Cornell editors.

The second problem has to do with the focus or scope of annotation in some of the Cornell volumes and is of consequence only as one more manifestation of bias favoring early texts over later. Whether inadvertently or as a matter of principle, there is, in facing-texts situations, a tendency to regard the earlier version (on the left) as the main text at hand and the later (on the right) as a variant having inferior status. My example here will be *The Borderers,* edited by Robert Osborn (Wordsworth 1982), in which the last sentence of the editorial introduction to the parallel reading texts explains, "Beneath the early version are critical and interpretive notes, most of which apply equally to the late version" (69). This is reasonable procedure as far as it goes, but it means that passages of revised text where there is no corresponding early text on the left-hand side necessarily go unannotated.

Thus "some natural tears" in the late version, line 762 (echoing the same phrase in *Paradise Lost* 12.645), "not a nerve would tremble" in line 779 (echoing *Macbeth* 3.4.101–2), and "fallen, / Like the old Roman, on their own sword's point" in lines 2310–11 (cf. *Macbeth* 5.8.1–2), each of which gets a note in de Selincourt's Oxford English Texts *Poetical Works,* are presented without commentary in the Cornell volume. (They are not especially striking parallels but nevertheless are exactly the kind of citation that Osborn provides in hundreds of notes to the early version.) In two notes on page 104, to early version 1.3.5–23, Osborn refers to the "eighteenth-century tradition of mad maidens" and cites Cowper's "Crazed Kate" in *The Task* and parts of Wordsworth's *A Ballad* and *Dirge*. A more useful reference, especially relevant to lines 15, 18, and 22—"no one ever heard . . . in rain or storm . . . they say"—would have been Wordsworth's *The Thorn;* and the phrase "an Infant's grave" on the facing right-hand page, in late version line 393, suggests that the poet himself was aware of the echo. I think Osborn would have included such a reference (*The Thorn* has "many a time and oft were heard," "In rain, in tempest," "They say," "Some say," "an infant's grave" in lines 159, 79, 122, 205, 214, 55, 61) had he devoted more serious critical attention to his later text of the play.

The third problem—to my mind much more serious than either of the preceding—is the virtual exclusion of Wordsworth's final texts from the Cornell Wordsworth. The volume containing *Peter Bell*, edited by John E. Jordan (Wordsworth 1985b), is a handy example. Its parallel reading texts are an editorial composite of two manuscripts of 1799 on the left-hand pages (principally manuscript 2, with passages from manuscript 3 where the former is defective) and the text of the first edition of 1819 on the right-hand pages. As in most of the other volumes in the series, a complete collation of variants from lifetime (and, where appropriate, posthumous) printings allows readers to reconstruct—in their minds or on paper—any of the subsequent authoritative versions, including of course the last, with a high degree of accuracy. Nevertheless, these later versions are available here *only* via the apparatus readings, and this means that for all practical purposes they have dropped out of sight and, given the likely influence that the Cornell Wordsworth will exert in the future (see below), out of the Wordsworth canon entirely.

Wordsworth's composition of *Peter Bell,* in five distinct manuscript versions and a succession of printed texts thereafter, by no means ended with the publication of the poem in 1819. He made changes for the version printed in his *Miscellaneous Poems* in 1820; further changes for each of the three versions in his *Poetical Works* of 1827, 1832, and 1836; and still more for his *Poems* in 1845. Between the first edition of 1819 and the final lifetime printing in the *Poetical Works* of 1849–50, he altered the poem substantively in close to two hundred lines (roughly one-sixth of the total). From his point of view, of course, these later changes, just like those in the successive manuscripts earlier, were improvements, and it is fairly easy to find examples that seem to justify the process.

The ass's "loud and piteous bray" in the first edition (505) is replaced by "long and clamorous bray" in the final text (465), and this revision enabled

Wordsworth to strengthen another descriptive phrase three stanzas later, rewriting "long dry see-saw of his horrible bray" (520) as "hard dry see-saw . . ." (480). The following in the first edition (in which "He" refers to the ass) is purely narrative business:

> That Peter on his back should mount
> He shows a wish, well as he can,
> "I'll go, I'll go, whate'er betide—
> "He to his home my way will guide,
> "The cottage of the drowned man."
> (636–40)

The final version of the same stanza, more straightforward in narration, adds thematic implications in the last two lines:

> But no—that Peter on his back
> Must mount, he shows well as he can:
> Thought Peter then, come weal or woe,
> I'll do what he would have me do,
> In pity to this poor drowned man.
> (591–95)

For this passage describing Peter's thoughts in the first edition—

> And once again those darting pains,
> As meteors shoot through heaven's wide plains,
> Pass through his bosom—and repass!
> (783–85)

—the corresponding final text has more emotion ("ghastly" in place of "darting"), is more consistently located (within Peter rather than shooting through heaven), and is more substantial rhetorically ("and repass" in the earlier text seems merely to fill out the line):

> And once again those ghastly pains,
> Shoot to and fro through heart and reins,
> And through his brain like lightning pass.
> (733–35)

"Renounced his folly" at the end of the final text (1133) seems much more in keeping with the idea of Peter's conversion than the first edition's "repressed his folly" (1183). And so on.

I am not especially interested in arguing that the final text of *Peter Bell* is rhetorically, narratively, or thematically better than earlier printed versions (and in any case I am probably incapable of objective judgment in the matter simply because I have been reading and teaching the final text for several decades). But I am concerned to emphasize that the latest readable text of *Peter Bell* in the Cornell edition is the *first,* not the last, printed version, and that Wordsworth's subsequent revisions, in bits and pieces in the Cornell apparatus, can only be reconstituted fragmentarily—a substitution here, another there—in a process inconvenient to the trained textual scholar and, realistically considered, out of the question for the student and general reader. (In the Cornell edition, to arrive at the final text of lines 733–35, which I have quoted just above from my Riverside *Selected Poems and Prefaces,* one must combine line 783 of the 1819 text with the apparatus variant "ghastly," a revision that first shows up in the printing of 1836; add the variant lines to 784–85 that Wordsworth inscribed in his personal copy of *Poetical Works* of 1832; and then insert into *those* lines two further readings first appearing in 1836.)

Parrish, describing Wordsworth as a poet who strove "tirelessly for perfection of his art," says that the Cornell series will "make it possible . . . to follow the maturation of his poetic genius, and to honor his lifelong concern about his poems" (Parrish 1976, 90, 91). For readers using the Cornell *Peter Bell,* the poet's maturation may seem to come to an abrupt stop with the text of 1819. The rest of his lifelong concern is relegated to the apparatus. The same is true of Wordsworth's mature revisions in several other volumes—for example, *An Evening Walk* and *Descriptive Sketches,* where the latest reading texts are those of 1836; *Benjamin the Waggoner,* in which the latest text is, as with *Peter Bell,* the first edition of 1819; and the volume containing *Poems, in Two Volumes,* for which the latest texts are those of 1807. In all these volumes the apparatuses are remarkably full and precise. But they are not (nor are they intended to be) the equivalent of the poetic texts themselves.

The fourth and largest problem, a product and extension of everything I have so far discussed in this section, is the general effect that the Cornell emphasis on early texts may have on the study and understanding of Wordsworth in the next several decades. I shall use some examples from Jared Curtis's edition of *"Poems, in Two Volumes," and Other Poems* (Wordsworth 1983), which like all the others is an exemplary piece of scholarly editing. Let us imagine a student in the library seeking a respectable text of, say,

I wandered lonely as a cloud. Let us further imagine the student standing in front of the twenty or so grayish-green volumes of the Cornell Words-worth, clearly the handsomest, most substantial, most scholarly edition in sight, and somehow (by luck or by means of a general index in the final volume) managing to locate the poem in Curtis's volume, on pages 207–8. In this version the poem is eighteen lines long (not twenty-four, as formerly in the standard texts); has "dancing" instead of "golden" daffodils in line 4; has "Ten thousand dancing" instead of "Fluttering and dancing" in line 6; has a "laughing" instead of a "jocund" company in the fourth line of the second stanza (what standardly used to be the third stanza); and has lost entirely the following stanza that formerly constituted lines 7–12:

> Continuous as the stars that shine
> And twinkle on the milky way,
> They stretched in never-ending line
> Along the margin of a bay:
> Ten thousand saw I at a glance,
> Tossing their heads in sprightly dance.

Reading the shorter, plainer text in the Cornell volume, the student may well wonder how the poem came to be so famous. It is an attractive piece, certainly, but somehow not so vivid and imaginative as one had thought it would be.

It is mainly the inadvertent *standardizing* of these early texts that worries me.[14] This same hypothetical student, looking elsewhere in Curtis's volume, will unwittingly miss other lines and images that were formerly (back in the 1970s!) a familiar part of Wordsworth's best-known work—for example, "Beside a pool bare to the eye of heaven" in a couplet of *Resolution and Independence,* lines 53–54 (a later revision in place of 1807's "When up and down my fancy thus was driven"); "life's pilgrimage" in the same poem's line 67 (replacing 1807's "their pilgrimage," referring to the leechgatherer's "feet and head"); "Proteus rising from the sea" in the penultimate line of *The world is too much with us* ("coming from the sea" in 1807); "I listened, motionless and still" in *The Solitary Reaper,* line 29 ("I listen'd till I had my fill" in 1807); the cuckoo's "twofold shout . . . At once far off and near" in the second stanza of *To the Cuckoo* ("restless shout . . . About, and all about!" in 1807); and "fond illusion of my heart" in *Elegiac Stanzas,* line 29 ("fond delusion" in 1807). The long title of the Intimations ode—*Ode: Intimations of Immortality from Recollections of Early Childhood* (simply "Ode" in 1807) —and the epigraph from *My heart leaps up* are other later additions by

Wordsworth that are absent from the texts (though of course present in the apparatus) in Curtis's volume.

My notion of the imminent standardization of early texts is less hypothetical than the student I have just described.[15] There is already in print, well established in the Oxford Authors series, a 750-page *William Wordsworth* edited by Stephen Gill (Wordsworth 1984c), in which, to quote the editor's preface, "for the first time a selection of Wordsworth's work is offered in which the poems are ordered according to the date of their composition, and presented in texts which give as nearly as possible their earliest completed state" (v). Here we have the early readings that I just cited from *Poems, in Two Volumes,* plus (along with much else) early versions of *Lyrical Ballads,* a manuscript text of *Peter Bell* (which, in lacking the Prologue stanzas that banish "dragon's wing, the magic ring" and extol the "nobler marvels [of] the mind . . . in life's daily prospect," is even barer than the first printed text), a manuscript text of *The Ruined Cottage* (again, manuscript D, which came *after* the "earliest"), and of course the 1805 *Prelude.* In his 1983 essay on Wordsworth's texts, Gill argues that the effect of the traditional procedure (e.g., in the de Selincourt-Darbishire Oxford English Texts edition) of printing Wordsworth's final versions, while recording earlier readings in apparatus and notes, "is to *efface* a poem's earlier existence," and he thinks that a chronological order employing final texts "*completely destroys* the usefulness of the chronological arrangement" (Gill 1983, 181; italics added).[16] But surely Gill's own procedure in the Oxford Authors *William Wordsworth* even more effectively (because there is no apparatus) effaces the later texts. The new chronological arrangement reveals a poet who, instead of declining, was all along less brilliant than we had remembered.

It is possible to see the beginnings of the present situation in de Selincourt's publication of the early *Prelude* seven-plus decades ago and to trace its development in scholars' increasing interest in what, from a skeptical point of view, sometimes seems to have become novelty for novelty's sake. Meanwhile, the once standard texts are on the verge of becoming rare books. The de Selincourt-Darbishire Oxford English Texts edition of *Poetical Works* has long been out of print. Perhaps one day someone will be making yet another startling discovery—the later Wordsworth!

*   *   *

The shifting attitudes toward Wordsworth's texts in the twentieth century are not exactly a credit to Wordsworth scholarship. Initially the critics were interested mainly in the poet's ideas, and their motives were political in a broad sense: Wordsworth's later conservatism in politics and religion was to be rejected (as de Selincourt's introduction to *The Prelude* in 1926 made clear), and the late text of *The Prelude,* when an alternative became available in the 1805 version, was to be scorned as an embodiment of contemptible, even dangerous, beliefs. Scholars for a long time seem not to have noticed that by 1805 Wordsworth had already arrived at practically all his "later" ideas. Expressions of the hated piety of old age (as in Arac's phrase quoted earlier, "the piously revised text of 1850") actually occur in Wordsworth's earliest surviving correspondence—for example, this sentence of September 1790, when he was twenty: "Among the more awful scenes of the Alps, I had not a thought of man, or a single created being; my whole soul was turned to him who produced the terrible majesty before me" (Wordsworth 1967, 34)—and they are especially frequent in letters referring to John Wordsworth's death in February 1805, just when the poet was completing the thirteen-book *Prelude.* The notion that the 1805 version must be more reliable than the later texts as a record of Wordsworth's politics (etc.) in the 1790s is not logically valid, and the known biographical facts go against it.

The gradual equation of supposed bad politics (etc.) with bad poetry is similarly untenable. The following, from the ascent of Snowdon in the 1850 text, book 14, is a familiar battleground:

> —It was a close, warm, breezeless summer night,
> Wan, dull, and glaring, with a dripping fog
> Low-hung and thick, that covered all the sky.
> But, undiscouraged, we began to climb
> The mountain-side. The mist soon girt us round,   15
> And, after ordinary Travellers' talk
> With our Conductor, pensively we sank
> Each into commerce with his private thoughts:
> Thus did we breast the ascent, and by myself
> Was nothing either seen or heard that checked   20
> Those musings or diverted, save that once
> The Shepherd's Lurcher, who, among the crags,
> Had to his joy unearthed a Hedgehog, teased
> His coiled-up Prey with barkings turbulent.
> This small adventure, for even such it seemed   25
> In that wild place, and at the dead of night,
> Being over and forgotten, on we wound
> In silence as before. With forehead bent

Earthward, as if in opposition set
Against an enemy, I panted up   30
With eager pace, and no less eager thoughts.
Thus might we wear a midnight hour away,
Ascending at loose distance each from each,
And I, as chanced, the foremost of the Band:
When at my feet the ground appeared to brighten,   35
And with a step or two seemed brighter still;
Nor was time given to ask, or learn, the cause;
For instantly a light upon the turf
Fell like a flash; and lo! as I looked up,
The Moon hung naked in a firmament   40
Of azure without cloud, and at my feet
Rested a silent sea of hoary mist.
A hundred hills their dusky backs upheaved
All over this still Ocean; and beyond,
Far, far beyond, the solid vapours stretched,   45
In Headlands, tongues, and promontory shapes,
Into the main Atlantic, that appeared
To dwindle, and give up his majesty,
Usurped upon far as the sight could reach.
Not so the ethereal Vault; encroachment none   50
Was there, nor loss; only the inferior stars
Had disappeared, or shed a fainter light
In the clear presence of the full-orbed Moon;
Who, from her sovereign elevation, gazed
Upon the billowy ocean, as it lay   55
All meek and silent, save that through a rift
Not distant from the shore whereon we stood,
A fixed, abysmal, gloomy breathing-place,
Mounted the roar of waters—torrents—streams
Innumerable, roaring with one voice!   60
Heard over earth and sea, and in that hour,
For so it seemed, felt by the starry heavens.

Only twenty of these fifty-two lines are substantively identical with the corresponding text in 1805; that is to say, Wordsworth changed the wording, in some places revising entire sentences, in more than three-fifths of the lines.[17] The handful of single-word revisions may seem indifferent: 1805 has "mist" for "fog" in line 12, "silently" for "pensively" in line 17, "stood" for "hung" in line 40 (though this change probably should be considered related to a larger revision in lines 50 ff.), and "its majesty" for "his majesty" in line 48 (an alteration that, had it been in the opposite direction, from "his" to "its," no doubt would have been displayed by critics as one more instance of Wordsworth's "covering up" his earlier animism). At the next level up, the revisions of phrases may seem mainly to illustrate de Selincourt's characterization (in his introduction of 1926) of later stylistic improvements: "Weak phrases are strengthened, and the whole texture is more closely knit" (Wordsworth 1959, lvii). The 1805 version of the first of the quoted lines—"It was a Summer's night, a close warm night"—could be considered somewhat repetitious; in revision Wordsworth got rid of the extra "night," thereby making room for an additional adjective: "breezeless." Further examples of the same process may be seen in line 32 (1805: "perhaps an hour"; 1850: "a midnight hour"), line 45 (1805: "the vapours shot themselves"; 1850: "the solid vapours stretched"), and line 47 (1805: "Into the Sea, the real Sea"; 1850: "Into the main Atlantic").

The 1805 equivalent of lines 14–15 has a detail that Wordsworth later deleted: "having faith / In our tried Pilot" (which, had it been added rather than omitted in the later text, might have been censured as further evidence of the aging poet's orthodoxy). The 1805 description of the dog and the hedgehog (corresponding to 1850's lines 22–24)—

> The Shepherd's Cur did to his own great joy
> Unearth a hedge-hog in the mountain crags
> Round which he made a barking turbulent

—might be deemed agreeably plainer than the elaborate (indeed nearly mock-epic) passage of 1850. The 1805 version of lines 40–42 is also plainer:

> The Moon stood naked in the Heavens, at height
> Immense above my head, and on the shore
> I found myself of a huge sea of mist,
> Which meek and silent, rested at my feet.

But in this instance the later poeticizing (and condensing) might be thought to result in a more impressive picture ("firmament," "azure," "without cloud," and "hoary" have no counterpart in the 1805 version, while 1805's "meek and silent" appears further on in the 1850 text, at line 56).

The most interesting (and, in the scholarly literature, the most controversial) difference has to do with the last thirteen lines of the passage (50–62). The corresponding text of 1805 consists of two sentences:

Meanwhile the Moon look'd down upon this shew
In single glory, and we stood, the mist
Touching our very feet: and from the shore
At distance not the third part of a mile
Was a blue chasm, a fracture in the vapour,
A deep and gloomy breathing-place thro' which
Mounted the roar of waters, torrents, streams
Innumerable, roaring with one voice.
The universal spectacle throughout
Was shaped for admiration and delight,
Grand in itself alone, but in that breach
Through which the homeless voice of waters rose,
That dark deep thorough-fare had Nature lodg'd
The Soul, the Imagination of the whole.

The 1805 text emphasizes the chasm ("rift" in 1850) and the roar of the waters emanating from it, symbolic of "The Soul, the Imagination of the whole." In the 1850 text, the focus has shifted from the ground to the sky, and it is the moon, unencroached upon and sovereign, that becomes emblem of the imagination. It is an open question, in these revisions, whether Wordsworth was clarifying his original idea (and emblematization) of the imagination or consciously expressing a different idea by means of the difference of emphasis among the details of the scene. There are many concepts and images of imagination in *The Prelude*, not all of them compatible with one another, and we can never know for sure (perhaps Wordsworth himself did not know) whether the 1805 and 1850 versions of the passage should be considered one more or two.

I should think that both passages, early and late, would qualify as beautiful and moving descriptions introducing Wordsworth's powerful conclusion to the poem. Yet the Norton Critical Edition's footnote to the 1850 lines is niggling in the extreme: "None of the other great passages of *The Prelude*—indeed of Wordsworth's poetry as a whole—suffered in revision as did the Ascent of Snowdon. From the earliest reworkings (*1850*, 50–53, e.g., belong to 1816/19) to the final concession to orthodoxy in 61–62 (1839 or later), alterations are consistently for the worse" (Wordsworth 1979b, 461). Lines 61–62 are no more a "concession to orthodoxy" than the earlier images of earth-sky reciprocity (ennobling interchange!) in the opening paragraph of *Tintern Abbey* and the final lines of Coleridge's *Frost at Midnight*. With this note in the Norton edition, as with all such statements based on "the worst of Wordsworth," we are in the realm of aesthetic politics, about which "team" is going to be right.

What "suffers most in revision," what is better or worse—even, in such a matter, what constitutes consistency ("consistently for the worst")—can hardly be demonstrated, much less proven. What *is* demonstrable is that Wordsworth did revise his poems—*The Prelude* and all the others. One can, in the manner of the disapproving tradition beginning with de Selincourt, call his revising "obsessive" and "compulsive." One can also, taking a different view (and tone), see a great deal to admire in Wordsworth's craftsmanly improvements. But regardless of our evaluations, we do have at hand the reality of a major poet, one of the greatest in English, writing and repeatedly revising his poem.

The textual primitivists—the long line from de Selincourt to Hobsbaum and Jonathan Wordsworth—have reacted to this reality in the worst possible way. They hate revisions, considering anything later than the "earliest complete state" a deterioration.[18] They wish that the revised texts would disappear and probably are glad that the de Selincourt-Darbishire *Poetical Works* is out of print. A healthier reaction would be to stop this nonsense about "the worst of Wordsworth" and grant the legitimacy and interest, intrinsic or in connection with other texts, of *all* the versions of *The Prelude* and the rest of the poems in the canon. More recent textual theory—in the writings of James Thorpe and Hans Zeller, for example[19]—favors this more catholic view, and it has the additional support of common sense: Wordsworth did, after all, write the 1805 version *and* the 1850; the 1798 *Peter Bell* and the rest of the versions including those of the printed texts of 1819, 1820, 1827, 1832, 1836, and 1845; *The Ruined Cottage, The Pedlar*, and *The Excursion*—and each of these versions (and of course others that I have not mentioned) embodies some degree of the poet's intention and authority. It is possible to argue that some versions carry more authority than others. It is not possible, I think, to argue that authority resides only in a single version and that the rest of the texts in a series, whether early or late, should be banished to some limbo of poor relationship. Least of all is it possible to bestow authority on a text merely because the critic prefers it over all other versions—especially if it is a text with only a hypothetical existence.

The most interesting work on Wordsworth's texts and revisions argues or assumes this more fluid notion of literary authority. Raymond Carney, reviewing the first four volumes of the Cornell Wordsworth in 1981, ponders "the extent to which the concept of a final text is itself a critical fiction" and answers with major statements concerning writing and revision as a continuous process. For example, "It is the concept of the well-made text that needs jettisoning. We need to begin to talk about writing as a process with significance in and of itself, composition as an activity of consciousness and not merely as a means of producing ultimate meanings. Can we begin to understand manuscripts and revisions not as imperfect or approximate versions of some unrealized final event, but as events unto themselves with their own self-satisfying logic and rationale?" (Carney 1981, 634–35). Robert Young (1982), replying to Baker's "Prelude and Prejudice," defends the equally legitimate claim to authority of each of the three versions of *The Prelude* in the Norton Critical Edition. Clifford Siskin, in a 1983 study of "literary change," uses Wordsworth as a principal example of the "complementary relationship between revision and spontaneity": "What Wordsworth did was to innovate upon the idea of change, and thereby to valorize the formal procedure of revision, by positing a new relationship between parts and wholes. . . . In Wordsworth, process and product fuse as parts and wholes enter a mutually interactive relationship" (Siskin 1983, 10, 7–8). And Susan Wolfson, in a 1984 essay comparing the 1799, 1805, and 1850 versions of the drowned man of Esthwaite, begins with the statement that "Recent critical studies in a variety of fields have encouraged us to revise our understanding of what constitutes an authoritative version of a work and to regard textual variants and the dynamics of revision as significant events in the shape of a career" (Wolfson 1984, 918). Her admirable essay studies revision as a continuous process of self-reading, self-reconstructing, and *The Prelude* as a poem constituted by all of its texts at once.

These examples from the criticism, alike in viewing revision as an ongoing endeavor, with authorial intention residing in all the successive versions of a work, are the best possible justification for the Cornell Wordsworth. Regardless of the primitivist ideals that prompted the project in the first place, the Cornell volumes are giving us more and more versions, along with much new information, to complicate and enrich our picture of the development of Wordsworth's poetry. We shall still need de Selincourt and Darbishire's *Poetical Works* or another, more accurate printing of the latest texts. These, if not the ultimate scholarly goal that they once were, do have their legitimacy. They were, after all, what put Wordsworth among the English poets.

9

Pictorialism and Matter-of-Factness in Coleridge's Poems of Somerset

COLERIDGE WROTE ONLY A FEW POEMS of the first rank—perhaps no more than a dozen, all told—and he seems to have taken a very casual attitude toward them. He originally published *The Eolian Harp* under the title "Effusion"; he gave *Reflections on Having Left a Place of Retirement* the subtitle "A Poem Which Affects Not to Be Poetry"; he described *Fears in Solitude* as "a sort of middle thing between Poetry and Oratory"; and he kept *Kubla Khan* in manuscript for nearly twenty years before offering it to the public "rather as a psychological curiosity, than on the ground of any supposed *poetic* merits" (Coleridge 1912, 1:100 n., 106 n., 257 n., 295). *Christabel* and *This Lime-Tree Bower My Prison* are two other items that he delayed publishing in book form, and *The Nightingale* and *The Rime of the Ancient Mariner,* which came out anonymously or seemingly as Wordsworth's in *Lyrical Ballads* beginning in 1798, did not appear under Coleridge's own name until the *Sibylline Leaves* volume of 1817. My thesis in this chapter is that, despite his own lack of interest and confidence in them, Coleridge's handful of first-rate pieces exerted a powerful influence on the language of subsequent English poetry, right up to our own time.

I want to develop this thesis by way of a Keatsian view of Coleridge's poems. One of my special interests over the years has been the realistic elements of Romantic poetry. When I was in graduate school several decades ago, Romanticism was still under attack by the New Humanists as a literature of escape, and so there was, for me, an attractive alternative in seeing Porphyro (in Keats's *The Eve of St. Agnes*) as a pilgrim intent on getting not into heaven but into Madeline's bed and in arguing that Wordsworth's principal sphere of interest was, as Wordsworth himself said it was,

> Not in Utopia,—subterranean Fields,—
> Or some secreted Island, Heaven knows where!
> But in the very world, which is the world
> Of all of us,—the place where in the end
> We find our happiness, or not at all!
> (Fourteen-book *Prelude*, 11.140–44)

I turned Aristotle's description of plot, with its parabola of rising and falling action, into a graphic representation of the structure of many of Keats's poems, both narrative and lyric, using a simple horizontal line to mark a division between an actual world of mortal experience (below the line) and an ideal world of nonmortal perfection (above the line).[1] Keats's speakers in the best of the odes, and his heroes and heroines in at least some of the narratives, take off from the real world in quest of an imagined ideal but then are afflicted by what Endymion at one point calls "homeward fever" (*Endymion* 2.319). Their excursions into the ideal are inevitably failures, and they long to return to the reality that, at the beginning of the action, had seemed so faulty. *Ode to a Nightingale* is a handy epitomizing example: its structure takes the form of an imaginative excursion to join an unseen bird in a forest followed by return to reality and the speaker's "sole self." But the scheme has widespread application, describing Endymion's quest for Cynthia, Madeline's quest for union with her lover in a dream, the initial situation of the "Bright star . . . in lone splendor hung aloft the night," the wretched knight's temporary happiness in La Belle Dame's grot, and the hypothetical remedies of Psyche's temple, the permanently frozen pastoral of the Grecian Urn, the lovers' magical palace in *Lamia,* and the "songs of spring" in *To Autumn.*

I want to apply this scheme to Coleridge. Coleridge is not, of course, generally regarded as one of the realists among the English poets. In the common opposition between the mysterious, high-flying, metaphysical tendencies of one kind of Romanticism and the plain, down-to-earth, commonsensical tendencies of another, Coleridge is decidedly with the mysterious, high-flying, and metaphysical. Xanadu is a type of Shangri-la, the Ancient Mariner's voyage is full of miraculous events, and *Christabel* is a tale of vampirism; the Conversation poems celebrate blurry abstractions about "the one Life within us and abroad," "the Almighty Spirit," "God . . . [teaching] Himself in all." Yet Coleridge's poems also have structural elements of Keatsian and Wordsworthian "homeward fever." In some of the best of them, there is a conflict between the upward tendency of the ostensible subject matter and the downward tendency of the "plots." The themes seem to go in one direction, the stories in another.

Take *The Eolian Harp* as an early example. The theme of *The Eolian Harp* is sometimes said to be Coleridge's vision of "all of animated nature" as "organic Harps" played upon by "one intellectual breeze, / At once the Soul of each, and God of all" (44–48). But the story of the poem is something quite different—a dramatic confession of a man who allows himself to indulge in "idle flitting phantasies," "shapings of the unregenerate mind" (40, 55) amounting to heresy, and who is glad to return from these flights of fancy to the reality of his wife and cottage. *Reflections on Having Left a Place of Retirement* affirms "the bloodless fight / Of Science, Freedom . . . the Truth in Christ" (61–62) and the coming of God's kingdom, but the story is about a reluctant departure and the solace of imaginative return. *This Lime-Tree Bower My Prison* likewise has a thematic "message": "Henceforth I shall know / That Nature ne'er deserts the wise and pure" (59–60). Read for its story, however, *This Lime-Tree Bower* is about a man who, because of a trivial domestic accident, cannot go on a walk with his friends, imaginatively accompanies them to view a wide prospect from the top of a hill, and then returns to the comfortable reality of his actual surroundings—lime trees, a walnut tree, ivy, elms, a bat, a solitary humble-bee. *Frost at Midnight* is thematically about "The lovely shapes and sounds intelligible / Of [God's] eternal language" (59–60). Structurally the poem involves excursions into the past (to the speaker's schooldays in the city) and into the future (to a time when the speaker's infant son will grow up to "wander like a breeze / By lakes and sandy shores," 54–55), and again there is a solacing return to a present reality, this time to "the secret ministry of frost," the shining icicles, and the quiet moon (72–74). The story in *Frost at Midnight* is not perfectly clear, but the speaker is unhappy with his situation at the beginning, and in some way he solves his problem through the imagined excursions. *The Rime of the Ancient Mariner* is loaded—almost (as Coleridge himself felt) overloaded—with religious, social, moral, and psychological themes: the sacredness of God's creatures, the hapless plight of the inheritors of Original Sin, the difference between the working and the nonworking of imagination, and so on. As a story, the poem is, once again, an excursion into some kind of fantasy world and a glad return to the Mariner's native land: "Oh! dream of joy! . . . Is this mine own countree?" (464–67).

I think there is a connection between the "homeward" tendencies of these poems and some important qualities of Coleridge's poetic style.

Before the 1790s, the most notable characteristic of the language of English poetry was its artificiality. Wordsworth sets this forth in detail in his preface to the second edition of *Lyrical Ballads* (1800) when he makes a distinction between words and things and condemns various types of language that do not represent things—personifications, poetic diction, clichés, and the rest. He uses one of Thomas Gray's sonnets to illustrate the emptiness and insubstantiality of the eighteenth-century style he is attacking. Here is another example from the same poet, the opening of Gray's *Ode on the Spring:*

> Lo! where the rosy-bosom'd Hours,
> Fair Venus' train appear,
> Disclose the long-expecting flowers,
> And wake the purple year!
> The Attic warbler pours her throat,
> Responsive to the cuckow's note,
> The untaught harmony of spring:
> While whisp'ring pleasure as they fly,
> Cool Zephyrs thro' the clear blue sky
> Their gather'd fragrance fling.

On this side of the 1790s, we no longer have "rosy-bosom'd Hours," "Venus' train," "purple year," "Attic warbler," "Cool Zephyrs," and the like. The language of poetry becomes plainer, more concrete, more straightforward, more natural (seeming, at least, to represent what Wordsworth called "the real language" of ordinary speakers). A serious and moving poem about mid-nineteenth-century religious crisis and the disappearance of God begins with some chat about the weather: "The sea is calm tonight. / The tide is full, the moon lies fair / Upon the straits. . . ." A famous poem of the 1920s pondering the nature of human life begins with very homely description of a schoolroom:

> I walk through the long schoolroom questioning;
> A kind old nun in a white hood replies;
> The children learn to cipher and to sing,
> To study reading-books and history,
> To cut and sew, be neat in everything
> In the best modern way—the children's eyes
> In momentary wonder stare upon
> A sixty-year-old smiling public man.

A not-so-famous poem of the 1960s about the unreliability of perception begins with a person on a train addressing a stranger sitting next to him:

> How it should happen this way
> I am not sure, but you
> Are sitting next to me,
> Minding your own business
> When all of a sudden I see
> A fire out the window.[2]

I don't, of course, mean to suggest that all poetry before the 1790s was as artificial and prettified as the lines about "rosy-bosom'd Hours" quoted from Gray or that all poetry after the 1790s was as plain and straightforward as Matthew Arnold's weather report or Yeats's schoolroom or Mark Strand's questioning of the reality of a fire outside the window. But as a general tendency, with a preponderance of the one kind of poetry before the 1790s and a preponderance of the other kind after the 1790s, the change is quite remarkable and, I would argue, quantitatively demonstrable. The 1790s may be seen as *the* crucial decade, a kind of watershed in the history of English poetry. I suggest that Coleridge played a central role in the change.

Let me focus this change with a passage of nature description from the opening paragraph of *This Lime-Tree Bower My Prison,* where Coleridge pictures a "roaring dell" that he had told his friends about:

> [That] roaring dell, o'erwooded, narrow, deep,
> And only speckled by the mid-day sun;
> Where its slim trunk the ash from rock to rock
> Flings arching like a bridge;—that branchless ash,
> Unsunn'd and damp, whose few poor yellow leaves
> Ne'er tremble in the gale, yet tremble still,
> Fann'd by the water-fall! and there my friends
> Behold the dark green file of long lank weeds,
> That all at once (a most fantastic sight!)
> Still nod and drip beneath the dripping edge
> Of the blue clay-stone.
>
> (10–20)

In contrast with Gray's stanza from *Ode on the Spring,* these lines from *Lime-Tree Bower* are quite sharp and specific. Gray gives us numerous embellishments in the form of classical allusion but no help whatsoever toward visualizing ("Lo!"—behold, see!) the rosy-bosom'd Hours, Venus's train, the purple year, and the rest. One could, however, easily draw (or mentally re-create) a picture of Coleridge's dell, giving a proper angle to the sides, adding the branchless ash tree in front of the waterfall, and sketching in the trembling leaves, the long lank weeds, and the blue clay-stone. Coleridge's syntax is a little awkward, but the images are concrete, highly detailed, and presented in clear relationships to one another. *This Lime-Tree Bower* has, or can be read as having, a lofty theme about the ubiquity of beauty and God's presence in nature. Its descriptive passages, especially at the beginning and end, are quite literally down-to-earth, full of particularities, and eminently visualizable. They are matter-of-fact in the manner of good passages of Wordsworth and pictorial in the manner of good passages of Keats.

Coleridge did not always write such pictorial and matter-of-fact descriptions. Much of his verse is in the style that Byron characterized as "turgid ode and tumid stanza" (*English Bards and Scotch Reviewers,* 256)—a lucky choice of interchangeable terms meaning swollen or bloated and, at the same time, empty of significant content. It is easy, in the early pages of Coleridge's chronologically arranged *Complete Poetical Works,* to find expressions such as "soft Compassion," "Furies fell," "Vengeance drunk with human blood," "dragon-wing'd Despair," "sorrow-clouded breast of Care," "Fancy's high career," "Life's gilded scenes," Hope's "cheering beam," "Fancy's vivid colourings," "Glory's blood-stain'd palm," "Morning's wing," "Memory's Dream," "Love's pale cheek," and the like. There are fervent exhortations to *see* what no one can possibly see (just as in Gray's *Ode on the Spring*), and for sentiments we have to slog through such extravagances as this from an early version of *Monody on the Death of Chatterton:*

> Thy corpse of many a livid hue
> On the bare ground I view,
> Whilst various passions all my mind engage;
> Now is my breast distended with a sigh,
> And now a flash of Rage
> Darts through the tear, that glistens in my eye.
> (Coleridge 1912, 1:13)

A selected edition of Coleridge from the 1950s that I regularly used as a course textbook in the 1960s and 1970s has a telling juxtaposition between the worst of Coleridge in the turgid/tumid vein and some of the best of Coleridge in the conversational matter-of-fact.[3] In this edition, *Ode to the Departing Year* ends in the middle of a verso page with these lines:

I unpartaking of the evil thing,
   With daily prayer and daily toil
   Soliciting for food my scanty soil,
Have wail'd my country with a loud Lament.
Now I recentre my immortal mind
   In the deep Sabbath of meek self-content;
Cleans'd from the vaporous passions that bedim
God's Image, sister of the Seraphim.

And then just below, on the same page of this selected edition, comes the opening of *This Lime-Tree Bower My Prison:* "Well, they are gone, and here must I remain, / This lime-tree bower my prison! . . ."

Passages in the homely, conversational style of "Well, they are gone, and here must I remain" are relatively rare in Coleridge's poetry, and so are passages of pictorial, matter-of-fact description of the sort that I quoted about the roaring dell, the waterfall, the ash tree, and the leaves and weeds. There are plenty of matter-of-fact details to cite—for example, the precise measurement of Kubla Khan's enclosure ("twice five miles," 6) and the Second Voice's straight-faced explanation of the mechanism that drives the Ancient Mariner's ship ("The air is cut away before, / And closes from behind," 424–25)—and some of the most memorable pictures in English poetry. Think of the transfixed Wedding-Guest, the "ice, mast-high," the "bloody Sun, at noon," the skeleton ship, the "silly buckets on the deck," and the Pilot's boy going crazy in *The Ancient Mariner* (53, 112, 297); or the poet's "flashing eyes" and "floating hair" at the end of *Kubla Khan;* or the "redbreast sit[ting] and sing[ing] / Betwixt the tufts of snow on the bare branch / Of mossy apple-tree" and the rest of the dozen or so extremely sharp visual details at the close of *Frost at Midnight;* or this description of Christabel praying in the forest:

It was a lovely sight to see
The lady Christabel, when she
Was praying at the old oak tree.
   Amid the jagged shadows
   Of mossy leafless boughs,
   Kneeling in the moonlight,
   To make her gentle vows;
Her slender palms together prest,
Heaving sometimes on her breast. . . .
              (279–87)

But such passages occur in fewer than a dozen poems in the Coleridge canon—notably, among pieces written (or at least begun) before Coleridge and the Wordsworths departed for Germany in the autumn of 1798, *The Eolian Harp, Reflections on Having Left a Place of Retirement, This Lime-Tree Bower, Kubla Khan, The Ancient Mariner, Frost at Midnight, Christabel, Fears in Solitude,* and *The Nightingale,* and among pieces written after 1798, only *Dejection: An Ode* (1802) and *To William Wordsworth* (1807). The works that put Coleridge "among the English poets" are so few that if one wants to know what happened to Coleridge as a poet, it makes more sense to inquire what happened when he was successful rather than, as with a writer such as Wordsworth, what happened when he wasn't. What is it that caused Coleridge to write his few good poems?—or, since I am connecting Coleridge's good poems with certain qualities of style (plainness, substantiality, concreteness, particularity: the pictorialism and matter-of-factness of my title), what is it that caused Coleridge to produce those memorable passages of visualizable detail?

One ready answer that might pop into the minds of readers of the first chapter of *Biographia Literaria* is the influence of Coleridge's schoolmaster at Christ's Hospital, the Reverend James Boyer. Coleridge writes that "In our own English compositions . . . [Boyer] showed no mercy to phrase, metaphor, or image, unsupported by sound sense, or where the same sense might have been conveyed with equal force and dignity in plainer words. Lute, harp, and lyre, muse, muses, and inspirations, Pegasus, Parnassus, and Hippocrene, were all an abomination to him. In fancy I can almost hear him now, exclaiming '*Harp? Harp? Lyre? Pen and ink, boy, you mean! Muse, boy, Muse? your Nurse's daughter, you mean! Pierian spring? Oh 'aye! the cloister-pump, I suppose!*'" (*BL,* 1:9–10). This certainly points toward the plainness and concrete detail that I have been emphasizing. But Coleridge had the advantage of this lesson at the very start of his poetry writing and didn't heed the lesson until six or eight years later. His surviving early poems, from 1787 through the middle of 1795, are, in effect, full of harps, lyres, and muses and are conspicuously short on pens, ink, and the nurse's daughter.

How about early literary influences? We know from both *Biographia Literaria* and the letters that Coleridge was greatly moved by the poetry, especially the sonnets, of William Lisle Bowles, who combined, as Coleridge wrote in a note to his sonnet to Bowles published in the *Morning Chronicle,* "exquisite delicacy of painting . . . tender simplicity . . . [and] manly pathos" (Coleridge 1912, 1:84 n.). We also know that William Cowper was one of his favorite poets and that he composed the opening paragraph of *Frost at Midnight* with pointed reference to a well-known passage of Cowper's *The Task*. Then there were the poems of close friends and associates—Charles Lamb, Robert Southey, and, after a while, Wordsworth. But Bowles, Cowper, Lamb, and Southey do not create specific visual images in their poetry, any more than Gray did in the stanza quoted earlier. Bowles's sonnet *To the River Itchin*, for example, begins with reference to the river's "crumbling margin," its "silver breast, / On which the self-same tints still seem to rest." One imagines the Reverend James Boyer saying to Bowles: "*Crumbling margin, boy? Silver breast? Self-same tints?—You mean sides, surface, colors!*" Bowles, Cowper, Lamb, and Southey were all writing in the then standard eighteenth-century modes, using words to represent not things but abstractions—mental concepts, definitions, logical entities. And Wordsworth's earliest influence is confined to the first version of *Salisbury Plain*, which is nearly all that Coleridge knew of Wordsworth's poetry before he wrote his own first good poems toward the end of 1795.

Perhaps we can explain what happened to Coleridge in terms of his finding a proper audience. Much of Coleridge's early poetry in the turgid/tumid manner is addressed not to any actual auditors but to a vaguely conceived mass audience comprising all of England, or perhaps the entire population of the world. There are exceptions to this dramatic stance—for example, blank-verse lines addressed to his friend Charles Lamb and to his brother George—but in general, in his early poetry, Coleridge either writes to individuals whom he does not know personally (as in his "Sonnets on Eminent Characters") or else imitates Milton in addressing the nation from pulpit or public platform. The results are full of artifice and emptiness, just as one would expect in a writing situation where the audience does not exist and communication is a purely academic endeavor. Coleridge's turning to audiences whom he actually knew and loved—his wife in *The Eolian Harp*, Charles Lamb in *This Lime-Tree Bower*, his infant son in *Frost at Midnight*, William and Dorothy Wordsworth in *The Nightingale*—produced some amazingly good poetry. But the question of how Coleridge attained this more realistic and immediate poet/audience relationship is merely a variant of the question I started with: Why Sara and Charles Lamb and the Wordsworths at this particular time in his life?

Coleridge's marriage to Sara Fricker in October 1795 is a possible explanation. Marriage does entail an access of reality. Romance is the rising action of life, marriage the descent—or so it is frequently portrayed in fiction—and what was previously veiled, mysterious, and fervently desired becomes known and freely enjoyed. Because Coleridge's first poems in his pictorial, matter-of-fact style either mention Sara or are addressed to her, it is tempting to connect the change—what happened to Coleridge—to his change in marital status. Unfortunately for this explanation, Coleridge from time to time reverted to his former windy style, producing works in the turgid/tumid vein even while he was still happily married.

My own explanation of what happened to Coleridge has to do with rural Somerset, the ground on which we are meeting this morning and which we'll be trudging over tomorrow afternoon.[4] As a matter of chronological fact, Coleridge went to London after he left Cambridge University at the end of 1794, and shortly afterward he moved to Bristol, which was then, just as it is now, a metropolis, one of the major cities of Great Britain. He lived in Bristol from January through September 1795 and then went from the city to what he calls his "place of retirement," the cottage at Clevedon, a town some twenty-five or thirty miles to the northeast of here, where he resided for three months, from his wedding day, 4 October, until the end of the year. At the beginning of 1796 he left Clevedon to raise subscriptions for his new periodical, *The Watchman.* He was on the road for this purpose during January and February 1796 and then returned to Bristol in order to be closer to the printers who would produce *The Watchman.* He lived in Bristol for the rest of 1796 and then moved to Stowey on the last day of the year. The "Coleridge Cottage" (across the road) was his residence until he departed with William and Dorothy Wordsworth for Germany in September 1798.

There are, then, in Coleridge's adult life before the turn of the century two distinct periods when he was away from the cities that, as he says in *Frost at Midnight,* were an impediment to his union with nature. The first period consists of the final three months of 1795, when he and Sara lived at the cottage in Clevedon, and the second consists of all of 1797 and January–August 1798, when he, Sara, and their first child, Hartley, lived in Stowey. And it happens that Coleridge wrote (or, in the case of *Christabel,* began) practically all of the good poems he ever produced—*The Eolian Harp* and *Reflections on Having Left a Place of Retirement* in Clevedon in 1795, and *This Lime-Tree Bower, Kubla Khan, Frost at Midnight, The Ancient Mariner,* the beginning of *Christabel, Fears in Solitude,* and *The Nightingale* in and around Stowey in 1797–98—in these relatively homely situations. It may look like a gross simplification to connect Coleridge's intermittent periods of good poetry with these two periods of retirement amidst rural surroundings. But further support for just such a simplified view exists in the fact that in the year separating the two periods, when he traveled for two months and then returned to live in Bristol again for the remainder of 1796, Coleridge mainly wrote long bad poems in the old turgid/tumid vein—*Religious Musings, The Destiny of Nations,* and *Ode to the Departing Year,* his principal accomplishments of 1796.

I suggested at the beginning of this chapter that Coleridge's handful of good poems exerted a major influence on the style of subsequent English poetry. Now at the conclusion I'd like to say a little about Coleridge's influence on the poetry of two important contemporaries, Wordsworth and Keats.

It is sometimes forgotten, when Coleridge and Wordsworth are studied together, that in the early years of their relationship Coleridge had much more of a reputation than his older associate. A two-volume reference work published in 1798, David Rivers's *Literary Memoirs of Living Authors of Great Britain,* notices Coleridge among the 1,112 living authors but does not include Wordsworth.[5] Before 1798, Wordsworth had published just the two slender volumes containing *An Evening Walk* and *Descriptive Sketches* (they came out together in January 1793). Neither was a critical success, and there was no call for a second edition of either. Coleridge, in contrast, was the author of a play, *The Fall of Robespierre,* published in 1794; ten numbers of a periodical, *The Watchman,* issued between March and May 1796; a substantial collection of *Poems on Various Subjects,* published first in 1796 and then in a second, enlarged edition a year later; a slim quarto containing *Fears in Solitude, France: An Ode,* and *Frost at Midnight,* which came out in 1798; and some single poems published here and there separately. He was a well-established writer, mostly in poetry, at a time when Wordsworth was still just getting started.

Coleridge, however, had no sense of this superiority. In the presence of Wordsworth, he felt himself, as he told a friend in June 1797, "a *little man by his* side"; and he wrote to another friend a month later that "Wordsworth is a very great man—the only man, to whom *at all times* & in *all modes of excellence* I feel myself inferior" (*CL,* 1:325, 334). Coleridge's self-abasement vis-à-vis Wordsworth has caused some scholars to overlook the fact that while Coleridge's best achievements in poetry go hand-in-hand with Wordsworth's, seemingly joined in an interinvolved process that has been likened to biological symbiosis and lyrical dialogue,[6] they in fact *precede* Wordsworth's own productions at almost every point where documentary chronological evidence exists. Coleridge's conversational blank verse anticipates Wordsworth's first efforts in the same manner by at least a year and a half; *Frost at Midnight* precedes *Tintern Abbey,* a poem that resembles it in many aspects of theme and structure, by four or five months; the Mariner's tale in Coleridge's *Rime* precedes Wordsworth's mariner's tale in *The Thorn* by a few days or, more probably, a few weeks; *The Prelude* can be (and has been) read as a long Coleridgean Conversation poem. A perceptive writer on the literary relationship of the two poets says flatly that "Coleridge's poetry was the prime influence on Wordsworth's from the first days of their association until the winter of 1799–1800" (Magnuson 1988, 10). And Wordsworth's preface to *Lyrical Ballads,* at least according to Coleridge, grew out of mutual conversations between the two and was begun on the basis of notes by Coleridge.

The influence of the *Lyrical Ballads* experiment—first as a jointly authored anonymous volume published in Bristol and London in the autumn of 1798; then as a second edition, in two volumes, with the famous preface at the beginning of volume 1, in 1800; then in two more editions, in 1802 and 1805; and in printing after printing of Wordsworth's collected poems beginning in 1815 and continuing to the present day—has been incalculable. And Coleridge's role, as a theorist about the language of poetry but much more significantly as the poet who wrote the earliest of the Coleridge-Wordsworth lyrical ballads, was considerable. We can take Wordsworth's familiarity with Coleridge's poems for granted, and I think we should take Coleridge's influence on Wordsworth for granted as well.

In the case of Keats, there is no question about who influenced whom, but again it is possible to sharpen the account of the relation of the earlier poet's works to the later. We of course place Coleridge with the earlier generation of Romantics—I have just suggested that he played a leading role in the *Lyrical Ballads* experiment—but, apart from *The Ancient Mariner,* his most significant poems were first made widely available in the midst of the activities of the second generation of Romantics, in particular in 1816 and 1817, when Keats was at a most impressionable stage of development as poet and thinker. *Christabel* (written mainly between 1798 and 1800) and *Kubla Khan* (written during 1797–98) were first published in May 1816 in a pamphlet that was much anticipated, widely noticed by the critics, and reissued in two subsequent editions before the year was out. (Reviewers of the pamphlet included Keats's friends John Hamilton Reynolds, William Hazlitt, and George Felton Mathew.) *Sibylline Leaves,* Coleridge's most important collection of poems before the later 1820s, came out in July 1817 containing, among other works, *The Ancient Mariner, The Eolian Harp, This Lime-Tree Bower, To William Wordsworth, The Nightingale, Frost at Midnight,* and *Dejection: An Ode.* Most of these poems were composed between 1795 and 1802; for several of them, *Sibylline Leaves* represents the first publication in book form, if not the first publication ever. Coleridge was also getting considerable public notice from another work that he issued at this time, the two-volume *Biographia Literaria*, published in the same month as *Sibylline Leaves*.

Keats mentions Coleridge several times in his letters and actually met him once, on Hampstead Heath on a Sunday morning in April 1819 two weeks before he drafted his own best-known literary ballad, *La Belle Dame sans Merci*, and about a month before he wrote his own "greater Romantic lyric" to a nightingale, the most admired of his odes. It is also a matter of biographical record that Keats owned a copy of the 1797 second edition of Coleridge's *Poems*, and he certainly was familiar with *Sibylline Leaves*.

There are frequent echoes of Coleridge in Keats's poems and some important general likenesses as well.[7] Perhaps most prominent is Coleridge's influence on Keats's Gothicism. Both *The Eve of St. Agnes* and *Lamia* show numerous similarities with *Christabel* in plot, character, theme, motif, image, and atmosphere, some of them so close in detail as to constitute pointed allusions, as if Keats were retelling (or completing) Coleridge's fragment. The well-known Keatsian pictorialism owes much to Coleridge—as, for example, in these lines from *The Eve of St. Agnes* when Madeline kneels to pray in her moonlit bedchamber. (Compare the passage quoted earlier in this paper in which Coleridge describes Christabel "praying at the old oak tree . . . Kneeling in the moonlight . . . Her slender palms together prest, / Heaving sometimes on her breast," and so on.)

> Rose-bloom fell on her hands, together prest,
> And on her silver cross soft amethyst,
> And on her hair a glory, like a saint:
> She seem'd a splendid angel, newly drest,
> Save wings, for heaven. . . .
>
> (220–24)

Then there is the generic influence of Coleridge's Conversation poems on the younger poet's odes. Keats's best odes figure prominently in the genre that M. H. Abrams (1965) has named "the greater Romantic lyric." But Coleridge's *The Eolian Harp, Frost at Midnight,* and *Fears in Solitude* are the earliest of Abrams's defining examples, all three of them written before *Tintern Abbey,* which is the first of the Wordsworth items in Abrams's list. It is not too much to say that Coleridge single-handedly invented the type. The *Sibylline Leaves* volume, containing these and other Conversation poems, was published just two years before Keats wrote his odes. The earlier works were unquestionably an influence on them.

My conclusions from this cursory survey should be self-evident. Words-worth, through his example in the lyrical ballads and other narrative, conver-sational, and autobiographical poems, as well as through his theorizing about the proper language of poetry in the landmark preface, exerted a tremendous influence on the course of subsequent English poetry, especially in the direc-tion of plainness, simplicity, and matter-of-factness. Keats too, as his reputa-tion expanded in the latter half of the nineteenth century, had a powerful impact on the Victorians (Tennyson and the Pre-Raphaelites in particular) and later upon modern poets such as Wallace Stevens and William Carlos Williams, who themselves became important influences on more recent writ-ers right up to the present. Coleridge, best known in his day primarily as a theologian, social critic, literary theorist, and talker, after a while became one of the standard Romantic poets in his own right and began to exert as much influence directly as he did through those whom he influenced. All this adds up to a considerable result from a handful of poems that Coleridge in effect tossed off, paid very little attention to, and for the most part didn't even bother to publish until long after they were written.

10

The Multiple Versions of Coleridge's Poems

HOW MANY *MARINERS* DID COLERIDGE WRITE?

EACH OF COLERIDGE'S BEST-KNOWN POEMS exists not just in a single text but in several separate versions, some of which differ drastically from others, and every one of which is independently authoritative in the sense that it was authored by Coleridge himself.[1] Thus we have sixteen or more manuscript and printed texts of *The Eolian Harp,* twelve distinct texts of *This Lime-Tree Bower My Prison,* eighteen or more texts of *The Rime of the Ancient Mariner,* and similar numbers for *Frost at Midnight, Kubla Khan, Christabel,* and the Dejection ode. The multiplicity of versions considerably complicates any attempt to read and interpret the poems. In this chapter I shall describe some of the versions of Coleridge's most frequently anthologized poems and discuss some of the complications that these versions introduce into Coleridge criticism.

One of our most deeply ingrained notions about Coleridge's poetic texts is that there should be—somewhere, whether already existing or yet to be constructed by scholars—a single "best" or "most authoritative" text for each of Coleridge's poems and that it is the job of the modern textual scholar to determine what that single best or most authoritative text is (and, if the scholar is doing an edition of the poems, to construct and print that text as the standard to which all earlier variant texts lead up and from which all later variant texts descend).

Traditionally, the best or most authoritative text of an author's work has been thought to be some form of "final" version, most often the latest text written or printed during the author's lifetime—the last that the author *could* or *might* have had a hand in. All earlier versions of the work, whether in manuscript or printed form, were routinely assigned inferior status, as so many temporary stages on the way to the final version. When they were given any recognition at all, these earlier versions were usually reported fragmentarily, in textual apparatuses at the foot of the page or in the back of an edition. In the rare instances where an edition presented early and late versions on facing pages, it was usually understood that the version on the left-hand side was some kind of incomplete preliminary text that stood as a milepost on the way toward the perfection of the text on the right-hand side.[2] Thus in the case of *The Rime of the Ancient Mariner,* the text in one or another of Coleridge's late *Poetical Works*—1828, 1829, or 1834 (this last in the year in which the poet died)—was *the* best, *the* most authoritative, version. All earlier versions were viewed as texts preliminary to the one Coleridge most wanted us to read ever after, the version of the late *Poetical Works.*

Another, more recent view of textual authority—a view associated in Romantic studies with Jonathan Wordsworth, Stephen Parrish, and the Cornell edition of Wordsworth's poems, and in the field of American literature vigorously argued by Hershel Parker—is the idea that the most authoritative version of a work is the *earliest* rather than the latest and is usually (where manuscripts are available) a manuscript form of the work rather than an early printed text. Thus Wordsworth's tale of poor Margaret is seen as "best" in the early text called *The Ruined Cottage,* and this form of the story is (aesthetically as well as theoretically) preferred over the more complicated versions in *The Pedlar* and book 1 of *The Excursion.* In the much-discussed instance of *The Prelude,* a number of influential critics are on record as preferring one or another earlier version rather than the latest recoverable text in which Wordsworth himself had a hand—that is, the thirteen-book text of 1805 over the fourteen-book text of 1850, and then a hypothetical five-book version of 1804 over the thirteen books of 1805, and, to move even further backward, a two-part version of 1798–99 over the hypothetical five books of 1804.[3] (Jeffrey Baker [1982, 79] commented some years ago that the best text of all, earlier than any known manuscript, would be the version heard by Wordsworth's dog as the poet composed orally during his walks.) In the example of *The Rime of the Ancient Mariner,* for which we have no extant manuscript, the best—because earliest—version would be that of the first edition of *Lyrical Ballads,* and this is the basis of the text that William Empson and David Pirie concocted, without marginal glosses but with modernized spelling and passages taken over from later versions, in their selected edition, *Coleridge's Verse,* published by Faber in 1972.

Both of these views—the preference for the author's final text and the countering preference for a first or early text—alike depend on the belief that there is, whether late or early, some single version that is best or most authoritative. This is a belief that is being challenged, and gradually replaced, by an idea first proposed by James Thorpe in the 1960s and then developed and championed in Germany by Hans Zeller; in the United States by Jerome McGann, Donald Reiman, Peter Shillingsburg, and myself (among others); and in Britain by James McLaverty and the most recent serious editor of Coleridge's poems, J. C. C. Mays.[4] This newest idea is that every individual version of a work is a distinct text in its own right, with unique aesthetic character and unique authorial intention.

The concept of multiple versions has more practical relevance to some writers than to others. Keats, who died young and had no time to revise over a long lifetime the way Wordsworth and Coleridge did, is generally a single-version author. He does not seem to have been interested in revising even where he had plenty of time to make changes, and frequently when one is looking around for the best, most authoritative version of a Keats poem (say, of *Ode on a Grecian Urn*) there is really only a single substantive text to choose.[5] But with Wordsworth and Coleridge, compulsive revisers who lived three or four decades after first drafting their most admired poems, there are plenty of versions competing for attention. The theory of versions—the idea that every separate version is a work in its own right and that all authoritative versions are equally authoritative—allows for some interesting new ways of looking at their works.

Thus, where before we might have thought we had only one or two *Rimes of the Ancient Mariner*—for example, the well-glossed, well-epigraphed text of one of the late *Poetical Works* (or of J. D. Campbell's and E. H. Coleridge's editions based on one or another of those late texts) and the sparer, more archaic version of the first printed text in the *Lyrical Ballads* of 1798—it is now possible to say that Coleridge authored (and, in authoring, *authorized*) a great many separate versions of *The Ancient Mariner*. I count at least eighteen but feel certain that there are others still to be discovered.

Let me go into a little detail concerning the multiple versions of Coleridge's major poems. Every student of Romanticism knows that Coleridge modernized the spelling and some of the language of *The Ancient Mariner* for the second publication of the poem, in the next edition of *Lyrical Ballads* in 1800, and that he added the Latin epigraph and the prose marginal glosses fifteen or more years after that. It is similarly well known that he added the lines celebrating "the one Life within us and abroad" to *The Eolian Harp* twenty-two years after he completed the first version of that poem and that there are striking differences between the original and revised texts of the Dejection ode, which at one time or another was addressed to Sara Hutchinson, Wordsworth, a fictional character called "Edmund," and an unnamed "Lady." And the best critics working on individual poems—say, *Frost at Midnight* or *Kubla Khan*—regularly make use of the manuscripts, successive printings, and annotated copies to support their interpretations. Even so, I think that students of Coleridge in general have very little idea of the frequency of variation among the texts or of the multiplicity of versions of the works they are studying and the complexity of relationships among the versions. And I also think that these same students continue, in large numbers, to regard the so-called final texts as the principal versions, slighting or entirely ignoring the earlier authoritative versions.

Here are some textual facts concerning the seven best-known works in the canon.[6] For *The Eolian Harp* we have sixteen or more separate manuscripts and printed versions dating from 1796 through 1828. Coleridge drafted at least part of the poem in August 1795, a few weeks before his marriage to Sara Fricker, and had a complete first version in hand sometime before the end of the year. The earliest surviving forms of the poem are the first printed text, in Coleridge's *Poems on Various Subjects,* published in April 1796, and the holograph manuscripts associated with that text at the University of Texas and Haverford College (*CoS* 119, 120, 124). Subsequently there are attempts at revision by Coleridge in other holographs at Texas and Cornell (*CoS* 121–23); then a second printed text, in the next edition of Coleridge's *Poems,* published in October 1797; a version constituted by Coleridge's request to his publisher to cancel three lines comparing melodies to footless birds of Paradise (*CL,* 1:331); and another printed text, in the third edition of Coleridge's *Poems,* published in 1803. After the *Poems* of 1803, there are Coleridge's manuscript alterations of the text in a copy of the 1797 *Poems* now at Yale (*CoS* 515), then two distinct versions in the volume published in 1817 titled *Sibylline Leaves*—the first version consisting of the original printed text in the body of the book, the second consisting of this text as corrected and expanded in the errata items listed at the front of the book (errata items that included, among other things, the insertion of the lines about "the one Life within us and abroad"). The latest authoritative version is that in Coleridge's *Poetical Works* of 1828 (though there are additional changes in minor details in the final lifetime edition, the *Poetical Works* of 1834).

These amount, as I said, to sixteen different versions of the poem, ranging from fifty-one to sixty-four lines in length—sometimes written or printed as a single paragraph, sometimes divided into three, four, or five paragraphs—and variously titled "Effusion XXXV" or "Composed at Clevedon, Somerset-shire" or "The Eolian Harp." There are too many differences to enumerate in this essay. In general terms, they change the tone, the philosophical and religious ideas, and the basic structure rather drastically. The first recoverable version, "Effusion XXXV," recounts an amusing incident of early married life, while the latest version is a much more serious affair—and one of the most frequently discussed poems of the Coleridge canon.

For *This Lime-Tree Bower My Prison,* which Coleridge first drafted in the summer of 1797 and then revised and expanded over the next year or so, there is a much simpler array—only twelve separate versions. The first of these is in a letter to Robert Southey of July 1797, the same month in which Sara Coleridge spilled the boiling milk on Samuel's foot (*CL*, 1:334–36). The second is in a letter to Charles Lloyd now in the Berg Collection of the New York Public Library (*CoS* 680). The third version is represented by an extract of lines 38–43 quoted in a letter to John Thelwall, October 1797 (*CL*, 1:349–50). The fourth is the earliest printed text, in Southey's *Annual Anthology* in 1800, and the fifth is constituted by manuscript alterations that Coleridge made sometime between 1800 and 1810 in a copy of the *Annual Anthology* now at Yale (*CoS* 682).[7] The sixth version is a text reprinted with only very minor changes from the *Annual Anthology* in William Frederick Mylius's *The Poetical Class-Book* (1810). The seventh and eighth versions are the uncorrected and corrected texts in *Sibylline Leaves* of 1817, and the ninth is constituted by Coleridge's further alterations of the poem in a copy of *Sibylline Leaves* now at Harvard (*CoS* 606). There are still more minor substantive changes in the *Poetical Works* of 1828, 1829, and 1834.

These versions vary from fifty-five to seventy-seven lines in length. The most interesting differences among the versions appear in the manuscript texts, in two of which (the letters to Southey and Lloyd) the exquisitely detailed description of the roaring dell that we admire so much in the printed texts is mostly left out and the wide prospect—the second of the three landscapes described in the standard text—is missing entirely. But manuscript and printed versions alike show important differences concerning the spiritual significance of nature: in several earlier texts, all nature is "a living thing / Which acts upon the mind"; a middle version replaces this idea with a description of the "soul / Kindling unutterable Thanksgivings / And Adorations" (*CoS* 682); and in subsequent texts Coleridge dropped both the idea of nature as a "living thing" (*Sibylline Leaves* errata) and the lines about "the Almighty Spirit . . . [making] Spirits perceive his presence" (*CoS* 606).

For *Frost at Midnight,* written in 1798, I know of ten distinct versions beginning with the first printed text, in the quarto volume containing *Fears in Solitude, France: An Ode,* and *Frost at Midnight* published in the fall of 1798. After this comes a version constituted by manuscript changes that Coleridge made probably about a decade later in an annotated copy of the 1798 quarto.[8] Subsequently, we have two different printed versions in 1812 (in the *Poetical Register,* vol. 7, and the pamphlet *Poems, by S. T. Coleridge, Esq.* issued by Law and Gilbert), three others in the proofs and the uncorrected and corrected published texts of *Sibylline Leaves* in 1817, a substantial set of variants in a letter that Coleridge wrote in 1820 (*CL,* 5:111–12), and the texts of the *Poetical Works* of 1828, 1829, and 1834 (1828 agrees substantively with the corrected *Sibylline Leaves;* 1829 and 1834 together constitute the final lifetime version).

These versions range from eighty-five to seventy-three lines in length, and in this case Coleridge shortened the poem, cutting out half a dozen lines from the end so as to conclude with the "silent icicles, / Quietly shining to the quiet Moon." He continually worked at revising the description and evaluation of the speaker's mental activity in the first paragraph of the poem. One text mentions the speaker's "delights . . . volition . . . deep faith" and emphasizes the playfulness of the interaction of the speaker's mind with the objective world (1798 quarto). Another text describes this playfulness as "wild reliques of our childish Thought" and associates it with the speaker's life in the past rather than his situation in the present (*Poetical Register*). A still later text removes all the self-belittling phrases of the description (*Sibylline Leaves*). And the latest text substitutes an almost negative description for the positive, with emphasis on the triviality of the experience and the bizarre, solipsistic character of the "puny flaps and freaks" of the idling spirit, everywhere seeking of itself, making a toy of thought.

The eighteen versions that I mentioned of *The Rime of the Ancient Mariner* consist of the first printed text, in the original *Lyrical Ballads* of 1798; then a version constituted by revisions that Coleridge requested in a letter to the publisher of mid-July 1800 (*CL,* 1:598–602), and another version, earlier or later than this, represented by Coleridge's annotations in a copy of *Lyrical Ballads* now at Trinity College, Cambridge (*CoS* 577). Subsequently there are three more printed texts, each different from the others, in the *Lyrical Ballads* of 1800, 1802, and 1805; two more versions in the uncorrected and corrected texts of *Sibylline Leaves;* at least six further versions represented by Coleridge's handwritten changes in copies of *Sibylline Leaves* at Columbia, Harvard, Yale, Duke, Stanford, and in a private collection (*CoS*

598–603, 605);[9] and finally the versions of Coleridge's late *Poetical Works* in 1828, 1829, and 1834.

The poem loses some thirty-nine lines in the course of revision, most of its archaic spellings, and the prose "Argument" that was printed on a separate page before the beginning of the poem in the first two editions of *Lyrical Ballads;* undergoes changes of title; gains a Latin epigraph from Thomas Burnet; and gains fifty-eight prose glosses printed in the margins beside and beneath the verses. (All commentators, regardless of whether or not they approve of Coleridge's addition of the glosses, agree that the glosses produced major changes in our reading of the poem.)[10]

Kubla Khan has the smallest number of versions among the major poems. It is not difficult to imagine an initial stage of the work consisting of the first thirty-six lines—the description of Kubla Khan the triumphant creator, or arrogant tyrant, decreeing his stately pleasure dome in a place sacred to the river Alph, producing a miracle of rare device—and then a later stage of composition in which Coleridge added the remaining eighteen lines expressing a fervent desire to re-create "that dome in air." Among extant versions, however, as opposed to imagined ones, there are only five: the holograph fair copy in the British Library (*CoS* 288); the first printing of the poem, in the *Christabel* volume of 1816; a slightly altered version in the form of a marked copy of this printed text at Harvard (*CoS* 62); and the texts in Coleridge's *Poetical Works* of 1828 and 1834.

The manuscript differs in wording from the first printed text in about one-fifth of the lines, but the manuscript variants, like those that occur in later printings, are of relatively minor importance. The more interesting differences among the versions have to do with the organization (rather than the wording) of the lines—in particular, the successive changes in the structure of the poem that are created by the changing positions of the paragraph divisions—and with Coleridge's prose accompanying the verse. Concerning this first matter, the manuscript text consists of two paragraphs of verse, the 1816 text is in four paragraphs, the final versions are printed as three or four paragraphs (there is an ambiguous page-break in 1834)—and each scheme of divisions produces a different way of reading the poem.[11] Concerning the other matter, Coleridge's first (extant) explanation of the circumstances, in a short note at the end of the manuscript, gives the place and date and mentions the influence of opium but says nothing about Purchas's *Pilgrimage,* or the composition of "two to three hundred lines," or the interruption by a person on business from Porlock. This is then expanded into the much longer version, containing all those now-famous details, that formed the preface to the poem in the first printing of 1816. It has been sensibly remarked that were it not for the preface we would never know that the poem was a fragment. The preface controls our reading from beginning to end: when it is removed, the poetic lines clearly emphasize creativity and inspiration, but coming after the preface, the lines emphasize the poet's *failure* at creativity.[12]

For *Christabel,* which Coleridge began in 1798, expanded in 1800, further enlarged in 1801, and then tinkered with, but never completed, all the rest of his life, I have identified eighteen versions, but probably there are several more than that number. To begin with, we know of nine manuscript versions (or partial versions) earlier than the first printed text, which was in the *Christabel* volume of 1816.[13] That first printed text can count as the tenth version. Then there are at least five subsequent versions in the form of manuscript changes that Coleridge made in copies of the edition of 1816.[14] Three more versions are constituted by the texts in the *Poetical Works* of 1828, 1829, and 1834.

Christabel is the longest of Coleridge's best-known works, and it is not possible here to go into the numerous details of substantive difference among the manuscripts and printed texts. I shall just mention a couple of interesting revisions in two annotated copies of the 1816 text that survive at Harvard and Princeton. In the first (*CoS* 62), at the point at which the witch Geraldine removes her robe and vest and the narrator exclaims, "Behold! her bosom and half her side," Coleridge inserted a rhyming line to describe what Christabel saw: "It was dark and rough as the Sea Wolf's hide." In the annotated copy at Princeton (*CoS* 63), Coleridge added a series of prose glosses in the margin, written in the same style as those in *The Ancient Mariner,* to explain what was happening in the lines of verse beside them. For lines 204–9, for example, Coleridge writes, "The Mother of Christabel, who is now her Guardian Spirit, appears to Geraldine, as in answer to her wish. Geraldine fears the Spirit, but yet has power over it for a time." And for lines 262–70: "As soon as the wicked Bosom, with the mysterious sign of Evil stamped thereby, touches Christabel, she is deprived of the power of disclosing what had occurred." There are five such glosses for the text of part 1, and four for the text of part 2, and in them Coleridge assumes the role and the voice of one of the earliest interpreters of the action taking place in the verse.

Finally (in this skimming survey) we come to the Dejection ode, which Coleridge wrote and rewrote several times in 1802 and then, just as with his other poems, continued to revise over the next three decades. For this work we have at least fifteen distinct versions—the first four in manuscripts and a transcript written before the initial publication of the poem, in the *Morning Post* of 4 October 1802; then several more versions in manuscripts and transcripts of late 1802, 1803, and 1804–5;[15] a partial version constituted by two long quotations in an essay by Coleridge in *Felix Farley's Bristol Journal* in 1814; then three more versions in the proof sheets and the uncorrected and corrected published texts of *Sibylline Leaves;* further revisions in some annotated copies of *Sibylline Leaves;* and finally, as usual, the texts included in the late *Poetical Works.*

The earliest version of *Dejection* is 339 or 340 lines long—two and a half times the length of the latest version—and it is so different in theme and tone from the latest that some scholars consider it a separate work in the Coleridge canon. John Beer, for example, in his Everyman edition of Coleridge's poems, prints both an early and a late text, with separate titles (Coleridge 1974), and Stephen Parrish, in the preface to his study of the manuscripts, insists that the earliest version is "an altogether different poem" (1988a). These scholars are quite right. One of the points of the present chapter is simply that all the other versions of *Dejection* are separate works as well. Not least among the interesting revisions is the changing identity of the person addressed in the poem: the famous lines at the beginning of what we usually think of as the fourth stanza—"O Lady! we receive but what we give, / And in our life alone does Nature live"—are successively uttered to Sara, to Wordsworth, to Edmund, to William, to Edmund again, and finally to the unnamed "Lady." The revisions change the poem from a passionate love lament to an almost academic dissertation on the shaping spirit of imagination. The beloved Sara of the letter becomes something like a Spenserian or Miltonic muse in the shorter, more dignified text of the late *Poetical Works.*

My enumeration of the multiple versions of Coleridge's seven best-known poems adds up to ninety-four separate texts. But even this expanded canon of versions does not take into account the thousands of differences in the lesser details of punctuation, capitalization, spelling, and paragraphing among the texts. Such lesser differences can have considerable effects. The first printing of *The Eolian Harp,* for example, made frequent use of the old long *s,* while the second printing, just a year later, uses only the modern *s*—with the result that the first text looks much more like an eighteenth-century poem and the second looks much more like a work of the nineteenth century. The paragraph divisions in *Christabel* continually change from version to version, and so, as a result, does the reader's idea of how Coleridge structured this narrative fragment.[16]

This multiplicity of versions constitutes a type of textual *instability* that makes interpretation of Coleridge far more difficult than it would be if we had only one version per work. Practical criticism—the day-to-day business of reading and interpretation—has always needed two things: first, a single author of the work that is being read and interpreted, and, second, a single text. Notwithstanding its far greater literary sophistication, critical theory also depends on single authors and fixed texts. With Coleridge there is no problem about the single author. But with so many versions of his poems, there does seem to be a problem in identifying the work that the critic is to read and interpret. Coleridge is usually the sole author of the poems we are concerned with, but he himself undermines the concept of a stable text by his continuous revising.

Coleridge made no secret of his idea that revision is an essential part of the creation of poetry. In his twenty-year plan for an epic poem, as he outlines it in a letter of early April 1797, the final five years were to be devoted to revision—an amount of time equal to the five years that he says he would give to the original drafting of the work (*CL*, 1:320–21, 6:1009). In another letter, this time in early October 1800, he says that his "taste in judging" is "far more perfect than [his] power to execute": "I do nothing, but almost instantly it's defects & sillinesses come upon my mind, and haunt me, till I am completely disgusted with my performance" (*CL*, 1:629). The implication is that he immediately sets about to remedy, by revising, what he perceives as "defects & sillinesses."

But while these remarks in Coleridge's letters would cover the ordinary practices that we see in many poets who want to alter and improve their works, there is something extraordinary about the frequency with which Coleridge revised his texts. I suggest that Coleridge changed his texts at least partly in order to create the very instability that would make his poems and their meanings elusive. Certainly his public practice called attention to textual fluctuations in his poetry.

He was, for example (as I pointed out at the beginning of chapter 9), conspicuously casual about his poetic accomplishments. He classed the first version of *The Eolian Harp* among his "Effusions" when he published it in his volume of 1796; he gave *Reflections on Having Left a Place of Retirement* the subtitle "A Poem Which Affects Not to Be Poetry"; he characterized *Fears in Solitude* as "a sort of middle thing between Poetry and Oratory"; he offered *Kubla Khan* to the public, as he says in the preface, "rather as a psychological curiosity, than on the ground of any supposed *poetic* merits" (Coleridge 1912, 1:100 n., 106 n., 257 n., 295). *Sibylline Leaves* begins with a preface mentioning "the fragmentary and widely scattered state" of the poems herein collected, and the final piece in the volume, *The Destiny of Nations,* is pointedly fragmentary, breaking off almost in midsentence with the beginning of a wild and desolate landscape that is never further described.[17] In such practices Coleridge intentionally presents himself to the public as a writer who is not wholly serious in his endeavors and perhaps not even competent. The emphasis is on the amateur qualities of the performance, its rough and unfinished character—the transitory, provisional nature of the work that the reader is holding in hand.

This public casualness seems to go together with Coleridge's almost flaunting display of the instability of his texts. As he kept revising his works, he also called attention to his revising in notes and prefaces to the poems. And he frequently changed his texts right before the reader's eyes (as it were) by means of printed errata lists, which both emphasize the fact that the revisions were made since the poems were set in type for the book and also provide a second version of the printed poem to accompany the first. In *Sibylline Leaves,* where the errata revisions are the most extensive of all, the errata pages are prominently placed at the beginning rather than the end of the volume. Then there are the handwritten changes and revisions that Coleridge wrote in the margins and above and beneath the lines in copies of his works that he gave to friends and acquaintances. The abundance of such annotated copies—J. C. C. Mays has located two dozen annotated copies just of *Sibylline Leaves*—suggests that Coleridge was typically unwilling to give away his works without making changes by hand to show that the printed text alone would not do.

For the critic who inherits this entire poetic ensemble, the existence of these many versions creates a number of important theoretical and practical problems. In the first place, it certainly has the potential of expanding the Coleridge canon dramatically (this is the issue implied in the subtitle of this chapter, "How Many *Mariners* Did Coleridge Write?"). If every separate version is a work in its own right and all authoritative versions of a work are equally authoritative, then the Coleridge canon contains not just a single *Eolian Harp* but sixteen or more works variously entitled "Effusion XXXV" or "Composed at Clevedon, Somersetshire" or "The Eolian Harp"; contains twelve separate works titled "This Lime-Tree Bower My Prison"; contains at least eighteen works titled "The Rime of the Ancient Mariner"; and so on through the list.

Another way of thinking about the Coleridge canon is to question the *identity* of any specific work in it. When we speak of *The Eolian Harp* or *The*

Ancient Mariner, are we speaking of a single version of a work or of all the versions taken together? And if we are speaking of all the versions taken together, are we thinking of a series of stages in which the work is defined by the *process* of its successive revisions, or are we thinking of all the versions as existing simultaneously, as they might in a variorum edition giving a complete account of successive readings? Theorists who worry about the identity of a literary work are primarily concerned with the elements of the work that make the same impression on all readers alike (as opposed to elements that impress each reader differently according to the individual reader's interpretation).[18] But these theorists always start with some specific text at hand. The more basic question raised by a theory of versions is how to identify a work in the first place so as to have a specific text to theorize about.

There are of course practical questions about editorial procedure—most obviously the question of which version we shall choose for reprinting (for example, in a standard edition or in an anthology) when we are allowed only one version per title. The old concept of choosing or constructing a text according to the author's final intentions was a handy solution to the problem. But as James Thorpe remarked more than three decades ago, saying that the author's final text is the most authoritative "is much like saying that an author's last poem (or novel, or play) is . . . [the author's] best one; it may be, and it may not be" (1972, 47). The newer idea of taking the earliest text as most authoritative is similarly handy but also similarly suspect when several versions exist.

The newest idea that all authoritative versions are equally authoritative makes editing considerably more difficult, because scholars now have to make choices not necessarily indicated by the authors—involving themselves in what Thorpe called "the aesthetics of textual criticism" (1965, 1972) or choosing versions on such grounds as historical importance or "representativeness." John Beer defied convention by printing the earliest (rather than the latest) text of *The Eolian Harp* in his Everyman edition of Coleridge's poems, and, as I have already mentioned, he included there both early and late versions of *Dejection.* Many more such departures from the old standard may be predicted, and future editors will have some tough choices to make in presenting a single reading text for each of the several hundred titles in the Coleridge canon.

Most important, there are a number of ways in which these multiple versions complicate the problems of interpreting the poems, whether individually or all the poems taken together as a unified (or, as the case may be, *dis*unified) body of work constituting the poet "Coleridge." The editorial choice of the latest texts may well be artistically justifiable. Coleridge, just like Wordsworth, seems to have been an amazingly shrewd reviser, and I think most critics would agree, even if they couldn't logically defend their preferences, that his later versions are almost always richer, more complex, better structured, more pleasing aesthetically. But when we come to interpretation (as opposed to reading and admiring), there are serious liabilities in working—as we usually do—solely or even primarily with those latest texts.

For one thing, any view of Coleridge's poetry based only on the latest texts—a view that one might get, for example, from reading selections in an anthology that arranges them in chronological order—certainly results in a distorted idea of Coleridge's development as a poet. We conventionally read *The Eolian Harp* in its chronological position for the summer or autumn of 1795, *This Lime-Tree Bower My Prison* in its chronological position for July 1797, *Frost at Midnight* and *The Ancient Mariner* in their positions for the spring of 1798, and so on, all the while imagining that Coleridge wrote what we are reading in just this order and at just the times represented by the dates of original composition. In fact, in such a situation, we are reading a text of *The Eolian Harp* that dates either from 1817 or from 1828 (depending on when the 1817 errata revisions are considered to have become a part of the complete poem), but in any case a text that Coleridge first arrived at some twenty or more years after the first-draft date of August 1795. Similarly we are reading a *Lime-Tree Bower* and an *Ancient Mariner* that date not from 1797 and 1798 but again from 1817 or later—that is, from a time when Coleridge was in his forties rather than in his twenties—and a *Frost at Midnight* that dates not from 1798 but from 1829, when Coleridge was in his later fifties. (And since I am supposing that many of us are still reading texts based on E. H. Coleridge's Oxford edition, in matters of punctuation and other accidentals we are reading versions that date from the very end of Coleridge's life—and even beyond, since there were numerous further small changes introduced into Coleridge's poems by the twentieth-century editor and the Oxford printers.)

In a like manner, by working with the latest texts we run the risk of misunderstanding or even being entirely ignorant of Coleridge's changes of interest and emphasis in subject matter, idea, and theme. We customarily read *The Eolian Harp* as a serious meditation on "the one Life within us and abroad," while the poem in fact began as a relatively frivolous "effusion" and only gradually developed into the philosophical poem that we have today. *Lime-Tree Bower* undergoes significant changes in religious sentiment in the course of revision. The structural and thematic opposition that makes *Frost at Midnight* so successful a poem was arrived at only toward the end of

Coleridge's life. *The Ancient Mariner* seems to become a much more theologically minded work in its later versions. And so on through the list.

It is clearly a mistake to think that all these latest texts existed together before the end of Coleridge's career, and any idea of unity in Coleridge's work that is based on these latest texts can apply only to the late period in which they were perfected. With an understanding of multiple versions, the critic can begin to grasp the biographical and historical reality of Coleridge's work—can do a kind of archaeological excavation, as it were, in which versions actually existing at the same time can be connected to form layers of Coleridgean textual history.[19]

For an example of such a Coleridgean archaeological layer, consider the following. In the early summer of 1798, just before Wordsworth wrote *Tintern Abbey,* the canon of major poems that I am surveying stood as follows: *The Eolian Harp* was in the state represented by the text in Coleridge's *Poems* of 1797—no longer an effusion but still a long way from the more serious philosophical meditation that we read in the standard text. The state of *Lime-Tree Bower* is somewhat in question. Coleridge may have arrived at the text with the three successive landscapes that he published in 1800, but it is possible that the work was still in the more rudimentary form represented by the letters of the summer and autumn of 1797. *Frost at Midnight* at this time was presumably in the state represented by the quarto text of 1798—more ambiguous in its attitude toward the speaker's mental activity in the opening lines and concluding not with the "silent icicles, / Quietly shining to the quiet Moon" but with the infant Hartley's shouts of eagerness as he tries to escape his mother's arms (a rather discordant note in relation to the tone of the rest of the midnight meditation). The just-completed *Ancient Mariner* was probably in its earliest known form—sans epigraph, sans gloss, sans everything except the plot itself (which Wordsworth criticized as "having no necessary connection") and the imagery (which Wordsworth thought "somewhat too laboriously accumulated").[20] Presumably at least some of the lines of *Kubla Khan* had been drafted by this time, perhaps the first thirty-six, as I surmised earlier in this chapter. Some or all of part 1 of *Christabel* had been drafted. The Dejection ode would not begin to take shape for another three years.

Such an array as I have described is a far more accurate representation of the state of Coleridge's poetry just before Wordsworth wrote *Tintern Abbey* in the summer of 1798 and presumably is more useful as a background for discussion of such topics as Coleridge's influence on Wordsworth and Coleridge's development of the blank-verse meditation that marks the beginning of what we now admire as the so-called greater Romantic lyric.

Coleridge, as he himself was well aware,[21] did invent the greater Romantic lyric, because *The Eolian Harp, This Lime-Tree Bower,* and *Frost at Midnight* are all earlier than *Tintern Abbey* and other works in this mode by Wordsworth, and also earlier than any that we single out by other writers, such as the odes of Keats. But *The Eolian Harp, Lime-Tree Bower,* and *Frost at Midnight* as they existed in the early summer of 1798 were quite different poems from the ones we know today.

It is of course the late texts that we read, interpret, and find unity in (and among). There remains, however, for author-centered critics, a nagging question concerning the poet's intentions in his continuous remaking of the poems. A favorable view of Coleridge as artist and thinker might wish to take the line that he had a deliberate plan in his revisions: to create, in his poems taken all together, the kind of unity in multeity—the harmonious whole made out of the separate parts—that he described in *Biographia Literaria* and elsewhere as the ideal of poetic art and that has become, not coincidentally, the kind of unity that critics have generally placed a high premium on ever since (Deconstruction notwithstanding).

Coleridge changed his poems at every period of his life, but he did some especially significant revising in 1815, when he was preparing his works for publication in *Sibylline Leaves.* The date coincides neatly with two important publications by Wordsworth around the same time: first, *The Excursion,* perhaps just a few months earlier (August 1814), with the highly publicized preface in which Wordsworth explains the unity and interrelatedness of all his works together, and second, Wordsworth's first collected *Poems* (April 1815) with another preface explaining the principles by which the poems were classified and arranged into categories. It would be a nice piece of biographical and textual criticism to explain Coleridge's most significant revisions as a reaction to these publications by Wordsworth. Such an explanation would inevitably involve seeing Coleridge the critical theorist turning theory into practical self-criticism as he revises to achieve in his own work the same kind of unity of effect that Wordsworth was in the process of accomplishing in his.

It requires only a medium amount of ingenuity to see Coleridge's alterations as tending toward this unity of effect. In *The Eolian Harp* Coleridge adds the lines celebrating "the one Life within us and abroad," thus giving us ever afterward a memorable passage to help explain the action and theme of *The Ancient Mariner:* the Mariner's abrupt and seemingly motiveless shooting of the albatross now becomes a violation of the "one Life" principle. Similarly, this same passage added to *The Eolian Harp* helps explain why it is that the poet's lime-tree bower, in the next Conversation poem, can be correctly seen as no prison at all but instead as a part of the "one Life" available wherever one looks. *This Lime-Tree Bower My Prison* is revised to make the religious significance of nature more compatible with that conveyed in *The Eolian Harp* and *Frost at Midnight*. *Frost at Midnight* is revised so as to place more emphasis on the interactions between the human mind and nature and to strengthen the contrast between what is in effect a failure of imagination in the opening paragraph and the successful working of the same faculty later on in the poem, a contrast that parallels the nonfunctioning and subsequent functioning of imagination in *The Ancient Mariner* and relates to similar concerns with the imagination in other works.

The Ancient Mariner itself is made much more complex by the addition of voices, most notably the voice of the theologically minded, scholarly annotater who supplies commentary in the margins and thereby sharpens the logic of the story, expands the religious and moral significances, and adds to the unity of the work. *Kubla Khan* becomes, with the addition of Coleridge's preface, a poem not so much about Kubla's glorious (perhaps we should say arrogant) decree of the stately pleasure dome as it is a poem about creating, or failing to create, unity. Kubla Khan did create a unity, as we can tell from all the images of mingling and merging in the first part of the poem, culminating in the shadow of the dome floating midway on the waves of the sacred river and the "mingled measure" heard from fountain and caves: "It was a miracle of rare device, / A sunny pleasure-dome with caves of ice" (31–36). The question suggested by Coleridge's preface is whether the speaker, desperately wanting to "build that dome in air," can accomplish a similar act of unification. The most important revisions of the Dejection ode heighten the emphasis on Coleridge's concerns with perception of nature, with imagination, and with creativity and thus make that poem more obviously relatable to principal concerns of the others.

Only *Christabel*, at this level of medium ingenuity, does not conveniently connect with the others I have discussed, though I feel sure that a slightly greater-than-medium degree of ingenuity could make suitable connections there as well. Perhaps one could solve the problem for the time being simply by exempting all fragments of any sort in this scheme. *Christabel* is the only real, as opposed to purported, fragment among the works I have mentioned so far. One could give it a place similar to that occupied by *Hyperion* among Keats's otherwise well-integrated poetical works: *Hyperion* fails to fit any scheme for the unity of Keats's poems taken all together, and so, we might say, *Christabel* doesn't have to fit either.

In this favorable view that I have sketched out, Coleridge appears to have been a genius at revising his poems. The main tendency of his changes, with or without the model of Wordsworth before him, was to create unity out of the diversity of his compositions in their numerous earlier forms, and the unity that he created provides license and authority for modern critics to explain—however diversely—the unity they discover as a quality that genuinely exists in the poetry.

A less favorable view of the poetry as a unified body is also possible. In this view, the revisions do not really support the progress of unity out of diversity after all. The alterations were made randomly, some much earlier than others, and some in an opposite or contrary direction (for example, the religious sentiments of one of the later versions of *Lime-Tree Bower* actually conflict, rather than harmonize, with the tendency of changes made in other Conversation poems, and the insertion of the lines about "the one Life within us and abroad" seriously damaged the structure and therefore the meaning of *The Eolian Harp*). Coleridge as reviser seems compulsive, willful, out of control, and the bulk of the revisions have to be judged as arbitrary tinkering, minor adjusting, alteration for the mere sake of alteration, rather than the results of any sober attempt to integrate the poems in the way I described just above. The bottom line of this kind of thinking is that Coleridge the famous advocate of unity may in fact have been one of the most scattered and *dis*unified poets in all of English literature.

Yet a third, and again favorable, view of the alterations may be constructed on the basis of my earlier observations about Coleridge's conspicuous featuring of his poetry's instability. Coleridge may have wished to imply that his poems were always in progress toward a never-to-be-attained but increasingly approached perfection. Or, equally, he may have wished to suggest that the perfect poem was a chimera and that authority itself was therefore a fiction. That is to say, he may have been either a Whig or a Deconstructionist, for both of these positions could require a demonstration of textual instability.

There is evidence to support all three of these different views of Coleridge as reviser. But judgments of this kind are ultimately critical constructs—at best, informed opinions—while the multiplicity of versions, being a matter of textual fact, is in a different category of information. It is a matter of fact with which Coleridgeans should become better acquainted.

11

Wordsworth, Coleridge, and the Shaggy Dog

THE NOVELTY OF *LYRICAL BALLADS* (1798)

COLERIDGE'S *CHRISTABEL* OPENS AT MIDNIGHT, near a castle, in chilly weather, with a full moon shining dimly in the sky and some owls hooting so raucously that they awaken a rooster, who starts crowing, thinking that it is morning. In the midst of these details comes an elaborate description of an old dog who lives in the castle and marks the time of day by howling precisely four times for each quarter hour and then, on the stroke of the hour, once for each hour, which means that at midnight, when the poem begins, the dog gives out sixteen howls—as Coleridge explains, "Four for the quarters, and twelve for the hour . . . Sixteen short howls, not over loud" (10–12). Admirers of *Christabel* tend not to dwell on these lines about the dog. The poem is a serious allegory about witchcraft, seduction, and the power of evil to triumph over the seemingly lesser power of good. But the description of the dog, read slowly and literally, is ridiculous. The question in these early lines is not what is going to happen to the people in the castle, but what is this weird dog doing in the poem?

Near the beginning of the fourth book of Wordsworth's *Prelude*, describing the poet's return home after his first year at Cambridge, we read about another dog, a "rough terrier of the hills" who helps Wordsworth compose his poetry. The dog does this in two ways. First, it acts as audience and absorber of the poet's excitement when he comes up with an image that he thinks is really good:

A hundred times when, roving high and low,
I have been harrassed with the toil of verse,

> Much pains and little progress, and at once
> Some lovely Image in the Song rose up
> Full-formed, like Venus rising from the Sea;
> Then have I darted forwards and let loose
> My hand upon his [the dog's] back, with stormy joy;
> Caressing him again and yet again.[1]
>
> (4.110–17)

And second, the dog looks after Wordsworth's public appearance and reputation in the local society. The poet characteristically composes aloud, talking to himself as he walks along, oblivious of his surroundings. The dog lets him know when people are approaching so that he can "give and take a greeting, that might save / My name from piteous rumours, such as wait / On men suspected to be crazed in brain" (128–30).

This too is ridiculous. Wordsworth is returning to the Lake District nature that he grew up in, and while out walking with this dog he has one of his transcendental experiences, amounting to a much-needed restoration of his soul.

> . . . Gently did my soul
> Put off her veil, and, self-transmuted, stood
> Naked, as in the presence of her God. . . .
>
> (150–52)

The passage goes on at some length and is one of the most elevated spiritual experiences of the poem. It concludes with a sound made by the wind in the trees,

> . . . a breath-like sound,
> Quick as the pantings of the faithful Dog,
> The off and on Companion of my walk;
> And such, at times, believing them to be,
> I turned my head, to look if he were there;
> Then into solemn thought I passed once more.
>
> (185–90)

In this way, one of the loftiest passages of *The Prelude* is framed by the low comedy of Wordsworth's dog—who in aesthetic sensibility is portrayed as the equal of the poet and socially is much more adept because it is better in touch with the surrounding reality.

Neither of these dogs is the subject of this essay. But they can set a tone and suggest a theme for the "shaggy dog" of my title. They are instances of a kind of comic incongruity or misfittingness that can result when a writer brings together humor and serious subject matter. It is an important quality: many of the most esteemed literary works have comic misfittingness of this sort—the ridiculous mixed in with high seriousness. And it figures prominently in the poems of Wordsworth and Coleridge, two of the most profound writers in all of British literature.

On 4 October 1998, we celebrated the two hundredth anniversary of the first publication of Wordsworth and Coleridge's *Lyrical Ballads*, which all agree is a landmark volume in our literature. For people who are into commemorating anniversaries, this was a big one. Through much of the twentieth century, the 1798 publication was considered the initiating event of British Romanticism. The beginning date of the Romantic period in the *Norton Anthology of English Literature* was 1798 as recently as a decade ago, even though the first author in the Romantics section, William Blake, had written some of his most important works a dozen or more years earlier, in the 1780s. The large survey course in the second half of British literature that I teach at the University of Illinois is still called "English Literature from 1798 to the Present," even though, again, we actually start with writings from the 1780s.

Lyrical Ballads is notably the only literary publication (as opposed to political event or turn of a century) that has been used to mark the beginning of a period in either British or American literature. And if one observes that the Romantic period is routinely the first section in the second of two volumes in almost any standard anthology for the survey, it is not difficult to see the *Lyrical Ballads* date of 1798 as marking the division between the first and second halves of all of British literature. And, further, since the writers in volume 2 are conspicuously more "modern" than those in volume 1, it is similarly not extravagant to see *Lyrical Ballads* as signaling the beginning of modern literature itself. One literary historian calls *Lyrical Ballads* "the most important poetical publication in the English language since the appearance of *Paradise Lost*." Two others describe the book as "the most important volume of verse in English since the Renaissance, for it began modern poetry" (Wordsworth 1992, 3, xi).[2]

I wish to consider why literary historians get so excited, still, about this literary event that happened more than two hundred years ago. *Lyrical Ballads* did reasonably well in its own time, once people got used to its deviations from what were then the approved ways of writing poetry. It went through four editions between 1798 and 1805, more than most books of poetry achieved at the time. Nowadays it is honored as the first publication of two of the most admired poems in canonical British poetry—Coleridge's *The Rime of the Ancient Mariner*, the first of the twenty-three pieces in the volume, and Wordsworth's *Tintern Abbey,* the final item, which was added as an afterthought when the rest of the poems were already in place. But the importance of *Lyrical Ballads* is greater than both its contemporary popularity and the high quality of its two best poems. It exerted tremendous influence on the style, subject matter, and some of the techniques of modern poetry—by which I mean the kind of writing that has been filling literary magazines and volumes ever since, right up to the present day.

I shall single out four things that were new in *Lyrical Ballads* of 1798 and suggest that these, taken together, are the real reason that critics, literary historians, and poets made such a fuss over the two hundredth anniversary.

1. *Lyrical Ballads* initiated (or, more accurately, legitimized and prominently exemplified) a new kind of subject matter for poetry—a subject matter of ordinary people and ordinary events.
2. The volume gave major emphasis to a new plain style in poetry.
3. The volume put into print a new kind of poem—what I shall call the shaggy-dog story in verse.
4. The volume established a new relationship between author and reader in a literary transaction. Here is the beginning of a kind of interpretive democracy in which it is the individual reader, rather than the author, who determines the meanings in a literary work.

The first two of these novelties—ordinariness of subject matter and plainness of style—are the two best-known literary characteristics of *Lyrical Ballads.* Wordsworth himself was the first to point them out, in the prefatory "Advertisement" at the beginning of the volume. The earliest reviewers exclaimed over them in the periodical press, and critics have been making much of them ever since. The third and fourth items in my list are not so well established, and it is mainly these that I address in this chapter.

Wordsworth's and Coleridge's Shaggy-Dog Stories in Verse

There is a large element of mystery about the happenings of the poems in *Lyrical Ballads,* starting with *The Rime of the Ancient Mariner,* when an old sailor stops a person on his way to a wedding, grabs him by the arm, fixes him with a glittering eye, and says, without any preliminaries, "There was a Ship." Probably the first-time reader is just as shocked and uncomfortable as the Wedding-Guest is in the poem. In the next piece in the volume, *The Foster-Mother's Tale,* we do not know who is speaking, what the occasion is, or what to make of the story: a foundling baby is brought up with books and religion, apparently goes crazy from too much reading, becomes a heretic, is thrown into prison, then escapes to become a sailor and is last seen sailing away by moonlight, "And ne'er was heard of more." Is this supposed to be background and sequel to *The Ancient Mariner?* The poem is subtitled "A Dramatic Fragment," and it just sits there, the second item in the contents, a total bewilderment. The third poem, titled *Lines Left upon a Seat in a Yew-Tree . . . ,* tells the life story of another person who came to a bad end—an idealist who, unappreciated by the world, learns to despise humankind and ends up a recluse, with no accomplishment other than having built a seat in a yew-tree on his property. There is an extended moral in the final seventeen lines, but it is muddled and contradictory, and we are unable finally to tell what the man did that was wrong or what the moral is. And so it goes pretty much through the volume. Time and time again, lacking conventional explanations, transitions, some kind of logic to hold things together, the poems end as puzzles.

Because they are mysterious and puzzling especially in their conclusions—or *non*conclusions—I want to liken the poems, for the sake of illustration, to the kind of joke called a shaggy-dog story, a type that dates from around the time I was in high school in the 1940s. Two definitions from standard dictionaries will establish the main idea. According to one, a shaggy-dog story is "a long and involved story, regarded as humorous by the narrator, often told with extraneous detail that culminates in an absurd or irrelevant punch line" (*Random House,* 1230). In the other, it is "a long-drawn-out circumstantial story concerning an inconsequential happening that impresses the teller as humorous but the hearer as boring and pointless; also: a humorous story whose humor lies in the pointlessness or irrelevance of the punch line" (*Webster's Ninth,* 1080). I could illustrate the shaggy-dog story by telling one, but it would take more space than I have available, and the main result would be serious doubt about my sanity. That of course would be exactly my purpose: the hearer of the story is mystified both by the story being told and by the seemingly misdirected energy and intensity of the person telling the story.

Some of the *Lyrical Ballads*—about a third of them—have intentionally humorous elements to go with the serious. The horse in *The Idiot Boy* is a good example: this is "a horse that thinks," the smartest character in the poem, and it plays an important role in the joyful reunion between the idiot boy and his mother at the end of the poem. But I am less interested in the humor (or nonhumor) of the shaggy-dog story than I am in the other characteristics of the definitions that I just quoted: the inconsequentiality of the happening, the puzzlement over the extraneous detail, and the pointlessness of the punch line.

Here are some details from five of the poems to illustrate the shaggy-doggedness of the *Lyrical Ballads.*

(1) *The Rime of the Ancient Mariner* tells a great story. The Mariner commits a horrible crime in shooting the albatross, gets into serious trouble, and then, when he is able to love and bless the slimy sea-creatures that he had earlier despised as ugly, some of his punishment—though not all of it—is lifted. Little children love to hear this story. It would make a terrific video cartoon. It is a simple story, and the materials are quite primitive. But a great many questions are left undecided in the text. Everything is symbolic, but there is very little explanation of what the symbols mean. For example: What is the albatross supposed to represent? Why does the Mariner shoot it? Why is the Mariner's punishment so severe for such a trivial action? What causes the Mariner to bless the slimy sea-creatures? What are we to make of the various supernatural spirits in the poem?

Almost every detail raises questions about what is going on. At the end of the Mariner's story, the listener in the poem, the unfortunate Wedding-Guest, turns *from* the bridegroom's door and goes off to be by himself:

> He went, like one that hath been stunn'd
> > And is of sense forlorn:
> A sadder and a wiser man
> > He rose the morrow morn.

> (655–58)

"Sadder" means more sober, that is, more serious; "wiser" means just what the modern reader would expect: the Wedding-Guest has learned something. But what he has learned is never specified. Interpretations of *The Ancient Mariner,* one of the most frequently read and most written-about poems in all of British literature, run into the thousands. There are questions everywhere and almost no answers in the text itself.

(2) Wordsworth's *Simon Lee*—which has for its full title *Simon Lee, the Old Huntsman, with an Incident in Which He Was Concerned*—is mainly description of a decrepit old man who formerly managed fox hunts and was the fastest person in the hunt, outrunning the people, horses, and dogs altogether. Now he is sick, half-blind, and has ankles so swollen that he

can hardly walk. Toward the end of the poem, the speaker pauses to address the reader:

> My gentle reader, I perceive
> How patiently you've waited,
> And I'm afraid that you expect
> Some tale will be related.
>   (69–72)

This is a reasonable expectation, since the title of the poem mentions "an incident in which [the old man] was concerned."

> O reader! had you in your mind
> Such stores as silent thought can bring,
> O gentle reader! you would find
> A tale in every thing.
> What more I have to say is short,
> I hope you'll kindly take it;
> It is no tale; but should you think,
> Perhaps a tale you'll make it.
>   (73–80)

The anticlimactic "incident" occupies the final three stanzas. The speaker comes upon Simon vainly attempting to hack through the root of an old tree stump. He takes Simon's tool and severs the root with a single blow— and this brings tears of thanks and praise from Simon. The last four lines sum up the speaker's feelings about the incident:

> —I've heard of hearts unkind, kind deeds
> With coldness still returning.
> Alas! the gratitude of men
> Has oftner left me mourning.
>   (101–4)

This seems an extreme or irrelevant reaction to an event in which nothing more impressive has occurred than severing the root of a tree stump. The reader is left hanging—feeling tricked, perhaps—trying to understand how the story connects to the feelings.

(3) *The Idiot Boy* is a longer poem in which, again, nothing much happens, or at least not as much as the reader might expect from the excitement of the narrator and the agitation of the people in his story. The main characters are Betty Foy; her mentally defective son, Johnny, whom she loves

dearly; and an old neighbor woman named Susan Gale. At the beginning of the story, Susan Gale is very sick, somebody has to go to town to fetch the doctor, and there is nobody to send but Johnny. So they put him on a horse, tell him how to find the doctor's house, and off he goes. And then he fails to come back. The clock strikes eleven at night, and he has not returned. And then twelve—still no Johnny. Betty Foy abandons the ailing Susan and runs into town looking for her son. She wakes up the doctor, who grumpily reports that Johnny never arrived there. She runs around looking for Johnny everywhere, and at last finds him, sitting on his horse by a waterfall not far from their home, looking up at the moon (which he thinks is the sun) and listening to the hooting of the owls (which he thinks is the crowing of roosters). It is a wonderful reunion, and Susan Gale is able to take part, because in her concern for the absence of Johnny she has miraculously gotten over her sickness and gone out to join the search for him.

Just before Johnny is rediscovered, the narrator of the story, who presents himself as an apprentice poet, addresses both the reader and the muses directly, asking permission to invent some wonderful adventures to explain Johnny's absence—for example, that he has been traveling through the sky to catch a star, or has been turned into a horseman-ghost, or has become a mighty sheep-hunter, or has been transformed into a fiery devil, threatening all the neighbors. But the stern muses refuse to let him tell any such fantastic story. He has to tell what actually happened, which is that Johnny has sat on his horse by the waterfall pretty much ever since he left home. That is, practically nothing has happened—the events are all in the minds of the people worried about Johnny. *The Idiot Boy* is the only other poem in the volume besides *The Ancient Mariner* that is set off with a separate half-title page, and it is the second longest poem in the book, about seven-tenths the length of *The Ancient Mariner*. This makes for a conspicuously long poem—and a great deal of fuss on the part of the characters and the narrator—for so little in the way of actual events. Once again, readers are left shaking their heads: What *is* this story about, anyhow?

(4) Then there is Wordsworth's *The Thorn*, which is probably the most interesting for teaching and criticism after *The Ancient Mariner* and *Tintern Abbey*. This is a question-and-answer dialogue concerning, first of all, a stunted thornbush on a high mountain ridge, a little muddy pond near by, and a small hill of brilliantly colored moss beside the pond, and, in connection with these, a story about a woman named Martha Ray who is said to have been jilted by her lover, borne a child out of wedlock, and murdered the baby—either by hanging it from the thornbush or by drowning it in

the pond—and then buried the baby's body under the hill of moss. We are told that she regularly goes up the mountain to sit beside the hill of moss and cry, over and over, "Oh misery! oh misery! / O woe is me! oh misery!" (65–66, 76–77).

The main speaker telling this story, Wordsworth makes clear in the preface to the volume, is "not . . . the author's own person: the character of the loquacious narrator will sufficiently shew itself in the course of the story." In later editions of *Lyrical Ballads,* he explains more lengthily in an endnote to the poem:

> The character which I have here introduced speaking is sufficiently common. The Reader will perhaps have a general notion of it, if he has ever known a man, a Captain of a small trading vessel for example, who being past the middle age of life, had retired upon an annuity or small independent income to some village or country town of which he was not a native, or in which he had not been accustomed to live. Such men having little to do become credulous and talkative from indolence; and from the same cause . . . they are prone to superstition. On which account it appeared to me proper to select a character like this to exhibit some of the general laws by which superstition acts upon the mind. (Wordsworth 1992, 350–51)

The story of Martha Ray, unwed motherhood, and child murder makes this a poem about crime and social morality. But Wordsworth's comments about superstitious imagination invite closer scrutiny of the details, and when one gets into those, it turns out that possibly none of the events really happened: that there was no murder, no baby, not even a Martha Ray; that "Oh misery! oh misery! / O woe is me! oh misery!" is actually the sound of the wind on the mountain; and that the only realities of the poem are the stunted thornbush, the pond, and the hill of moss—plus, of course, what the speaker's superstitious imagination creates and attaches to these natural objects.[3] This may be another poem in which, for all its length and high emotions, nothing much actually happens.

(5) The most difficult poem of *Lyrical Ballads* is not a narrative but a lyric, the final poem in the volume: *Tintern Abbey,* formally titled *Lines Written a Few Miles above Tintern Abbey, on Revisiting the Banks of the Wye during a Tour, July 13, 1798.* This is a tourist poem in which the center of attraction, the famous ruined abbey, is out of sight "a few miles" downstream. It is a nature poem in which, after the opening paragraph, there are almost no images of nature. It is a political poem in which most of the speaker's political, social, and economic beliefs lie unexpressed between the

lines. It is a religious poem in which what seems to be unmediated contact with a pantheistic deity is soberly, even logically, explained in terms of tourist-postcard chitchat.

Tintern Abbey is a texture of contradictions from beginning to end: simultaneously a celebration and a lament over the speaker's maturing, a depiction of both the harmony and the disharmony of humans and nature, an alternately successful and unsuccessful attempt to reconcile the "two consciousnesses" of past and present selves that Wordsworth was always writing about,[4] and a view of the speaker's and his sister's future that is at once tenderly optimistic and funereal. Four decades ago, I wrote that "it is sometimes difficult, even after many readings, to decide what the poem is primarily about" (Wordsworth 1965, 516). Wordsworth criticism since then has not simplified the business. We know that *Tintern Abbey* is about nature, time, mortality, memory, imagination, society, the city, humanity, and God (to name a few of the more frequently mentioned possibilities). But it is a challenge to sort out the combinations and emphases among these, and this still leaves innumerable problems concerning specific details (as in the famous lines about "a sense sublime / Of something far more deeply interfused," 96–97, where the question "more deeply interfused than what?" has no apparent answer). At almost every point, the poem raises questions that the text fails to answer. Unlike some of the other poems just described, it has what looks like a solid enough conclusion, when Wordsworth, speaking to his sister, says:

> Nor wilt thou then forget,
> That after many wanderings, many years
> Of absence, these steep woods and lofty cliffs,
> And this green pastoral landscape, were to me
> More dear, both for themselves, and for thy sake.
>
> (156–60)

But if one asks what, exactly, Wordsworth has said in the 150 lines leading up to this final sentence, it is hard to come up with a clear answer. This is another Romantic poem, like *The Ancient Mariner,* on which there is an enormous literature of critical interpretations.

The Advent of Individual Reader Response

I think that Wordsworth and Coleridge gave strong impetus to a new kind of poem in English literature. I have called it the shaggy-dog story in verse in order to emphasize its relative pointlessness and lack of decisive conclusion. But regardless of generic label, it is a poem that puzzles the reader with serious questions about structure, meaning, and motive that are not resolved. The most interesting and important consequence of this kind of poem is the new relationship that it brings into being between the authorship side of the literary transaction and the reader. This is nothing less than the transferal of the meaning of a work from the author to the reader.

Readers of these poems have not, in their readings of the last two hundred years, simply observed the puzzles and unanswered questions and then told their friends, or written in papers and articles and books, that these poems are puzzles and the questions are unanswered. Rather, they have done what readers have done—and have had to do—with practically all the best poems ever since: they have created unities out of the materials of the texts; they have individually, on an ad hoc basis, supplied logic and closure where these things are lacking in the texts themselves; and, in effect, they have solved the puzzles and answered the questions. That is to say, from 1798 on to the present, the structures of the poems, the meanings, the logic, and the closure have in fact been the creations of the readers rather than the writers.

Wordsworth and Coleridge themselves were among the first to be consciously aware of the reader's creativity in reading their poems. Wordsworth writes in several places about the process and psychology of reading, starting with the shorter and then the longer preface to *Lyrical Ballads,* where he acknowledges and appeals to the reader's independent feelings and judgment. His preface to *The Excursion* in 1814, describing the connectedness of his various works into one grand project, says in effect that readers are on their own to construct a system out of the several parts. Two prefaces that he published in 1815 describe the reading process in detail, with the reader acting imaginatively on the poet's texts to create unity and meaning. There is a passage in book 5 of *The Prelude* to the same effect, speaking of "the great Nature that exists in works / Of mighty Poets" (5.586–607), implying that the reader's mind operates creatively upon poetry in the same way that the spectator's mind acts creatively upon nature. And Coleridge, in *Biographia Literaria* and other writings, is the principal theorist of unity in a literary work—the acknowledged basis for the thinking and practice of twentieth-century critics who have constructed unity in poem after poem where it was previously not thought to exist. In his theorizing, Coleridge was talking about creative reading as much as he was talking about creative writing. He is still the best modern theorist about what readers do in the act of reading.

What I am suggesting in this chapter is that for the last two hundred years—in very general terms, for something as large as the second half of British literature (using the two volumes of a standard anthology as the dividing point)—our poems have tended to be about ordinary people and events; the language has tended to be simpler, plainer, more conversational, more down-to-earth and concrete than it had been before; the poems have become puzzles of ambiguity, unresolved questions, and inconclusiveness; and, most important, the place where the meaning is determined has conspicuously shifted from author to the reception side of the transaction—the individual reader.

Now how, it may be asked, could one test out these enormous generalizations, and especially the last one—the idea that before 1798 the meaning of a poem was in the text, put there by the author, and after 1798 the meaning was in the individual reader's construction based on the text? The answer is that one does just what scientists do when they test out a hypothesis: one keeps one's eyes and ears open to observe what happens. Let us focus for a moment just on the endings of poems. If I had enough space, I could quote several hundred good poems from medieval times on up through the eighteenth century that end decisively—with a "clinch," as Barbara Herrnstein Smith says in *Poetic Closure* (1968, 2)—that is, with a point that sums up the poem's meaning, or "moral," or rounds out the story. Here, as a tiny array of data, are a handful of concluding couplets from Shakespeare's Sonnets:

> So long as men can breathe or eyes can see,
> So long lives this, and this gives life to thee. (Sonnet 18)

> For thy sweet love rememb'red such wealth brings,
> That then I scorn to change my state with kings. (Sonnet 29)

> This thou perceiv'st, which makes thy love more strong,
> To love that well, which thou must leave ere long. (Sonnet 73)

> For sweetest things turn sourest by their deeds;
> Lilies that fester smell far worse than weeds. (Sonnet 94)

> So shalt thou feed on Death, that feeds on men,
> And Death once dead, there's no more dying then. (Sonnet 146)

I propose, in very general terms, that this is the way poems tended to end before 1798. The ending tells us what the author was trying to say, or at least wraps up the poem so that the reader feels it to be satisfactorily concluded.

Poems this side of 1798 do not end so decisively. Many of the best of them conclude with real or implied questions. Think of Keats's "Was it a vision, or a waking dream? / Fled is that music:—Do I wake or sleep?" at the end of *Ode to a Nightingale;* or Tennyson's monologue spoken by Ulysses, ending heroically with the line "To strive, to seek, to find, and not to yield" but also with the suggestion that the aging hero is essentially on a quest for suicide, taking his men down with him; or Matthew Arnold's pointed lack of resolution in the final lines of *Dover Beach,* "And we are here as on a darkling plain / Swept with confused alarms of struggle and flight, / Where ignorant armies clash by night"; or the lack of explanation of practically everything at the end of Christina Rossetti's *Goblin Market;* or the last three lines of Gerard Manley Hopkins's most famous poem, *The Windhover,* "No wonder of it: shéer plód makes plough down sillion / Shine, and blue-bleak embers, ah my dear, / Fall, gall themselves, and gash gold-vermilion" (a nonexplanation if there ever was one); or the terrifying image at the end of Yeats's *The Second Coming,* "And what rough beast, its hour come round at last, / Slouches towards Bethlehem to be born?" This also is a small array of data, but if they are representative, they show that poems after 1798 do not end decisively in the way that poems did earlier. In each example, it has to be the reader, not the author or the text, who decides the meaning.

I shall add two poems by twentieth-century Americans to the database—picked almost at random from many hundreds of good possibilities for illustration. The first, written in the early 1920s, is Wallace Stevens's *Anecdote of the Prince of Peacocks,* a Romantic encounter poem in which a speaker, the Prince of Peacocks, meets a character named Berserk, asks him two questions ("Why are you red / In this milky blue? . . . Why suncolored, / As if awake / In the midst of sleep?"), and gets for an answer, "I set my traps / In the midst of dreams." Just as in Romantic poems a century earlier, the speaker gains new knowledge from the encounter:

I knew from this
That the blue ground
Was full of blocks
And blocking steel.
I knew the dread
Of the bushy plain,
And the beauty
Of the moonlight
Falling there,

Falling
As sleep falls
In the innocent air.

Stevens's poem can be interpreted to be logical and meaningful, but the interpreting is done by the reader in the act of reading. What does Wallace Stevens's poem have to do with Wordsworth and Coleridge? It just happens that those two poets, along with Keats, were Stevens's principal models all through his career.

My second American example is a short poem by Mark Strand written in the 1960s and published in *Reasons for Moving* (1969). It is titled *The Whole Story:*

How it should happen this way
I am not sure, but you
Are sitting next to me,
Minding your own business
When all of a sudden I see
A fire out the window.

I nudge you and say,
"That's a fire. And what's more,
We can't do anything about it,
Because we're on this train, see?"
You give me an odd look
As though I had said too much.

But for all you know I may
Have a passion for fires,
And travel by train to keep
From having to put them out.
It may be that trains
Can kindle a love of fire.

I might even suspect
That you are a fireman
In disguise. And then again
I might be wrong. Maybe
You are the one
Who loves a good fire. Who knows?

Perhaps you are elsewhere,
Deciding that with no place
To go you should not
Take a train. And I,
Seeing my own face in the window,
May have lied about the fire.

These are ordinary people on a train, though we are not sure how many there are. The language is extremely plain and conversational. There are numerous questions about what is going on and what the poem is about. The one who decides these questions and determines what the poem is about is the reader, obviously. Mark Strand also is an admirer of Wordsworth and Coleridge.

Actually the little book that was so influential on the subject matter, style, and greater complexity of poetry of the last two centuries, from Keats to Stevens and Strand and beyond, came about quite by accident. Wordsworth and Coleridge needed some pocket money to finance a walking tour, so they decided to write a poem that they could sell for five pounds to a magazine. Coleridge proposed a sea voyage for the subject. Wordsworth suggested shooting an albatross. And the poem took off—growing in size and seriousness until it was too important just to sell to a magazine. They decided to put together a volume containing *The Ancient Mariner* and whatever other poems and fragments they had on hand. Then Wordsworth, in a burst of energy at practically the last minute, produced a series of narrative poems to help fill out the volume. And even later he wrote *Tintern Abbey* and stuck that on at the end. They had a hard time finding a publisher for the book, and when it finally appeared, without any author's name on the title page, they did not see a copy right away and actually did not even know who the publisher was. But it did come out, on 4 October 1798, and British poetry was never the same afterward.

PART III

Romantics and the Classroom

12

Fifty-nine Ways of Reading
Ode on a Grecian Urn

EVEN WITHOUT SEEING A LIST of contributors to the collection of essays in which this chapter was originally published, I think I can safely claim to have been acquainted with *Ode on a Grecian Urn* longer than any of the others. I first read the poem in high school in the 1940s just after World War II. I reread it many more times between 1949 and 1958 in surveys, period courses, and seminars as an English major at the University of Texas, an MA student at Northwestern, and a PhD candidate at Harvard. Then I taught it at least once every semester—except when I was away on sabbatical leave—for the next four and a half decades at the University of Illinois, most recently in a large undergraduate survey of British literature since the 1780s and a graduate seminar on the topic "The New Romanticism" (the "old" being constituted by Keats and the five other currently canonical male poets of the period, the "new" consisting of those six plus a like number of more recently canonized women poets). I can report from this, first, that in all those years I have never seen students *not* get interested in Keats and his most famous ode—they walk and drive around listening to rock music or talking on cell phones and then, in class, become very serious about the difference between heard and unheard melodies, about the condition of eternal spring, and about the lovers never being able to kiss—and, second, that I myself have never tired of the experiences of reading and teaching the poem. On the contrary, *Ode on a Grecian Urn* continues to be rich and moving every time I read it—which ought to be remarkable, considering that I have known the fifty-line text (really, the several different fifty-line texts that are recoverable) word by word, mark by mark, for so many decades.

Teachers of my generation (and of the preceding and immediately fol-
lowing generations) were taught to read poetry according to the principles
of the New Criticism, the powerful movement initiated in the 1920s by
I. A. Richards and practiced influentially in the 1930s and 1940s by William
Empson and F. R. Leavis among others in Britain and by Cleanth Brooks,
John Crowe Ransom, and Alan Tate among others in the United States. The
New Critics were combating both the long-established "biographical"
method of criticism, which involved investigating and relating the facts of
authors' lives while paying hardly any attention to the works the authors
wrote, and a mindless kind of "appreciation" where works were admired, in
general terms, for their wisdom, brilliance, emotional power (*King Lear* was
"very moving"!) but were not actually read for either their content or the
artistic strategies by which that content was conveyed or, as was frequently
the case, subverted. The New Critics advocated a process of "close reading"
(sometimes called "slow reading"), examining a text one line, one phrase,
even one word at a time. They were interested not in authors' "messages"
but in the representation of dramatic (fictionalized) speakers in particular
circumstances and, above all, in structures of irony, paradox, ambiguity,
and contradiction. (If some of this sounds like the approach of the more
recent Deconstruction, that is simply because Deconstructionists, too,
learned their tactics from the New Critics.) Keats especially, because of the
prevalence of paradox and contradiction in his texts, was a frequent subject
of New Critical analysis. *Ode on a Grecian Urn* is an exemplary text in
Cleanth Brooks and Robert Penn Warren's extremely influential textbook,
Understanding Poetry (1938), where it is presented with a dozen questions
beginning "In what sense is the urn a 'sylvan historian' (line 3)?" and concluding "Are the last two lines a teasing utterance or not? What is their
truth? Do the preceding 48 lines serve to define it?" (474–76). As the subject
of a famous essay, "Keats's Sylvan Historian: History without Footnotes," in
Brooks's *The Well Wrought Urn* a decade later, it has a central place among
case studies assembled to demonstrate that "the language of poetry is the
language of paradox" (3).

We taught, in the good old days of the 1950s, 1960s, and 1970s—in courses
such as my department's English 101, "Introduction to Poetry" (required of
all English majors)—by posing Brooks-and-Warren-like questions about
specific details in the texts. My routine study questions for Keats's odes,
which still strike me as fundamentally sound, were a simple triad of (1) What
does the speaker want? (What is the speaker's problem?); (2) What contrasts,
tensions, ironies, etc., oppose the speaker's desire? (a question about the

poem's structure); and (3) Is the opposition resolved? (a question about closure). For class discussion of *Ode on a Grecian Urn,* I devised numerous specific questions, such as: Who is speaking? Who or what is being addressed? What is odd about an "unravish'd bride"? What do "unravish'd bride" and "foster-child" have in common? In what sense can "quietness" be a husband, or "silence and slow time" foster parents? Beginning in line 5, the poem's syntax itself poses Brooks-and-Warren-like questions that can stimulate class discussion—"What leaf-fring'd legend . . . ?"—and six or seven more questions are asked before the end of the first stanza. The complications multiply with the introduction of several impossible situations in the images of stanzas 2 and 3. In stanza 4 the speaker adds still further questions ("Who are these coming to the sacrifice? . . . What little town . . . ?"). And the poem concludes with the urn's (or someone's) totally incomprehensible "message" of the last two lines, "Beauty is truth" and so on.

The poem thus provides very rich materials for class discussion—I could on any occasion easily devise fifty or a hundred questions based on details of the fifty-line text—and for several decades my (and I assume many other teachers') standard procedure was to introduce a selection of such questions, get various frequently bright answers from the students, and consider the merits of the answers and their tendencies to nudge toward larger generalizations concerning tone, attitude, thematic meaning, and so on. But I'm sorry to have to report that we operated in a scheme where there were right and wrong answers to the questions. The commonest activity of class discussion in those days was a sequence of wrong answers 1, 2, and 3 (volunteered by three well-meaning students) corrected by right answer 4 (delivered by the teacher). Granted that New Criticism was a matter of an individual reader huddling together with an individual text, doing the line-by-line, word-at-a-time slow reading, when it came to class discussion—PhD professor in the front of the room, face-to-face with freshmen and sophomores who had hardly any experience of life or literature or even much knowledge of the English language—some individual readers were thought to be superior to some others.

Confident that I was perfectly justified in correcting students' wrong responses, for several decades I cheerfully carried on the inculcation of an interpretation of Keats's major poems, *Grecian Urn* among them, in which, to put it in the barest possible terms, the theme was skepticism concerning visionary imagination, the various characters (Madeline in *The Eve of St. Agnes,* Lycius in *Lamia,* the knight in *La Belle Dame,* the speakers in the odes) were hoodwinked dreamers, and the basic idea was that, as it is stated in the final stanza of *Ode to a Nightingale,* the imagination "cannot cheat so well / As she is fam'd to do." I regularly drew a "Keats Map" on the board in my classes, consisting of a horizontal line dividing an ideal world above the line (heaven, immortality, the supernatural, timelessness, etc.) from an actual world below (earth, mortality, the natural, time, etc.) and had the students position various elements of the poems above and below the line—Madeline's dream in her bedroom above the line, for example, and Porphyro, physical love, the rest of the castle, and the storm outside below the line; La Belle Dame's magical grot above the line, and the knight's cold hillside of reality below; the Nightingale's forest above, and "here," the world of "hungry generations," below; and so on.[1]

Ode on a Grecian Urn fit the scheme perfectly, with the initial perfection of the permanence depicted in the world of Tempe or the dales of Arcady above the line and the speaker's real world of process, change, passion, and death below (complicated, as the poem develops, by the speaker's gradual realization, especially evident in the negatives at the end of stanza 4, that the ideal permanence is itself a kind of death, in sharp contrast to the life of "breathing human passion" in the actual world that the speaker earlier wished to escape). In this way my class "discussion" inevitably turned into lecture. I had the truth about Keats's poems, and the students didn't seem to mind taking it in. Accepting my reading was much easier than doing their own interpreting. It saved time and effort in the long run, and the students too believed that the professor's reading was likely to be the correct one.

These were, as I said, the good old days, now superseded by much improved ways of understanding poetry. For one thing, the New Critical "slow reading," once so radical in its approach (because, in focusing on "the text itself," it barred from consideration not only history and biography but every other extrinsic source, including the dictionary meanings of words in the text), became everybody's ordinary way of approaching a text. For another, the coming-of-age of Literary Theory (here capitalized to give it thematic status like a float in a Fourth of July parade) in the 1970s, 1980s, and 1990s opened up many more possibilities than had hitherto been thought of for the kinds of meaning that a reader could be aware of in a literary text. Of the twenty or so serious theories that attracted interest (and enthusiastic adherents) in those decades, I'll single out four that I think have had the most influence on our reading of *Ode on a Grecian Urn.*

(1) *Deconstruction*—taking a view that literary works are disorganized, illogical, incoherent, essentially indeterminate, and employing a methodology of analyzing works to find mistakes, inconsistencies, gaps, and contra-

dictions—could, as a theory, have been based solely on *Ode on a Grecian Urn,* because Keats himself had already written into his text those very incongruities and discordances that Deconstruction was established to expose. The poem has in fact been deconstructing itself for more than 180 years, but for many readers it took 1970s' theorizing to make it permissible to say so in class. We now understand, even with the most admired poems, that some conflicts are *not* resolved into agreement, that some closures are not really achieved, and that readers who demand agreement and closure must supply them interpretively, compensating for lacks in the actual texts themselves.

(2) *New Historicism* is an approach based on the idea of literature as a social activity involving not only authors but publishers, editors, printers, booksellers, purchasers, readers, reviewers, critics, teachers, students, and a great deal of nonliterary historical context, including the political and social ideas of everybody involved, local and national and international events, and so on and on. In its political emphasis, New Historicism began as a delicate outgrowth of the Marxist criticism that had some influence in the 1920s and 1930s and then was revived in the 1960s. Politics have always been central in the writings of Blake, Byron, and Percy Shelley among the Romantics and, in a different way (because of their progress from youthful radicalism to middle-aged conservatism), in the writings of Wordsworth and Coleridge. But what, we used to ask, can there possibly be of political interest in *Ode on a Grecian Urn,* where a speaker is confronting an old Greek vase with pictures depicting lovers, piper, trees, and a sacrificial procession, and musing on vague abstractions about Beauty and Truth? As it turns out, critics beginning in the 1980s have discovered plenty of political concerns in the poem. Keats's centering the poem in Greek life and culture made a point about the ancient origins of the modern revolutionary spirit, for example, and publishing it in *Annals of the Fine Arts* constituted an attack on the art establishment of the time.[2]

(3) *Feminism,* which has been enabling readers to see so many imbalances that formerly were invisible, allows one not only to ponder the sexual politics of "unravish'd bride" and the "maidens loth" struggling to escape in stanza 1, as well as the gender of the sacrificial animal in stanza 4, but also to consider more clearly the critical suggestion that Keats chose to write about an urn because its curved shape resembled that of a woman (Patterson 1954, 211–12, 218). Margaret Homans (1990), to mention one of the most helpful critics in this context, does not cite the ode but provides excellent background commentary in her comprehensive account of Keats's relationships

with women (both those he knew and those he imagined as readers). Daniel Watkins gives an extended analysis of patriarchal morality in the poem (1989, 104–20, 206–11).

(4) *Reader-Response Criticism* (sometimes called Reception Theory) has been making it increasingly reasonable—in books and articles, in the classroom, and in social activity more generally—to accept the diversity of individual responses to complex poetic texts. The title of the present chapter, which for the occasion could more accurately have been phrased "*Teaching* Fifty-nine Ways of Reading *Ode on a Grecian Urn*," takes off from my 1999 book on multiple ways of interpreting *The Eve of St. Agnes,* which in a central chapter (accompanied by a list in an appendix) presents fifty-nine different interpretations of Keats's narrative, some of them in direct conflict with some of the others, and maintains that all fifty-nine are legitimate readings and none of them is "wrong" (Stillinger 1999, 35–77, 147–49; see also the appendix following chapter 6 in the present volume). In my preface I announce an ideal of "interpretive democracy," and in a chapter on how we individually process the profusion of stimuli received from Keats's lines I advocate a practice of "no-fault reading" whereby, again, responses cannot be right or wrong, merely more or less interesting (ix, 89–96).

I have been teaching undergraduates on these principles for a dozen or more years, ever since I became interested in the idea of "multiples" in the basic components of a literary transaction—multiple authorship of works that we usually assume to have been written by a solitary genius; multiple textual versions of famous works in the canon; and, what is most relevant to the present occasion, multiple interpretations of those works everywhere one turns in the critical literature (by the most sophisticated of readers) and the classroom (by some of the most naive). In general, students have responded favorably to my approach, several over the years even remarking—after the exams were finished and the grades turned in—that the idea of no-fault reading had changed their lives! Friends, colleagues, and reviewers have been similarly approving, though not exactly in the same extravagant language.

The chief question that arises (from colleagues and reviewers, if not from students) is how one teaches a complex poem in a scheme where there are no wrong answers concerning the points being raised. In *Reading "The Eve of St. Agnes"* I quote Alvin Kernan's contemptuous depiction of no-fault readers as a group of savages "who have a great deal of difficulty piecing out the broken signs on the printed page" (Stillinger 1999, 91; Kernan 1990, 144). I counter this with numerous situations where multiple responses—contradictory and even "wrong" assertions among them—enhance the richness and complexity of the reading experience (Stillinger 1999, 89–96). The text of *Ode on a Grecian Urn* provides conflicting stimuli in practically every line—"Fair youth . . . thou canst not leave / Thy song . . . Bold lover, never, never canst thou kiss . . . She cannot fade . . . thou hast not thy bliss . . . And, little town, thy streets for evermore / Will silent be," and so on. With lines like these, the responses *have* to be multiple and contradictory.

Keats's well-known ideal of poetic disinterestedness—"Negative Capability," he called it, "when man is capable of being in uncertainties, Mysteries, doubts, without any irritable reaching after fact & reason" (*KL*, 1:193)—can be usefully applied to the author-text-reader transaction in *Ode on a Grecian Urn*. We have in the first place a negatively capable author/speaker who asks a great many questions about activities depicted on the urn, gets no answers to his questions (unless "Beauty is truth" is supposed to be one), but remains content in his situation of uncertainties, mysteries, doubts. We know he is content simply because the final lines, while lacking the logic that would enable clear paraphrase, have an unmistakable *air* of resolution about them—the message is from "a friend to man" and its wisdom is "all ye need to know." We have in the second place a negatively capable text, in the sense that it is an epitomizing texture of uncertainties, mysteries, doubts—possibly the best example of comparable length in all of British poetry. And in the third place, with the help of reader-response thinking we can say that we have negatively capable readers as well, who, like the author/speaker, similarly don't know the answers to the questions but are satisfied without knowing, accepting at the end a kind of contented irresolution.

In recent years, in trying to position the poet himself on the Keats Map, I have imagined Keats standing outside *Ode on a Grecian Urn* looking on with his readers and wondering, with each successive reading, how the various conflicts will get resolved, with the possibility (for Keats and the readers alike) that they will be resolved a different way each time. This is not a bad premise on which to conduct class discussion of the poem. It certainly beats fifty minutes of interpretive dicta from the front of the class.

13
Refurbish or Perish

WHEN KARL KROEBER LAST SPRING sent around a letter inviting suggestions for this English 9 program, and I responded by proposing that we have a panel to discuss the future of the study of Romanticism, I did not intend that he should put *me* on the panel. I had suggested the topic because I was seriously worried about what I myself would be doing, and what my graduate students would be doing, five or ten or fifteen years from now. As a result of the so-called knowledge explosion—the product of our industry in investigating and publishing during the past several decades—it seemed to me that, in the realms of knowledge and information, we already knew just about all that is worth knowing about the Romantics. And I thought it impossible that we could continue indefinitely to produce dissertations, articles, and books of the sort currently recognized as our main type of professional activity outside teaching. I was aware also of the rapid enlargement of a difficulty we had from the beginning—our inability to locate and agree on what the important *problems* in our field are (we have been solving problems at a great rate, but without any consensus on the worth or relative significance of these problems). Anyhow, as I said, I was quite concerned about the future of professional work in our field, and my being put on this panel only increased my worry. If conventional scholar-critic types such as myself are to announce the trends for future study, then we are really in bad shape.

Nevertheless, I set to work doggedly to write down some of the things that can (and undoubtedly will) be done in the study of Romanticism in the 1970s, and I ended up with a list that would take me half an hour to read. This included several traditional kinds of work—editing projects, bibliographical compilations (especially in secondary bibliographies), source studies (in which, though it has been almost *the* main type of scholarly activity in the first four or five decades of the twentieth century, there is still plenty of room for further work), thematic study, new interpretation of individual poems, and the like—and some not so traditional, such as psychoanalytical investigation and the problem of dealing critically with tone in literary works. It may well be that all the things I listed will be done in the first six months of 1971—which would leave nine and a half years of the 1970s still to worry about—and in any event I do not regret being unable to read the full list. I would, however, select three items from it for brief consideration here.

(1) First, one of our principal needs, as long as we profess to deal in *literary history,* is to teach and write with a great deal more historical information and awareness than we have been employing in recent years. Let me ask some random questions to underline what I think represents a kind of falling-off in our historically oriented programs in English literature.

I assume that all of you teach some of the *Lyrical Ballads.* How many of you know that Malthus's *An Essay on the Principle of Population* was published in the same year as *Lyrical Ballads?* (Or, if you know it, how many of you bring up the fact in your classes?) Coleridge mentions "This populous village" in line 11 of *Frost at Midnight,* which was written in 1798. This really isn't of any importance, but the social conditions of England that underlie many of Blake's, Wordsworth's, and Shelley's poems *are* of some importance.

How many students in our courses in Romantic poetry are aware of, say, Jane Austen's, Jeremy Bentham's, or John Stuart Mill's literary activities at the same time—or of the French, German, and Italian writers of the same period? Or, to pick a very minor author, how many of you have heard of Robert Bloomfield, who was born in 1766 and died in 1823, and whose life is described succinctly in W. L. Renwick's Oxford History of English Literature volume as follows: "Born in Suffolk, but became a shoemaker in London; given small post in Seal Office 1802; failed as bookseller; poor all his life, though achieving some notice as a minor poet" (Renwick 1963, 106 n.)? Bloomfield produced six volumes of verse between 1800 and 1822, one of which, *The Farmer's Boy,* went through five editions in the first two years and nine others before the poet died. Subsequently there were published a two-volume *Remains* in 1824, at least half a dozen complete editions of his works with many reissues later in the nineteenth century, and a *Selection* of his poems in 1947. I don't by any means wish to start a Bloomfield revival, but the fact is that there were hundreds of such poets as Bloomfield writing in our period, and they are interesting to know about—why they wrote, how they got their poems published, who read them and why (and who preferred them to what we now think of as the major poets of the period), what light they throw on the literary milieu in which the major poets wrote, and so on. I think our current curricula, even in departments that have only historically oriented programs, very likely give the impression that Blake, Wordsworth, and Coleridge wrote in one semester, and Byron, Shelley, and Keats wrote in another—and that not only were these the sole writers of the period but that the poets of the first semester and those of the second semester had very little to do with one another.

As another example with the same sort of dark implications, take the year 1817, in which Keats published his first volume. Jane Austen died in that year; *Blackwood's Edinburgh Magazine* was started; there were major works in political economy by David Ricardo, James Mill, and Robert Owen, and the first volume of Joseph Priestley's *Theological and Miscellaneous Works* appeared; Maria Edgeworth, William Godwin, and Thomas Love Peacock all published novels, and Hazlitt published *Characters of Shakespear's Plays;* John Hookham Frere's *The Monks and the Giants* first appeared, and Southey's *Wat Tyler* embarrassingly reappeared; Byron published two works, *The Lament of Tasso* and *Manfred;* Coleridge published *Sibylline Leaves, Biographia Literaria,* and *Zapolya.* How much of this literary context gets into our lectures and seminars on Keats at the point where we discuss his 1817 *Poems?* If you ask how much *should,* I would take the last item in the list, concerning Coleridge, and enlarge just a little. *Christabel* and *Kubla Khan* were first published in 1816, and a number of Coleridge's other good poems—including *This Lime-Tree Bower My Prison* and *Dejection: An Ode* —first appeared in book form in the 1817 *Sibylline Leaves.* The fact is that Coleridge's major publications (not the writing but the publication of his works) come in the *second* half of the period as we customarily divide it up. It is demonstrable that Coleridge's publications during 1816–17, including *Biographia Literaria,* had a significant effect on Keats's career, though nobody has studied the topic at length.[1]

I would simply suggest that if we are to continue to profess the *history* of English literature, probably we can do a better job than we are doing. My impression is that, in general, we study Blake, Wordsworth, Coleridge, Byron, Shelley, and Keats in chronological order, and treat their poems also in chronological order, but that there is hardly any mention of the connections, relationships, and contexts of the sort I've briefly touched on above, and that consequently our historical approach is not very well grounded historically. I suspect that we shall improve in this regard in the 1970s.

(2) My second item is still in the realm of literary history, though it is a relatively new concern. There is a great deal of activity currently going on—set in motion by the work of Robert Langbaum, Morse Peckham, and Earl Wasserman, among others—connecting Romantic and modern (or twentieth-century) literature. There is good reason for this. Let me again give some random examples. William Carlos Williams opens a poem (*January Morning*) by declaring,

> I have discovered that most of
> the beauties of travel are due to
> the strange hours we keep to see them:
>
> the domes of the Church of
> the Paulist Fathers in Weehawken
> against a smoky dawn—the heart stirred—
> are beautiful as Saint Peters
> approached after years of anticipation.

Williams also speaks, in a later poem (*Shadows*), of

> two worlds
>   one of which we share with the
>   rose in bloom
>   and one,
> by far the greater,
>   with the past,
>   the world of memory,
> the silly world of history,
>   the world
>   of the imagination.

Wallace Stevens writes, in *Anecdote of the Jar,*

> I placed a jar in Tennessee,
> And round it was, upon a hill.
> It made the slovenly wilderness
> Surround that hill.
>
> The wilderness rose up to it,
> And sprawled around, no longer wild.

> The jar was round upon the ground
> And tall and of a port in air.
>
> It took dominion everywhere.

More recently, Adrienne Rich begins a poem (*The Knot*),

> In the heart of the queen anne's lace, a knot of blood.
> For years I never saw it. . . .

In a piece called *Encounter in the Cage Country,* James Dickey builds up an ordinary visit to the London Zoo into a long-awaited secret meeting of tremendous—even apocalyptic—significance, and he concludes:

>   I was inside and out
> Of myself   and something was given a life-
> mission to say to me hungrily over
>
> And over and over   *your moves are exactly right*
> *For a few things in this world; we know you*
> *When you come, Green Eyes, Green Eyes.*

These poets are all writing in ways that we are accustomed to think of as "Romantic." That is, their poems assume the intrinsic meaninglessness of the external world, and they show the human mind or human imagination providing unity, order, value, significance, and even beauty in that world. The poems in some cases involve the same kind of merging of dream and reality that we find in Romantic poems; they worry about the union of subject and object, about the mind's relation to the external world; they mythologize; they make much of the marvelousness of the ordinary; they give a supernatural or *near*-supernatural significance to things of every day; and they succeed—just as the best Romantics did—in transcending a kind of literal, things-as-they-are realism without investing in any of the outdated systems of belief that used to make such transcendence more readily possible. I could collect hundreds and hundreds of such examples in twentieth-century poetry, and the result would be to show that there are significant likenesses representing significant continuity between Romantic and more recent literature—so much so that a strong case can be made for saying either that we are still today in the Romantic period or that "modern" literature begins with the Romantics.

This sort of investigation is, as I said, currently going on and will continue and flourish in the 1970s. It may be that in the not-too-distant future we shall see a revision, or at least a simplification, of standard literary history. At present, we deal in binary oppositions—the Renaissance is played off against the Middle Ages, the seventeenth century against the sixteenth, the eighteenth century against the Renaissance, the Romantics against the Neoclassicists, and so on—and these binary oppositions sometimes (and maybe rather too often) lead to falsifications in literary history. Possibly we can look forward to a time when we shall have just two periods, *earlier* and *modern,* with the modern beginning about the time that Wordsworth and Coleridge were considering publishing a joint volume of their work to be called *Lyrical Ballads.*[2]

(3) Finally, let me suggest that a great many of the things I would have mentioned, and the ones that I did mention, even though they may be of interest to the audience here this afternoon, are not going to be of much interest to students in the 1970s. I think that we shall have to work very hard toward solving some basic teaching problems and relevance problems if we are to stay in business.

I was talking not long ago with the chair of the English department in my local high school. She is a graduate of the University of Illinois' Master of Arts in the Teaching of English program, and I asked her (since I rarely get a chance to talk to a genuine practicing high school English teacher) whether the education courses in her graduate program had been of any help to her in her work. She replied that they had not been of any help but also that the literature courses she had taken were of no help either. I was shocked, until I stopped to realize that at present we teach graduate (and even undergraduate) courses as if all the students were going after PhDs and as if all were intending to teach in college and ultimately in graduate school. Not only high school teaching but all sorts of other professional and nonprofessional concerns are left out of consideration in the way we standardly teach literature.

There is considerable interest showing up these days concerning the reading process, the differences between individual backgrounds and abilities in a classroom full of students and the tremendous complications of what is sometimes called "the dynamics of aesthetic response." I don't myself have any good ideas as to what to substitute for the kinds of professional activity we have become used to carrying on, but I would strongly recommend a look at some of the literature now being published on reading and teaching—I think especially of Walter Slatoff's *With Respect to Readers: Dimensions of Literary Response* (1970), which was issued a few months ago by Cornell University Press. And I would recommend that everybody worry a little about the future, not of the study of Romanticism but of the profession itself. It is one of the implications of Slatoff's book that we have no adequate critical vocabulary to deal with 95 percent of what is *important* in a literary work and that our teaching and scholarship have mainly concerned themselves with the describable 5 percent remaining—the textual problems, the details of biographical fact, sources and influences, and the like. I suggest that we get on more immediately to dealing with that other 95 percent, or we shall pretty soon be out of work.

14

Glossing the Romantics

THE PROBLEM IN ANNOTATION that I shall address here is what sorts of information to provide for students who need much more information than the annotator can possibly provide. Not long ago I taught two seminars in Coleridge in the same semester—one an undergraduate honors course that met on Tuesday afternoons, the other a graduate seminar that met on Thursdays. One of my objects was to study the differences between undergraduates and graduates reading English poetry, and, since the two courses closely paralleled one another in weekly topics and assignments, I thought that I could share with the graduate students each Thursday some of what I had experienced in the undergraduate class two days earlier. Sometime around the middle of the semester I assigned the Dejection ode to both groups and asked them (among other things) to ponder the location of "within"—within what or whom?—in the closing couplet of the third stanza: "I may not hope from outward forms to win / The passion and the life, whose fountains are within." I suggested to both classes that they might get some help from Coleridge's earlier *Lines Written in the Album at Elbingerode, in the Hartz Forest*, especially the generalizing passage of lines 16–19:

> for I had found
> That outward forms, the loftiest, still receive
> Their finer influence from the Life within:—
> Fair cyphers else. . . .

Imagine my consternation, at the next meeting of the Tuesday class, when it turned out that not a single student in the undergraduate seminar—ten honors seniors in all—had even a vague idea of the meaning of "cypher" in the passage from the Album lines just quoted. They could have looked up the word in a dictionary (where, directed to the entry under the American spelling "cipher," they would have found something like "the symbol 0, indicating a value of naught; zero . . . a person or thing of no importance or value; nonentity"). But the fact is that they didn't use the dictionary, and as a consequence, for my undergraduates on that Tuesday, Coleridge could have written "sithers" or "brizzles"—"Fair brizzles else"!—or any other two-syllable assemblage of letters that similarly made no sense. Now imagine my describing this experience to my graduate class two days later and my dismay and their discomfort when it became apparent that the entire class—another ten people, this time students working toward MA and PhD degrees in English literature—were likewise ignorant of the meaning of "cypher" and therefore were likewise totally cut off from even the simplest implications of Coleridge's phrase.

This is a true story. It happened not in some beginning course in remedial English but first in a senior honors seminar and then again in a graduate seminar in a large midwestern state university. And I think, in spite of the way I have just dramatized it (mentioning "consternation" and "dismay"), that it exemplifies a not untypical situation in classroom instruction in the 1980s: the students in our English courses don't know the meanings of a great many of what used to be the common words and phrases of the English language. My question in this brief paper is: What should the annotator of texts for students do about it?

I didn't fully grasp the magnitude of the problem until a few years ago when I came to do a reading edition of Keats's poems for Harvard University Press.[1] This was to be a follow-up of the textual edition of Keats's poems that I published in 1978, and Harvard and I agreed that the student reading edition should have clean texts of the poems with a modest section of commentary at the back—some fifty or sixty pages in small type—to keep the size of the book to under five hundred pages and the price in paperback to under ten dollars. At that point I had a difficult task. I had already written several hundred typescript pages of commentary for the textual edition of 1978 but had to scrap the entire section for lack of room there. Now, for the commentary in the student reading edition, I had to reduce those several hundred pages to about one-fourth of their length.

My new commentary that I then produced was, in different stages, read by several friends and several specialists acting as consultants for the press (the two groups were not mutually exclusive), and I learned a great deal in the process. I learned, for example (to make a generalization out of it), that if you ask ten English professors what they consider absolutely essential in the way of annotations to Keats's poems, you will get ten different lists with almost no overlap. And, as a corollary, that if you want to please all ten with the book that finally comes out, you have to write nearly ten times as many notes as you planned in the first place.

I had determined, as a principle of annotation, and had made clear in my preface to the new edition that I would not explain words and names that are included in the ordinary college or desk dictionary. Harvard Press neglected to send my preface to the reader-consultants, and they were, in some cases quite reasonably, puzzled at my omissions. One reader, looking at my meager commentary for Keats's early *Ode to Apollo,* wanted me to add a note explaining "Æolian lyre." I rechecked the dictionary and found substantial entries for "aeolian," "aeolian harp," the proper name "Aeolus," and of course "lyre." Another reader, for the same poem, wanted me to add a note explaining "the Nine" (in the line "But when *Thou* [= Apollo] joinest with the Nine"). Again the dictionary could serve the purpose: under "nine" one finds "*cap.* the nine Muses" (and there is, of course, an entry for "muse," though I gather that my reader wanted only the simplest sort of gloss: "the Nine" = the nine Muses).

One rather puzzling thing about the readers' reactions was not what they wanted glossed but what they seemed content to leave unglossed. The short poem at hand, *Ode to Apollo,* mentions "western halls of gold," "adamantine lyres," "Homer," "harps of war," "[Homer's] renovated eyes," "Maro's lyre," the verb "respire," "funeral pyre," "the spheres," "the laurel'd peers," "Milton's tuneful thunders," "The Passions," "[Spenser's] hymn in praise of spotless chastity," "Æolian lyre," "Tasso's ardent numbers," "the Nine," and "great God of Bards." Out of these seventeen names, words, and phrases—nearly all of which, I feel pretty sure, would be outside the knowledge of even our smartest undergraduates—one reader picked "Æolian lyre" and another picked "the Nine" as the only omissions worth mentioning in my commentary on the poem. Why did they pick just these two? Probably because "Æolian lyre" and "the Nine" are customarily glossed and the others are not.

Another worrisome thing that came up, when I was pondering the business, was the inadequacy of the kind of short gloss that the reader-consultants were explicitly or implicitly asking for. What in fact does a student know when he or she is told that an Aeolian lyre is a wind-harp, "a box-shaped musical instrument having stretched strings . . . on which the wind produces varying harmonics over the same fundamental tone"—this without reference to Wordsworth, Coleridge, Shelley, and the pervasive Romantic tradition that M. H. Abrams has summed up in "The Correspondent Breeze: A Romantic Metaphor" (Abrams 1957)? What in fact does a student understand when he or she is told that "the Nine" are "the nine Muses" but then knows nothing about *The Iliad* or *The Faerie Queene* or *Paradise Lost* or *The Rape of the Lock* or any other of the thousands of works referring to this long-established epic tradition?

Let me use part of the fourth stanza of Keats's *Ode to a Nightingale* as further exemplification of some of the same sorts of difficulty:

> Away! away! for I will fly to thee,
>   Not charioted by Bacchus and his pards,
> But on the viewless wings of Poesy,
>   Though the dull brain perplexes and retards:
> Already with thee! tender is the night,
>   And haply the Queen-Moon is on her throne,
>   Cluster'd around by all her starry Fays. . . .

Annotated editions usually explain four or five words in this passage: "Bacchus" (the Greek god of wine); "pards" (meaning "leopards"); "viewless" ("invisible"); "haply" ("by chance" or "perhaps"); and "Fays" ("fairies"). All of these words are in the ordinary dictionary, and the definitions there are at least as full as the explanations usually provided in the glosses in the reading editions. I worry about what goes on in the mind of an undergraduate who is given the notes to "Bacchus" and "pards" and then translates: "Away! away! for I will fly to thee, / *Not charioted by the Greek god of wine and his leopards*"! What's wanted, of course, is some kind of gloss that explains more complexly who Bacchus was, what he did, and how and where he traveled, and then refers to Keats's best-known passages about Bacchus elsewhere (in *Sleep and Poetry* and *Endymion*) and recreates some of the graphic details that Keats and his readers knew in pictures such as Titian's *Bacchus and Ariadne* and Nicolas Poussin's *The Indian Triumph of Bacchus*.[2]

There are additional obscurities in these seven lines from Keats's ode: the notion of flying to the nightingale on the viewless (invisible) wings of Poesy; the mental processes of the dull brain perplexing and retarding; the syntax and punctuation of "Already with thee! tender is the night"; the pageantry of the Queen-Moon on her throne surrounded by fairy stars. It is quite possible that the customary short glosses to "Bacchus," "pards," "viewless," and the other terms actually *hinder* the reading process by giving the student a false sense of understanding the meaning of the lines. In any case, a great many such glosses get in the way of both the reader's activity in grasping the details of the passage and the reader's pleasure in discovering and working out something independently.

So far I have been taking a kind of Susan Sontag line "against annotation." Let me now suggest some of the kinds of thing I think are worth annotating in Romantic texts.

In the first place, there are basic details of biographical and historical context—for example, the date or dates of composition of a work; the place where the author wrote it (if this is for any reason important and, at the same time, not obvious from the text itself); perhaps some interesting or revealing details concerning the process of composition (cancellations and variants from manuscripts, for example); and certainly the routine details of publication. As long as we continue to consider literary works as biographical, historical, and cultural phenomena, it seems reasonable to try to provide details of biographical, historical, and cultural circumstances.

In the second place, one probably ought to identify quotations and allusions that the author expected a large proportion of the readers to recognize. I'm thinking of such things as Wordsworth's allusion to *Lycidas* in *Simon Lee*—"But, oh the heavy change!" (25)—by which he introduces a note of classical elegy into his own much more homely pastoral; and Coleridge's allusion to *Samson Agonistes* in the Dejection ode ("My genial spirits fail"), by which he momentarily connects his plight with that of the doomed Samson, "hopes all flat" and "nature . . . In all her functions weary of herself" (594–96). I'm also thinking of source material when the author is consciously making some point about the relation of the new work to its predecessor—Keats's *Isabella,* for example, where the narrator makes much of the differences between the old prose of Boccaccio and his own tough-minded modernization of the story.

In the third place, one might offer help in the countless situations of ambiguity that occur. Keats in his verse epistle *To My Brother George* writes, "But there are times, when those that love the bay, / Fly from all sorrowing far, far away" (19–20). The most prominent meaning of "bay" in the dictionary is "laurel," "symbol of poetic fame." But still, at least for students in the Midwest, who (especially in the winter) are bombarded with magazine and television ads featuring jet air travel to warm beaches in Florida and the Caribbean, it might be a good idea to clear up what "love the bay"—especially in connection with flying "far, far away"—really was intended to mean.

In the fourth place, there are of course all sorts of words and names that are not included in the ordinary college or desk dictionary. Everybody can think of hundreds of these—biblical, mythological, historical, and literary characters and references; place names; foreign words; archaic words and spellings; slang terms; and so on. It is, however, worth emphasizing again how many of the words and names that one needs to know turn out to be in the ordinary desk dictionary.

I'd like to conclude with still one more kind of problem in annotation, this time a problem that can't easily be solved—a problem having to do with life experience and the degree to which students can relate to, and understand, elements from another culture than their own. Here are some examples in another passage of Keats, the twenty-fourth stanza of *The Eve of St. Agnes:*

> A casement high and triple-arch'd there was,
> All garlanded with carven imag'ries
> Of fruits, and flowers, and bunches of knot-grass,
> And diamonded with panes of quaint device,
> Innumerable of stains and splendid dyes,
> As are the tiger-moth's deep-damask'd wings;
> And in the midst, 'mong thousand heraldries,
> And twilight saints, and dim emblazonings,
> A shielded scutcheon blush'd with blood of queens and kings.

The two most widely used British editions of Keats provide five notes to this stanza, explaining "imag'ries" in the second line, "knot-grass" in the third, "damask'd" in the sixth, "emblazonings" in the eighth, and the blushing "shielded scutcheon" in the final line—all of which are in the ordinary dictionary.[3] But these are not the problem. The problem is what to provide for the American student who has never been in a Gothic building and has never seen a triple-arched casement window with the elaborate carvings, diamond-shaped panes, stained glass, and coats of arms that Keats refers to. What, for that matter, should be done for the American student who has never seen a tiger moth?[4]

One of the anonymous Harvard readers of my commentary expressed this problem very movingly in speaking of the difficulty of cultural difference that attends the reading of Keats's ode *To Autumn:*

> Most students (and even many teachers) have no idea what a farm looks like or what happens in a harvest. This is not a matter of annotating a single word (e.g., "winnowing" or "store" . . .) but of explaining that a farm had a cottage at the center, an orchard (with hives) and a kitchen-garden close by, that

barns and outbuildings came next, then ploughed and sown fields, and then unploughable hilly land used for grazing. And that a grain harvest consisted of reaping, then gleaning, then threshing, then storing in garners; the harvest of drink could be grape-crushing or apple-crushing. Without knowledge . . . of such agricultural geography and ritual, the ode is unintelligible.

In this broad sense, problems of cultural difference occur all through Romantic literature. What shall we do for the student reading Coleridge's *Frost at Midnight* who has never seen a real log fire in a fireplace (a gas log, which might convey some of the atmospheric effects, of course has no film of soot with "puny flaps and freaks" such as Coleridge describes) or for a student—say, in the Deep South or in a tropical country—who has never seen frost or an icicle? What shall we do for the student reading the boat-stealing episode in *The Prelude* who doesn't know, because of never having done it, that when you row a boat you sit backward facing the stern? And so on.[5]

I had planned to end this chapter by describing a practical field trip for students of Romantic poetry, a trip that might have included Mont Blanc and the Simplon Pass, the Wye River valley, the English Lake District, a sheepfold, a muddy pond with not very many leeches in it, a lime-tree bower, the Vale of Kashmir, the Protestant Cemetery in Rome—there are of course many possibilities. But when it came to traveling under the sea, soaring off to another world, and taking opium in a farmhouse near Porlock, I had to give up the idea. You can see, though, even without this elaboration, that there is much more to glossing the Romantics than just copying words out of a dictionary.

15

The Romantics and Sputnik

A LONG TIME AGO—on a morning in the middle of November 1957—I was flying from Boston to Charlottesville for a job interview at the University of Virginia. The Modern Language Association convention for that year, in a one-shot flouting of its post-Christmas tradition, had already been held two months earlier, in Madison, Wisconsin. By now we had had most of our interviews, and the offers were piling up. We would all, before the end of the academic year, get good jobs, some of them for the first time starting at the rank of assistant professor (rather than instructor), at what then seemed enormous salaries ranging from $4,750 to $6,000. I had just completed my dissertation—all 789 pages of it—and was beginning to type the final copy (original and *four* carbons) on a secondhand typewriter that I had had specially fitted out with grave and acute accents, square brackets, angle brackets, curly braces, and a British pound sign—all the devices used by my dissertation director, Hyder Rollins (with a little help from Harvard University Press), in *The Keats Circle.* I was in great shape for a job interview on that trip.

The Russians had successfully launched the first man-made earth satellite, now known as Sputnik 1, six weeks earlier. My seatmate on the airplane had a *New York Times* that was still full of the event, and he was quite excited, saying that the physical sciences (in which he obviously had some stake) had now come into their own for good, and nothing would ever be the same. In return I rather stiffly identified myself as a humanities type and opined that while science was all very well for practical jobs and day-to-day necessities, scientists—like everybody else—had to learn to read and write and think as well as know something about history and human culture in general. A little thing like an artificial satellite would not, in the long run, have a significant effect.

As a beginning specialist in the English Romantic period, I can now confess, I didn't know much about that, either. In the Harvard graduate program of the mid-1950s, Wordsworth was very little taught or read (for reasons recoverable in Douglas Bush's "Minority Report" in the volume titled *Wordsworth: Centenary Studies,* issued by Princeton in 1951); Shelley was mentioned only to be ridiculed; and Blake was practically unheard of (except, apparently, as the creator of some drawings in the Fogg Museum). Coleridge was taught, mainly as a literary critic and philosopher, and Keats of course was studied and written about by nearly everyone, and not just because Harvard owned or had custodial responsibility for three-fourths or more of the Keats manuscripts then extant. But interest in and coverage of the period were very uneven there, and I suppose they were similarly uneven in other academic institutions. After all, as an extreme example, it would be another three decades before Blake was admitted to the MLA's *English Romantic Poets: A Review of Research and Criticism* (Jordan 1985).

We did know how to learn, however, and just as the satellites got bigger and heavier, carrying a dog on the next trip and human beings not too long after that, so also have we been steadily gaining better understanding of English Romanticism. There have been large and impressive biographies and chronologies; major reeditings of the poetry, letters, journals, notebooks; and literally thousands of significant and influential critical interpretations, using structuralist, phenomenological, psychoanalytic, and many other approaches that were virtually unknown when I was a graduate student. Our knowledge has genuinely advanced, and specialists in the field today control (and take for granted) a hundred times more in the way of facts, ideas, and interpretations than their counterparts did in the 1950s.

What has *not* advanced, of course, is our professional status, our enrollments, and the degree of support from both within and outside our institutions. Almost as a consequence of our success, it might seem, our audience has fallen off. In its heyday the Illinois English department had more than a hundred full-time faculty and a graduate program of some three hundred students. Today the tenured and tenure-track faculty is less than half that size and the graduate program somewhat less than a third—and the number of undergraduate English majors is also reduced from what it was, as the students increasingly go where the employment opportunities appear most likely, namely to engineering, computer science, and business. I do not, for myself, mind assuming a curatorial role, to serve as a source of knowledge for any museum visitor (as it were) who shows interest. But I do miss those large, *multiple* sections of undergraduates happily working through the best of Wordsworth, Coleridge, Keats, and the rest. The poetry in our care seems much too good to be scanted in the way it is.

A strange thing happened on my return from Charlottesville, a day and a half later. I was on a night flight that had intermediate stops at Washington, New York, and Providence, and at each place passengers got off but none boarded, until on the last leg, from Providence to Boston, I was the sole passenger. My young family, meeting me at the Boston airport, were quite mystified when the plane taxied up, stopped, and I alone emerged, the stewardess smiling over my shoulder. I wish I could make this episode into some sort of symbol about the persistence and triumph of the humanities after the various competing enterprises have run their course. But I'm afraid that it is merely representative of a young, soon-to-be professor's ineptness in practical matters, in this case the practical matter of air travel scheduling. But I did get home, and I still think, after all these years, that scientists like everybody else need to read, write, think, and know something about history and human culture.

Abbreviations

BL	Coleridge's *Biographia Literaria* (Coleridge 1983)
CL	*Collected Letters of Samuel Taylor Coleridge* (Coleridge 1956b)
CoS	Manuscripts in the Coleridge section of Rosenbaum and White (1982)
KC	*The Keats Circle* (Rollins 1948)
KL	*The Letters of John Keats* (Keats 1958)
Poems of JK	*The Poems of John Keats* (Keats 1978)

Notes

Chapter 1: What Keats Is About

This essay was originally the introduction to Keats's *Complete Poems,* my "reading edition" (based on the textual edition of 1978) published by Harvard University Press in 1982. It describes the predominant subject matter and themes of his best work and speculates briefly on the causes of his greatness as a poet. In later pieces in this collection (in particular, chapters 6 and 12), I argue for the validity of each reader's separate response—and therefore many different, sometimes contradictory answers—to the question of what Keats is primarily "about."

Chapter 2: Keats and Wordsworth

Originally published (as "Wordsworth and Keats") in *The Age of William Wordsworth: Critical Essays on the Romantic Tradition,* ed. Kenneth R. Johnston and Gene W. Ruoff (Rutgers University Press, 1987), 173–95, 357–58.

1. The five are Hunt (1828, 1:417–18), Landor (Blunden 1925, 89), Milnes (1848, 1:86–87), Clarke (1861, 97), and Severn (Sharp 1892, 33).

2. See Bate (1963, 264–68), Gittings (1968, 167–68), Motion (1997, 215–16), Moorman (1965, 316–18), and Gill (1989, 326–27).

3. The number of scholarly works centering on Wordsworth and Keats together is surprisingly small in view of the importance of the relationship. The principal older items are C. D. Thorpe (1927), mainly biographical information; Murry (1955, 269–91), chap. 11, "Keats and Wordsworth" (first published in Murry's *Studies in Keats: New and Old*), biographical anecdotes plus scattered impressions concerning Wordsworth's influence; Balslev (1962), an undiscriminating collection and survey of verbal similarities; Stillinger (1971), especially the essay "Keats, Wordsworth, and 'Romanticism'" (120–49),

on the two poets' theories of imagination; Allott (1971), on the older poet's influence on Keats's style as well as ideas; and D'Avanzo (1974), on specific connections between the Grecian passages of Wordsworth's *Excursion* and the subject and "character" of Keats's Grecian urn ode. The one major book-length critical study is Wolfson's *The Questioning Presence* (1986a). The biographies by Bate and Gittings contain extensive commentary on the relationship. A great many "echoes and borrowings" from Wordsworth are cited in the annotated editions by Bush (Keats 1959), Allott (Keats 1970), and Barnard (Keats 1973). The most comprehensive and useful work on Wordsworthian echoes in Keats is by Lau (1987, 1991).

4. My quotations are from the 1819 text (Wordsworth 1985b).

Chapter 3: Keats and Coleridge

Originally published in a Festschrift honoring Walter Jackson Bate, *Coleridge, Keats, and the Imagination: Romanticism and Adam's Dream,* ed. J. Robert Barth and John L. Mahoney (University of Missouri Press, 1990), 7–28.

1. On Wordsworth's influence, see my "Keats and Wordsworth," chapter 2 in the present collection. In both that chapter and this, I am practicing what Jonathan Culler calls "source study of a traditional and positivistic kind." Readers may, if they wish, substitute the more up-to-date concept of intertextuality and consider the Coleridgean (and Wordsworthian) materials as "prior linguistic acts" that constitute a part of "the ground, the conditions of possibility of [Keats's] own discursive actions." See Culler's chap. 5, "Presupposition and Intertextuality" (1981, 100–118; quotations from 109 and 107).

2. Green tells that she discovered Frere's manuscript (entitled "Abstract of a discourse with Mr. Coleridge on the state of the country in December 1830, written at the time by John Frere") while staying with Frere's daughter. There is a shorter, better-known account by Coleridge in a conversation two years later (14 August 1832) with his nephew and son-in-law Henry Nelson Coleridge, but this is likely to be less accurate than the one of 1830, because here Coleridge is recalling not just the event of 1819 but his conversation with Frere in 1830:

> A loose, slack, not well-dressed youth met Mr. —— and myself in a lane near Highgate.
> —— knew him, and spoke. It was Keats. He was introduced to me, and stayed a minute or so. After he had left us a little way, he came back and said: "Let me carry away the memory, Coleridge, of having pressed your hand!"—"There is death in that hand," I said to ——, when Keats was gone; yet this was, I believe, before the consumption showed itself distinctly. (Coleridge 1865, 195)

Coleridge's daughter Sara adds a note to this passage identifying "Mr. ——" as Joseph Henry Green (he was, besides being demonstrator at Guy's Hospital, the son-in-law of Thomas Hammond, of Edmonton, to whom Keats had been apprenticed in 1811–15) and adding Green's own reminiscence of the meeting: "The hand of Keats felt to Coleridge clammy and cold [Green told her] . . . like the hand of a dead man. . . . On approaching us in the lane, he asked if I would introduce him to Mr. Coleridge. 'Yes, certainly,' I said. We talked of all this to Mr. Gillman on our return to the house." It is worth recalling that

Coleridge subsequently made a similarly self-dramatizing remark about his friend and disciple Adam Steinmetz, who died in the summer of 1832: "I have ever anticipated this event, and . . . have often, after his taking leave of me, said, 'Alas! there is death in that hand!'" (to Mrs. Gillman, 13 August 1832, *CL*, 6:920).

3. Beer makes a similar statement in "A Stream by Glimpses" (1974, 238–39).

4. Keats also quotes *Christabel*—"A thing to dream of, not to tell!"—in his article "Mr. Kean" in the *Champion*, 21 December 1817, and Woodhouse suggested as an explanation of *Sleep and Poetry* (231), "Allusion to Lord Byron, & his terrific stile of poetry—to Christabel by Coleridge &c." See Keats (1985c, 210, 252). Keats's line in *Sleep and Poetry*—"Strange thunders from the potency of song"—probably has nothing to do with *Christabel,* but Woodhouse's note shows that he knew of, or else assumed, Keats's familiarity with the poem.

5. Keats's echo of the prefatory note to *Kubla Khan* is mentioned by Levinson (1986, 169). There are of course other references to Coleridge in *KC* besides those connected with Keats. Taylor and Hessey published Coleridge's *Aids to Reflection* in 1825, for example, and Bailey corresponded with Coleridge's daughter Sara in the 1840s (see *KC*, 1:281, 2:310, 2:452, 2:453, 2:463–64).

6. There is also a seeming instance of verbal borrowing in the opposite direction—Keats's "poesy . . . 'Tis might half slumb'ring on its own right arm" (*Sleep and Poetry* 236–37) taken over by Coleridge in the 1817 revision of *The Eolian Harp* (32–33), "the mute still air / Is Music slumbering on its instrument." See Barnard (1977, 311–13).

7. The same phrasing, "Traces of . . . influence," is repeated in a general history of Romantic poetry by Jackson (1980, 40).

8. Twitchell's essay appears in revised form as part of chap. 3, "The Male Vampire in Poetry," in his *The Living Dead* (1981, 92–101).

9. The pioneering work on similarities between *Christabel* and *The Eve of St. Agnes* is Routh's (1910). The fullest modern studies are by Maier (1971) and Twitchell (1978). Routh (1910) also points out similarities between *Christabel* and *Lamia.*

10. In parenthetical documentation here, the numbers before the slash refer to *Christabel,* those after the slash to *The Eve of St. Agnes* (or, in a later paragraph below, to *Lamia*).

11. In his review of Keats's *Lamia, Isabella, The Eve of St. Agnes, and Other Poems* in the *New Times,* 19 July 1820, Lamb quotes lines 208–24 and 226–43 of *St. Agnes* with the comment, "Such is the description which Mr Keats has given us, with a delicacy worthy of 'Christabel'" (Matthews 1971, 157).

12. *Christabel* also seems to be echoed in *La Belle Dame*—in Geraldine's description of warriors and steeds (81–87) and the phrasings "And nothing else saw she thereby" and "low moaning" (161, 275; cf. Keats's "And nothing else saw all day long" and "made sweet moan" in *La Belle Dame* 22, 20)—and in *Ode to a Nightingale* (cf. Coleridge's "bell . . . Knells us back to a world of death," 332–33, with Keats's "bell / To toll me back . . . to my sole self," 71–72). Several scholars beginning with de Selincourt (Keats 1926, 526) have suggested that *Christabel* influenced the meter of Keats's fragmentary *The Eve of St. Mark.*

13. I first discussed and diagramed this excursion-return structure, citing *Peter Bell* and *The Ancient Mariner* among contemporary precedents, in my introduction to *Twentieth Century Interpretations of Keats's Odes* (Stillinger 1968b, 1–16), revised in *The Hoodwinking of Madeline* (Stillinger 1971, 99–119). For another use of it, see the second large section of chapter 1 in the present volume.

14. In the earliest essay treating the Conversation poems as a group, Harper (1925) listed and discussed eight "Poems of Friendship or Conversation"—the four just named plus *Reflections on Having Left a Place of Retirement, Fears in Solitude, The Nightingale,* and *To William Wordsworth.* I am aware that subsequent Coleridge scholarship has removed *Dejection* (along with *To William Wordsworth*) from the group—e.g., Dickstein (1972) and Schulz (1985), especially, in the latter, the division of categories on pp. 400–5—but I think this is illogical. The poems of Coleridge that I am interested in here are much more homogeneous as a group than Keats's "great odes" (which are themselves a selection—usually five—from a dozen poems at one time or another designated "ode" in the Keats canon).

15. Abrams (1965) discusses *The Eolian Harp, Frost at Midnight, Fears in Solitude,* and *Dejection* among Coleridge's works, and *Ode to a Nightingale* among Keats's.

16. On Keats's echoes of *Dejection* see Daniel (1953); on *Frost,* see Davenport (1958).

17. *Edinburgh Review* 28 (August 1817): 514; *Blackwood's* 2 (October 1817): 5–6. Hazlitt's comments are cited by Muir ("Keats and Hazlitt," in Muir 1958, 143); Wilson's comments, which include verbal connections with Keats's letter in "mysteries" and "Penetralia," are mentioned by Beer (1959, 305–6). (Incidentally, Keats very likely wrote "Penetralia" in the original letter. Our only source for this famous document is a transcript by Georgiana Keats's second husband, John Jeffrey, who was an extremely careless copier of Keats's manuscripts.) Hardy (1952) cites *Dejection* 89–93 ("And haply by abstruse research to steal / From my own nature all the natural man— / This was my sole resource, my only plan: / Till that which suits a part infects the whole, / And now is almost grown the habit of my soul") as evidence that Coleridge himself was aware of "the over-assertive life of the intellectual."

18. Kohli (1968), arguing that Coleridge influenced both Hazlitt and Keats, points out that Hazlitt had read and reviewed *Biographia Literaria* several months before he wrote these lectures.

19. The first two passages are cited in connection with Keats by Hardy (1952) and the last two by Wolfson (1976a, 200).

20. Bailey recalled the phrase that Coleridge italicizes when, more than three decades later, he told Richard Monckton Milnes about his and Keats's excursion to Shakespeare's birthplace at Stratford in October 1817: "[Keats] was struck, I remember, with the simple statue there, which, though rudely executed, we agreed was most probably the best likeness of the many extant, but none very authentic, of the myriad-minded Shakspeare" (*KC,* 2:272).

21. In their introduction and annotations to *BL,* Engell and Bate mention Keats in connection with the last of these passages (Coleridge 1983, 1:cxi, 2:27 n.).

22. Referring to this passage, Watson, in his Everyman's Library edition of *Biographia Literaria,* twice comments on Keats's "close echo of Coleridge's language" in the Negative Capability letter (Coleridge 1956a, xviii–xix, 256 n.).

23. I long ago attempted such an argument, using Wordsworth as the representative of naturalized imagination, in "Keats, Wordsworth, and 'Romanticism'" (Stillinger 1971, 120–49).

Chapter 4: Reading Keats's Plots

From *Critical Essays on John Keats,* ed. Hermione de Almeida (G. K. Hall, 1990), 88–102, a more exclusively Keats-focused revision of "The Plots of Romantic Poetry," *College Literature* 12 (1985): 97–112.

1. See Abrams, "Coleridge's 'A Light in Sound'" (1984, 159–91).

2. The phrase is of course absurd, but there is no polite term for sexual intercourse taking place when one of the partners is asleep or comatose (and "partners" in this sentence is similarly inappropriate).

3. Space limitations preclude the usual summarizing of critical positions for this and the other main examples below, four of which (all but *The Eve of St. Mark*) are among the most frequently discussed poems of the Romantic period. For a survey of older criticism, see Stillinger (1985).

4. This statement might seem inconsistent with Keats's highly circumspect line 320, both in the original text that was printed ("Into her dream he melted") and in the revised version surviving in transcripts by Richard Woodhouse and George Keats ("With her wild dream he mingled"). But most of the other details of lines 289–333 (text and variants alike) enforce the idea that Porphyro and Madeline continue in two different states until he awakens her with "This is no dream" in line 326.

5. Two still useful essays on the structure of the Romantic lyric, written about the same time but independently of one another, are Chayes (1964) and Abrams (1965).

6. See Langbaum (1957, 53).

7. See Lyon (1958, 48–50).

8. A practicing structuralist might argue that plot (as I have been discussing it here) lies *beneath* the surface. But students can be taught to identify protagonists, aims, and obstacles in a matter of seconds (sometimes more rapidly than their theme-oriented teachers). These things must, therefore, be relatively visible when such speedy analysis is possible. For a nonnarrative example of what I mean by focusing on surface meaning, consider *The Eve of St. Agnes*, lines 211–13, where the "panes of quaint device" in the casement window in Madeline's bedchamber are described as "Innumerable of stains and splendid dyes, / As are the tiger-moth's deep-damask'd wings." Most American students have never seen a tiger moth and without a dictionary do not know the color signified by "damask" (or even that "deep-damask'd" refers to a color). The lines are, at first glance, virtually unintelligible. But the meaning is still plainly "surface." All one has to do is show the class a picture of a tiger moth.

Chapter 5: Keats's Extempore Effusions and the Question of Intentionality

Originally published in *Romantic Revisions,* ed. Robert Brinkley and Keith Hanley (Cambridge University Press, 1992), 307–20.

1. I quote from the manuscript at Harvard, which can be seen, with all or parts of three dozen other holographs, in the 1990 facsimile edition of Keats's *Poetry Manuscripts at Harvard* (Keats 1990b).

2. The holographs and other manuscripts are listed and described in my *Texts of Keats's Poems,* chap. 2, "The Manuscripts and the Transcribers" (Stillinger 1974, 14–62), and in *Poems of JK,* appendix 5, "Summary Account of the Manuscripts," 741–52. Their variants, cancellations, revisions, and other peculiarities are discussed in the individual textual histories in Stillinger (1974, 84 ff.) and are recorded in the apparatuses and textual notes of *Poems of JK* (passim). Many of the manuscripts can be examined in

facsimile. In addition to the Harvard facsimile edition cited in the preceding note, I have edited seven volumes of Keats facsimiles in the Garland series, The Manuscripts of the Younger Romantics (Keats 1985a, 1985b, 1985c, 1985d, 1988a, 1988b, 1988c). (The Richard Woodhouse materials in Keats 1985b, 1985c, and 1988c are particularly relevant to the present subject. Woodhouse was centrally concerned with Keats's processes of composition and revision, and some of his variorum-like textual annotations draw on as many as three, four, and even five different sources for a single poem.) For other facsimiles see Gittings (1970) and the numerous references in Stillinger (1974) to individual reproductions in books, periodicals, and sale catalogues. The most useful sources for Keats's and his friends' comments about writing and revising are KL and KC. Finney collected and studied several hundred photocopies of manuscripts for his The Evolution of Keats's Poetry (1936), and there is of course discussion of Keats's methods of composition in the standard biographies, particularly Bate (1963) and Gittings (1968). The fullest critical account of Keats's work in the manuscripts is still Ridley's Keats' Craftsmanship (1933).

3. For otherwise undocumented quotations and facts of this sort, see the commentary section in my "reading" edition of Keats's Complete Poems (Keats 1982).

4. Gittings (1968, 311 n.) reasonably suggests that Brown in his recollection has confused Nightingale with Ode on Indolence. But Brown's description is useful in any case: clearly Keats wrote some important "fugitive" poem in such circumstances.

5. A couple of exceptions—Brown's remark that There is a joy in footing slow was composed "with more than usual care" (KC, 2:64) and Keats's description of Ode to Psyche as "the first and the only [poem] with which I have taken even moderate pains" (KL, 2:105)—simply emphasize the "fugitive" character of the rest. Keats continues his comment on Psyche: "I have for the most part dash'd of[f] my lines in a hurry."

6. This comment (in a manuscript at Harvard) is a rough draft with numerous abbreviations and cancellations. In quoting, I have expanded the abbreviations and made some other minor changes for the sake of readability.

7. In this and the next two paragraphs I draw on chap. 2 ("Keats and His Helpers: The Multiple Authorship of Isabella") in my Multiple Authorship (Stillinger 1991a, 25–49).

8. For a simplified explanation, see Stillinger (1991a, 194–200).

9. For background to the earlier years of the controversy, see the essays collected by Newton-De Molina (1976).

10. Quoted by George Watson (in a section headed "Is Intention Prior to Creation?") in The Study of Literature (1969), as excerpted in Newton-De Molina (1976, 170). Subsequent theorists who deny the existence of significant prior intention include John R. Searle (1983, esp. 92–95) and Hershel Parker (1984, esp. 21–26). Parker, however, makes an illogical leap to the position—a main point of his book—that an author's intentions are represented only in the first writing of a work and that every subsequent revision should therefore be thrown out as violation of the author's original intention.

11. See also Spurgeon (1928), p. 31 and plate 9 opposite p. 32. It is worth observing that Woodhouse, who was in some ways the best contemporary reader of Keats's poetry and who made many hundreds of biographical and critical notes about the poems, showed no interest whatsoever in the overall ideas, themes, and "meaning" of the texts that he was annotating.

Chapter 6: Multiple Readers, Multiple Texts, Multiple Keats

This essay began as the keynote address delivered at the John Keats Bicentennial Conference at Harvard, September 1995, and was first published in *Journal of English and Germanic Philology* 96 (1997): 545–66. It was further revised for the collected papers of the conference, *The Persistence of Poetry: Bicentennial Essays on Keats,* ed. Robert M. Ryan and Ronald A. Sharp (University of Massachusetts Press, 1998), 10–35—the principal source of the text in the present collection—and then served as the basis of my *Reading "The Eve of St. Agnes": The Multiples of Complex Literary Transaction* (1999).

1. For examples of these newer lines of thinking, see my *Multiple Authorship and the Myth of Solitary Genius* (1991a) and *Coleridge and Textual Instability* (1994).

2. Reviewing Keats's 1820 volume in the *Indicator,* Hunt described the poem as "rather a picture than a story" (Matthews 1991, 172). The idea gets general support from Keats's own comments in a letter to John Taylor of 17 November 1819, concerning "colouring" and "drapery" in the poem (*KL,* 2:234).

3. See Wasserman (1953). Wasserman drew especially on Keats's letters to Benjamin Bailey, 22 November 1817, and to John Hamilton Reynolds, 3 May 1818 (*KL,* 1:183–87, 275–83).

4. Each of the fifty-nine items represents a considered statement of what the poem is about, and most have been developed at article or book length in the accumulating criticism. Proper documentation, even without explanatory discussion, would double the size of this essay, and many of the items have multiple sources (another multiple!). For details, see chap. 3 of my book that followed this essay, *Reading "The Eve of St. Agnes"* (1999).

5. The question of closure was first raised significantly by Herbert G. Wright (1945). Scores of critics have registered their opinions on the matter since then.

6. The principal critics whom I draw on are the usual array of now-classical reception theorists—Stanley Fish (1970), Norman Holland (1968), David Bleich (1978), Wolfgang Iser (1974, 1978), and Umberto Eco (1984), among others—but especially Louise M. Rosenblatt, whose major work on reader response, *Literature as Exploration,* was first published almost seventy years ago (1938). Rosenblatt has been a tremendous influence on the teaching of literature in the schools and is cited everywhere by reading specialists in colleges. She has only recently begun to be noticed in university English departments. Her most important work relevant to the present chapter is *The Reader, the Text, the Poem: The Transactional Theory of the Literary Work* (1978).

7. Some of this is recorded in *John Keats, 1795–1995, with a Catalogue of the Harvard Keats Collection* (Anon. 1995b); *John Keats: Bicentennial Exhibition* (Anon. 1995a); and Woof and Hebron's *John Keats* (1995).

8. The most useful criticism on this topic is Halpern (1966).

9. See, for example, Gell-Mann (1994).

Chapter 7: The "Story" of Keats

Originally published in *The Cambridge Companion to Keats,* ed. Susan J. Wolfson (Cambridge University Press, 2001), 246–60.

1. For an overview of materials on the development of Keats's reputation, see Stillinger (1984, 711–16). The most useful collections of early reviews and other nineteenth-century comments are Matthews (1971), Reiman (1972), and Schwartz (1973). The best surveys based on these materials are MacGillivray's introduction to his *Keats: A Bibliography and Reference Guide* (1949) and Matthews's introduction to his *Keats: The Critical Heritage* (1971). For early editions and commentary on Keats in the United States, see Rollins (1946); for his influence on Victorian poetry, see Ford (1944); and for the early biographies of Keats, see Marquess (1985).

2. See the comprehensive account by Wolfson (1995a).

3. Joseph Severn's phrase, in a letter to Charles Brown of 17 July 1821 (Brown 1966, 78).

4. "The Galignani volume was . . . pirated in America, where various composite editions of Keats, reprinted or imitated from it . . . show clearly that in the decade from 1830 to 1840 he was much better known and more highly esteemed by the general reading public of the [American] East than by that of Great Britain" (Rollins 1946, 29). On its significance in the history of Keats's British reputation, see Grigely (1995, 31–32).

5. See Brown (1937). A slightly more accurate text from the same manuscript source is given in *KC*, 2:52–97.

6. See MacGillivray (1949, liv–lv).

7. My explanation of Keats's "canonical complexity" in this section is based on two more detailed accounts that I have given in "Multiple Readers, Multiple Texts, Multiple Keats" (chapter 6 in the present collection) and the last two chapters of *Reading "The Eve of St. Agnes"* (Stillinger 1999).

8. Harlan draws on, among others, Frank Kermode (1985, 75) and Wolfgang Iser (1974, 7, 8), but his own definition is clearer and more comprehensive than the statements he quotes from them.

9. For the first 125 years of criticism on the poem, see Lyon (1958), and for the slightly larger period 1820–1980, see Rhodes (1984).

10. In chapter 3 of *Reading "The Eve of St. Agnes"* (Stillinger 1999), I list and expound fifty-nine different ways of interpreting the poem, presented as a token representation of a theoretically infinite number of possible readings. These fifty-nine ways are also listed in the appendix to chapter 6 in the present volume.

11. The papers of the MLA session were collected by its chair, Susan J. Wolfson, for a forum in *Studies in Romanticism* 25 (1986). See also Watkins (1989) and Roe (1995, 1997).

Chapter 8: Textual Primitivism and the Editing of Wordsworth

Originally published in *Studies in Romanticism* 28 (1989): 3–28. Subsequently this provided the basis for much of chapter 4, "Multiple 'Consciousnesses' in Wordsworth's *Prelude*," in my *Multiple Authorship and the Myth of Solitary Genius* (1991a, 69–95).

1. Unless another version is specified, my quotations of *The Prelude* are from the latest authoritative text (mainly that of manuscript D) as edited by W. J. B. Owen in *The Fourteen-Book "Prelude"* (Wordsworth 1985a). For the shorter poems I have generally quoted from my Riverside edition of the *Selected Poems and Prefaces* (Wordsworth 1965), which gives more accurate texts from the same sources that Ernest de Selincourt and

Helen Darbishire used in their five-volume Oxford English Texts edition, *The Poetical Works of William Wordsworth* (Wordsworth 1940).

2. The best sources of information concerning composition of the work are the introduction in de Selincourt's edition of *The Prelude* (Wordsworth 1959), esp. xliii–liv; Reed (1975, 11–15, 628–55); the sections on "Composition and Texts" in the Norton Critical Edition, *The Prelude, 1799, 1805, 1850* (Wordsworth 1979b, 512–22); and the introductions to the three presentations of the poem in the Cornell Wordsworth: Parrish's *"The Prelude," 1798–1799* (Wordsworth 1977), Reed's *The Thirteen-Book "Prelude"* (Wordsworth 1991), and Owen's *The Fourteen-Book "Prelude"* (1985a).

3. Robin Jarvis has expressed reservations about the existence of this version in "The Five-Book *Prelude:* A Reconsideration."

4. The passages quoted here and in the preceding paragraph occur in the original edition (1926) on pages xliv, xlviii–li, liv, lvi, lix–lxii. All of them, even the most fanciful and rhetorically extravagant, are repeated verbatim in the revised 2nd ed. (1959) on the pages cited in text here in the present chapter, a fault that I noted in my review in *Journal of English and Germanic Philology* (Stillinger 1960). Herbert Lindenberger's wistful suggestion of "a popular, composite edition of *The Prelude,* an edition based principally on the 1805 text" but dropping some of its weaker lines and passages and incorporating some of the better lines and passages added in revision (1963, 299), rather closely resembles, especially in spirit, de Selincourt's "ideal text" of nearly four decades earlier.

5. In reprinting the substance of her review in *The Poet Wordsworth,* Darbishire changed "They generally mar the poetry; they always disguise the truth" to "they often mar the poetry; they more often disguise the truth" (Darbishire 1950, 123).

6. For another argument favoring a single Wordsworth, see Groom's *The Unity of Wordsworth's Poetry* (1966).

7. For example (to select four), Stone (1974), Schell (1975), Manning (1983), and Wolfson (1984). For a helpful guide to the scholarship on *Prelude* revisions, see the index to Jones and Kroeber's *Wordsworth Scholarship and Criticism* (1985)—pp. 302–4 (the *Prelude* entries that specify "revision") and p. 306 (the revision entries that specify "Prel.").

8. Similarly, Reeve Parker, in proposing that the "literary merits [of *The Excursion* book 1] . . . have been underestimated," feels obliged to add: "As I hope will be clear, this is not the same as saying that I prefer 'later' Wordsworth or that the poem espouses a 'philosophy' I find congenial" (Parker 1972, 90).

9. The sentence has a stirring ring to it and has been quoted many times, but neither of its clauses comes close to being literally true.

10. These passages are not in the earlier version of Jonathan Wordsworth's description, published as "'The Climbing of Snowdon'" (J. Wordsworth 1970). Apparently critics are to be allowed their revisions, even while they attack poets for theirs. Jeffrey Baker has an amusing comment concerning Jonathan Wordsworth's zeal for earlier and earlier versions: "a reader who was determined to push the matter *ad absurdum* might claim that the greatest *Prelude* was probably known only to Wordsworth's dog, who heard the rambling poet's earliest, unrevised 'booings'" (Baker 1982, 79). After a promising start, however, Baker's essay ends up revealing just as much prejudice in the opposite direction, in favor of 1850.

11. I quote from the Wordsworth Summer Conference brochure for 1984. In *The Wordsworth Circle,* Jonathan Wordsworth reports good-humoredly on the debate:

"Norman Fruman put the case for the early version, Bob Barth and Jeffrey Baker for the late. There was a large and lively audience, and a remarkably dispassionate Chairman. Both sides were clear that they had won. A transcript will be published so that readers of *TWC* may decide for themselves" (J. Wordsworth 1985, 45). Subsequently, the "transcript" occupied the whole of the winter 1986 issue (vol. 17, no. 1). Quite possibly readers will decide that both sides *lost.*

12. Jonathan Wordsworth's phrase (see note 9 above) is taken over in the title and opening sentence of Stephen Parrish's "The Worst of Wordsworth" (1976). Parrish is the originator and general editor of the Cornell Wordsworth, and this brief essay, along with his foreword in the first volume published, *The Salisbury Plain Poems* (Wordsworth 1975, ix–xiii), constitutes a rationale for the series. See also Parrish's "The Editor as Archeologist" (1983), esp. pp. 6–7 (on the "hardening" of Wordsworth's "social, religious, and political orthodoxies") and pp. 12–14 ("ageing Tory humanist," "orthodox piety," "hardening crust of middle and old age," "crusted layers of revision").

13. Given our present-day interest in narrative technique, the role of the narrator, and self-reflexivity, critics ought to prefer the more complicated later version—tale *plus* narrator in equal proportions—and surely would have preferred it all along if the chronology of versions had not biased the issue. See Philip Cohen's "Narrative and Persuasion in *The Ruined Cottage*" (1978).

14. It has worried others as well. For one statement of concern—though it dates from reports on the Cornell Wordsworth written for the Modern Language Association's Committee on Scholarly Editions in 1977—see Donald Reiman's *Romantic Texts and Contexts* (1987), chap. 8, "The Cornell Wordsworth and the Norton *Prelude,*" esp. pp. 135, 145–46.

15. James Chandler, in a lengthy review of five volumes of the Cornell Wordsworth, casually mentions that "this should . . . be an edition sufficiently long-lived so that libraries will not have to replace it for a while," and "this will be the way that many students and scholars read their Wordsworth for some time to come" (Chandler 1986, 207, 208). Kenneth Johnston and Gene Ruoff comment approvingly in their introduction to *The Age of William Wordsworth:* "The editions of de Selincourt and Darbishire . . . have been challenged and replaced, particularly by the volumes of the Cornell University Wordsworth project, which seek to restore the poems to their earliest forms and set forth for patient examination all the revisions and encrustations to which Wordsworth subjected his canon throughout his long life. . . . The results of this enterprise have reached into the college classroom, with the result that today our students read versions of poems, or even entire poems, not known to exist in the late fifties or early sixties" (Johnston and Ruoff 1987, x–xi).

16. It is worth noting that a companion Oxford Authors volume, *Samuel Taylor Coleridge,* edited by H. J. Jackson (Coleridge 1985), similarly offers a chronological arrangement but nevertheless prints the standard final texts throughout.

17. I have used Reed's *Thirteen-Book "Prelude"* (Wordsworth 1991, 1:314–15) for my quotations of the 1805 text of this passage.

18. The most extreme theorist of textual primitivism to date is Hershel Parker, who in *Flawed Texts and Verbal Icons* sounds very much like the Wordsworthian primitivists, even though he never mentions our poet: e.g., "revising authors very often betray or otherwise blur their original achievements in ways they seldom intend and seldom become aware of"; "In revising or allowing someone else to revise a literary work, especially after

it has been thought of as complete, authors very often lose authority, with the result that familiar literary texts at some points have no meaning, only partially authorial meaning, or quite adventitious meaning unintended by the author or anyone else" (Parker 1984, ix, 4). Parker studies the revision of works by Twain, James, Crane, and Mailer and finds the later texts vitiated by mistakes, inconsistencies, and incoherences. He uses words such as "wreck," "damage," "deface," "violate," "destroy," "sabotage," and "drain" to describe the process of rewriting, and in one place he contrasts "a clear and consistent" original version with a "hopelessly confusing" revision (29, 37, 39, 40, 41, 74, 173, 184, 307). Parker's basic premise, that "genuine art is coherent" (23), seems extremely dubious. See Gary Davenport's review of Parker, "Necessary Fictions" (1985).

19. See Thorpe (1972, 32–47) and Zeller (1975).

Chapter 9: Pictorialism and Matter-of-Factness in Coleridge's Poems of Somerset

Originally published in *The Wordsworth Circle* 20 (1989): 62–68. This was the opening paper at the first Coleridge Summer Conference, in Nether Stowey, Somerset, July 1988.

1. See, for example, Stillinger (1971, 101) and my introduction to Keats's *Complete Poems* (Keats 1982), chapter 1 in the present collection.
2. Mark Strand, *The Whole Story*, in *Reasons for Moving* (Strand 1969, 17).
3. See Coleridge (1951, 46).
4. This and the reference to the "Coleridge Cottage" at the end of the paragraph are details relating to the original delivery of this paper, at the town hall in Nether Stowey.
5. See John E. Jordan (1976, 118).
6. See McFarland (1981, chap. 1, "The Symbiosis of Coleridge and Wordsworth") and Magnuson (1988).
7. See "Keats and Coleridge," chapter 3 in the present collection.

Chapter 10: The Multiple Versions of Coleridge's Poems: How Many *Mariners* Did Coleridge Write?

Originally published in *Studies in Romanticism* 31 (1992): 127–46. The essay is a preliminary statement of details and theory later incorporated into my *Coleridge and Textual Instability: The Multiple Versions of the Major Poems* (1994).

1. In theoretical writings on the subject (see note 4 below), there is no agreed-on definition of the degree of difference necessary to distinguish one version of a work from another. On the present occasion, I have used Shillingsburg's definition in *Scholarly Editing:* "A version has no substantial existence, but it is represented more or less well or completely by a single text as found in a manuscript, proof, book, or some other written or printed form" (1986, 47). In my subsequent study, *Coleridge and Textual Instability* (1994, 130), I incorporated Hans Zeller's more specific idea ("A New Approach to the Critical Constitution of Literary Texts," 1975) that a single substantive variant is sufficient to separate one version from another.

2. Parrish (1988b, 344), making an analogy with "the Whig interpretation of history," has described this traditional thinking as "textual Whiggery." As, in Whig history, events progress to ever better states of existence, so textual Whiggery has a retrospective view of a succession of texts "moving in an ordered, coherent way by a process of 'unfolding logic' toward completion of a great design."

3. See my "Textual Primitivism and the Editing of Wordsworth," chapter 8 in the present collection.

4. See Thorpe (1965), esp. pp. 32–47; Zeller (1975); McGann (1983); Reiman (1987), chap. 10, "'Versioning': The Presentation of Multiple Texts"; Shillingsburg (1986), esp. pp. 44–55, 99–106; Stillinger (1991a), chap. 9, "Implications for Theory"; Stillinger (1991b); McLaverty (1984); and Mays (1992).

5. While this is true generally, there are still many situations of multiple versions with relatively minor differences among them. I discuss Keats's methods of composing (and not revising very much) in chapter 5 in the present collection and give details concerning his multiple texts in the second section of chapter 6.

6. In parenthetical documentation, *CoS* refers to items in the Coleridge section of Rosenbaum and White (1982). Mays (1992, 138) calculates that he has "uncovered some twenty to thirty per cent more material" than is listed in *Index of English Literary Manuscripts.*

7. The alterations are given in Coleridge's *Marginalia* (1980, 1:94–95).

8. See Evans (1935).

9. These annotated copies are described by Johnson (1975).

10. For example (among critics of the last three decades), Dyck (1973); Lipking (1977); Simpson (1979), esp. pp. 98–101; Mellor (1980), esp. pp. 143–48; McGann (1981); Wheeler (1981, 42–64); Wallen (1986); and Wall (1987).

11. None of these schemes agrees exactly with the three-paragraph arrangement in E. H. Coleridge's Oxford edition (Coleridge 1912).

12. See Perkins (1990).

13. The nine manuscripts are the lost holograph lent to J. P. Collier (see Coleridge 1856, xxxix–xliii) plus *CoS* 51–53, 55, 57–59 and Coleridge's quotation of lines 656–77 in a letter to Southey of May 1801 (*CL,* 2:728).

14. These are listed in Rosenbaum and White (1982) as *CoS* 60–64. The annotations in *CoS* 63, now in the Robert H. Taylor Collection at Princeton, and *CoS* 64, owned by John Murray, are given by Rooke (1974).

15. The manuscripts are *CoS* 82–85, prior to first publication, and *CoS* 86–88, afterward. Stephen Parrish (1988a) provides facsimiles and annotated reading texts of the most important versions.

16. As Paul Magnuson pointed out when I delivered an early version of this chapter at the 1990 Coleridge Summer Conference in Cannington, Somerset, versions can also differ significantly from one another—quite independently of verbal and accidental variants—according to differences in the *contexts* in which the versions appear: for example, newspaper versus collected works, rare book versus modern anthology, and a change in position (relative to the rest of the contents) within a volume or set of volumes. Magnuson's own paper at the same Coleridge Conference, on the political context of the 1798 version of *Frost at Midnight* (in a volume issued by the radical publisher

Joseph Johnson and containing, for the rest of the contents, two political pieces on the French Revolution, *Fears in Solitude* and *France: An Ode*) provided a telling illustration. For the paper, see Magnuson (1991), and for the larger study on the same idea, see Magnuson (1998).

17. See Dyer (1989).

18. See Jonathan Culler's introduction to Valdés and Miller's *Identity of the Literary Text* (1985, 3–15).

19. In the process of organizing my information, I constructed a large grid consisting of seven vertical columns (one for each of the seven works whose versions I was tracing) and a series of forty vertical lines across the columns (one for each year of Coleridge's life from 1795 to 1834) and entered notes detailing the successive revisions of the poems in the seven vertical columns. I could then, for any year of Coleridge's poetic career, by reading horizontally across the grid, see at a glance which version of a poem existed at the same time as which versions of the others. This simple device—which one might think would be used routinely by anyone engaged in critical work grounded in biography and history—seemed to arouse considerable interest when I explained it in a related lecture on Coleridge's texts ("The Unity of Coleridge's Poetry and the Instability of the Texts") at the 1990 Wordsworth Summer Conference in Grasmere.

20. Wordsworth's comments occur in a note at the end of vol. 1 of *Lyrical Ballads* in the edition of 1800 (only).

21. In a manuscript note written above the beginning of *The Eolian Harp* in the copy of *Sibylline Leaves* formerly owned by Arthur A. Houghton, Coleridge speaks of "having first introduced this species of short blank verse poems—of which Southey, Lamb, Wordsworth, and others have since produced so many exquisite specimens" (Johnson 1975, 472).

Chapter 11: Wordsworth, Coleridge, and the Shaggy Dog: The Novelty of *Lyrical Ballads* (1798)

Originally published in *The Wordsworth Circle* 31 (2000): 70–76. The chapter is based on a talk given at Southwest Texas State University, San Marcos, October 1998, as part of a week-long celebration of the two hundredth anniversary of the publication of *Lyrical Ballads*.

1. Lines from *The Prelude* are quoted from the late text of *The Fourteen-Book "Prelude"* (Wordsworth 1985a). My quotations from *Lyrical Ballads* (1798) in this chapter are taken directly from the first edition.

2. The statements originally appeared in George McLean Harper's introduction to *Poems by William Wordsworth* (1923) and Harold Bloom and Lionel Trilling's *The Oxford Anthology of English Literature* (1973).

3. This is S. M. Parrish's persuasive reading of the poem in "'The Thorn': Wordsworth's Dramatic Monologue" (1957).

4. The defining passage is *The Prelude* (2.19–33). In these comments on *Tintern Abbey* I am drawing on the final chapter of my *Reading "The Eve of St. Agnes"* (1999, 125), where I use the poem to illustrate "canonical complexity."

Chapter 12: Fifty-nine Ways of Reading *Ode on a Grecian Urn*

Originally published electronically in *"Ode on a Grecian Urn": Hypercanonicity and Pedagogy,* ed. James O'Rourke (2003), a collection of invited essays in the Praxis series on the University of Maryland's *Romantic Circles* website at *www.rc.umd.edu/praxis/grecianurn.* The contributors were asked to illustrate "how a cross-section of established and younger scholars talk about [Keats's most famous ode] to a non-professional audience—our students."

1. For elaboration, see the second large section of chapter 1 in the present collection and my *Reading "The Eve of St. Agnes"* (1999, 107–13).

2. See, among others, Kelley (1995, 221–32), Roe (1997, 85–87), Magnuson (1998, 167–210), Cox (1998, 165, 185–86), and O'Rourke (1998, 75–77).

Chapter 13: Refurbish or Perish

Originally published in *The Wordsworth Circle* 2 (1971): 46–50. This was a paper at the English 9 session of the Modern Language Association meeting in December 1970 on the topic "The Study of Romanticism in the 1970s."

1. I subsequently made a start, two decades later, with "Keats and Coleridge," chapter 3 in the present collection.

2. This idea is pursued in "Wordsworth, Coleridge, and the Shaggy Dog," chapter 11 in the present collection.

Chapter 14: Glossing the Romantics: Texts for Students

Originally published in *The Wordsworth Circle* 16 (1985): 22–25. The paper was read at the December 1984 Modern Language Association convention in a session chaired by Betty T. Bennett on "Editing the Romantics: Problems in Annotation." My original title, before Bennett substituted the present more decorous wording, was "Glossing the Romantics for Students Who Don't Know Anything."

1. Keats's *Complete Poems* (1982).

2. See Jack (1967, 130–31, 159–60, and plates XIII, XIX).

3. The two words of this passage *not* in the ordinary dictionary are never glossed—"'mong" in the seventh line and "twilight" as an adjective in the eighth. The British editions referred to are Miriam Allott's *The Poems of John Keats* (Keats 1970) and John Barnard's *The Complete Poems* (Keats 1973). Both provide slightly misleading notes to "imag'ries," which here means "images" or "representations" rather than "designs" (Allott) or "patterns, designs" (Barnard), and Barnard connects "damask'd" with "rich fabric (originally from Damascus)" rather than with the grayish-red color that seems indicated by the context ("stains," "dyes," "deep").

4. At the MLA session I distributed a sheet containing the principal quotations from Coleridge and Keats used in this paper along with a picture of the British common tiger

moth. The black-and-white photocopy showed the elaborate wing markings (illustrative of "panes of quaint device") but not, of course, the color.

5. Norman Fruman told me after the session that many of his students at California State College, Los Angeles, coming from places where all the trees are evergreens, had no firsthand knowledge of deciduous trees and therefore got no visual or auditory or tactile impressions from the leaf images—blowing, falling, dying, decaying—in Shelley's *Ode to the West Wind*.

Chapter 15: The Romantics and Sputnik

Originally published in *Studies in Romanticism* 21 (1982): 558–60, in a section of short contributions under the heading "How It Was." This was *Studies in Romanticism*'s twenty-first anniversary issue, and David Wagenknecht, as he explains in his "Editor's Note," had "asked a number of important critics interested in romanticism to remind us what the study seemed like" at that dim moment in the past when the journal made its first appearance.

References

Abrams, M. H. 1957. "The Correspondent Breeze: A Romantic Metaphor." *Kenyon Review* 19 (1957): 113–30. (Reprinted in Abrams's *The Correspondent Breeze*, 1984, 25–43, 261–62.)

———. 1961. "Five Types of *Lycidas*." In *Milton's "Lycidas": The Tradition and the Poem*, ed. C. A. Patrides, 212–31. New York: Holt, Rinehart and Winston.

———. 1965. "Structure and Style in the Greater Romantic Lyric." In *From Sensibility to Romanticism: Essays Presented to Frederick A. Pottle*, ed. Frederick W. Hilles and Harold Bloom. New York: Oxford University Press, 1965, 527–60. (Reprinted in Abrams's *The Correspondent Breeze*, 1984, 76–108, 267–71.)

———. 1984. *The Correspondent Breeze: Essays on English Romanticism.* New York: Norton.

Abrams, M. H., et al., eds. 1974. *The Norton Anthology of English Literature.* 3rd ed. New York: Norton.

Allott, Miriam. 1971. "Keats and Wordsworth." *Keats-Shelley Memorial Bulletin* 22: 28–43.

Anon. 1926. "The 'Prelude': 1805 and 1850." *Times Literary Supplement,* 29 April, pp. 309–10.

———. 1995a. *John Keats: Bicentennial Exhibition, September 19–November 22, 1995.* New York: Grolier Club.

———. 1995b. *John Keats, 1795–1995, with a Catalogue of the Harvard Keats Collection.* Cambridge: Houghton Library.

Arac, Jonathan. 1983. Review of three books on Wordsworth. *Studies in Romanticism* 22: 136–46.

Arnold, Matthew. 1880. "John Keats." In *The English Poets: Selections with Critical Introductions by Various Writers . . .* , Vol. 4, *Wordsworth to Dobell,* ed. Thomas Humphrey Ward, 427–37. London: Macmillan. (Reprinted in Arnold's *Essays in Criticism, Second Series.* London: Macmillan, 1888, 100–21.)

Baker, Jeffrey. 1982. "Prelude and Prejudice." *The Wordsworth Circle* 13: 79–86.

Balslev, Thora. 1962. *Keats and Wordsworth: A Comparative Study.* Copenhagen: Munksgaard.

Barnard, John. 1977. "An Echo of Keats in 'The Eolian Harp.'" *Review of English Studies,* n.s., 28: 311–13.

Barth, J. Robert, and John L. Mahoney, eds. 1990. *Coleridge, Keats, and the Imagination: Romanticism and Adam's Dream.* Columbia: University of Missouri Press.

Bate, Walter Jackson. 1945. *The Stylistic Development of Keats.* New York: Modern Language Association.

———. 1963. *John Keats.* Cambridge: Harvard University Press.

———. 1968. *Coleridge.* New York: Macmillan.

———. 1977. *Samuel Johnson.* New York: Harcourt Brace Jovanovich.

Batho, Edith C. 1933. *The Later Wordsworth.* Cambridge: Cambridge University Press.

Beer, John. 1959. *Coleridge the Visionary.* London: Chatto and Windus.

———. 1974. "A Stream by Glimpses: Coleridge's Later Imagination." In *Coleridge's Variety: Bicentenary Studies,* ed. Beer, 219–42. London: Macmillan, 1974.

———. 1977. *Coleridge's Poetic Intelligence.* London: Macmillan.

Bleich, David. 1978. *Subjective Criticism.* Baltimore: Johns Hopkins University Press.

Blunden, Edmund. 1925. *Shelley and Keats as They Struck Their Contemporaries.* London: C. W. Beaumont.

Brinkley, Robert, and Keith Hanley, eds. 1992. *Romantic Revisions.* Cambridge: Cambridge University Press.

Brooks, Cleanth. 1947. *The Well Wrought Urn: Studies in the Structure of Poetry.* New York: Harcourt.

Brooks, Cleanth, and Robert Penn Warren. 1938. *Understanding Poetry: An Anthology for College Students.* New York: Holt.

Broughton, Leslie Nathan. 1927. Review of *The Prelude.* Ed. Ernest de Selincourt. *Journal of English and Germanic Philology* 26: 427–32.

Brown, Charles Armitage. 1937. *Life of John Keats.* Ed. Dorothy Hyde Bodurtha and Willard Bissell Pope. London: Oxford University Press.

———. 1966. *The Letters of Charles Armitage Brown.* Ed. Jack Stillinger. Cambridge: Harvard University Press.

Burke, Kenneth. 1943. "Symbolic Action in a Poem by Keats." *Accent* 4: 30–42. (Reprinted in Burke's *A Grammar of Motives.* New York: Prentice Hall, 1945, 447–63.)

Burton, Mary E. 1942. *The One Wordsworth.* Chapel Hill: University of North Carolina Press.

Bush, Douglas. 1951. "Wordsworth: A Minority Report." In *Wordsworth: Centenary Studies,* ed. Gilbert T. Dunklin, 3–22. Princeton, N.J.: Princeton University Press.

Carney, Raymond. 1981. "Making the Most of a Mess." *Georgia Review* 35: 631–42.

Chandler, James K. 1986. "Wordworth Rejuvenated." *Modern Philology* 84: 196–208.

Chatman, Seymour. 1978. *Story and Discourse: Narrative Structure in Fiction and Film.* Ithaca, N.Y.: Cornell University Press.

Chayes, Irene H. 1964. "Rhetoric as Drama: An Approach to the Romantic Ode." *PMLA* 79: 67–79.

Clarke, Charles Cowden. 1861. "Recollections of Keats by an Old School-Fellow." *Atlantic Monthly* 7 (January–June): 86–100.

Clarke, Charles Cowden, and Mary Cowden Clarke. 1878. *Recollections of Writers.* London: Sampson Low, Marston, Searle, and Rivington.

Cohen, Philip. 1978. "Narrative and Persuasion in *The Ruined Cottage.*" *Journal of Narrative Technique* 8: 185–99.

Coleridge, Samuel Taylor. 1856. *Seven Lectures on Shakespeare and Milton.* Transcribed and introduced by J. P. Collier. London: Chapman and Hall.

———. 1865. *Specimens of the Table-Talk of Samuel Taylor Coleridge.* Ed. H. N. Coleridge. 1835; new ed., London: John Murray.

———. 1893. *The Poetical Works of Samuel Taylor Coleridge.* Ed. James Dykes Campbell. London: Macmillan.

———. 1912. *The Complete Poetical Works of Samuel Taylor Coleridge.* Ed. Ernest Hartley Coleridge. 2 vols. Oxford, UK: Clarendon.

———. 1951. *Selected Poetry and Prose.* Ed. Elisabeth Schneider. New York: Rinehart.

———. 1956a. *Biographia Literaria.* Ed. George Watson. Everyman Library. London: J. M. Dent.

———. 1956b. *Collected Letters of Samuel Taylor Coleridge.* Ed. Earl Leslie Griggs. 6 vols. Oxford, UK: Clarendon, 1956–71.

———. 1972. *Coleridge's Verse: A Selection.* Ed. William Empson and David Pirie. London: Faber.

———. 1974. *Poems.* Ed. John Beer. Everyman Library. London: Dent.

———. 1980. *Marginalia,* Vol. 1, ed. George Whalley. Princeton, N.J.: Princeton University Press.

———. 1983. *Biographia Literaria.* Ed. James Engell and W. Jackson Bate. 2 vols. Princeton, N.J.: Princeton University Press.

———. 1985. *Samuel Taylor Coleridge.* Ed. H. J. Jackson. Oxford Authors. Oxford: Oxford University Press.

———. 1987. *Lectures 1808–1819: On Literature.* Ed. R. A. Foakes. 2 vols. London: Routledge and Kegan Paul.

———. 2001. *Poetical Works.* Ed. J. C. C. Mays. No. 16 of *The Collected Works of Samuel Taylor Coleridge.* 3 vols. (in 6). Princeton, N.J.: Princeton University Press.

Collingwood, R. G. 1958. *The Principles of Art.* 1938; reprint, New York: Oxford University Press.

Colvin, Sidney. 1887. *Keats.* English Men of Letters Series. London: Macmillan.

Cox, Jeffrey N. 1998. *Poetry and Politics in the Cockney School: Keats, Shelley, Hunt and Their Circles.* Cambridge: Cambridge University Press.

Culler, Jonathan. 1981. *The Pursuit of Signs: Semiotics, Literature, Deconstruction.* Ithaca, N.Y.: Cornell University Press.

Daniel, Robert. 1953. "Odes to Dejection." *Kenyon Review* 15: 129–40.

Darbishire, Helen. 1926. "Wordsworth's 'Prelude.'" *Nineteenth Century and After* 99 (January–June): 718–31.

———. 1950. *The Poet Wordsworth: The Clark Lectures.* Oxford, UK: Clarendon.

D'Avanzo, Mario L. 1974. "'Ode on a Grecian Urn' and *The Excursion.*" *Keats-Shelley Journal* 23: 95–105.

Davenport, Arnold. 1958. "A Note on 'To Autumn.'" In *John Keats: A Reassessment,* ed. Kenneth Muir, 95–101. Liverpool: Liverpool University Press.

Davenport, Gary. 1985. "Necessary Fictions." *Sewanee Review* 93: 499–504.

De Almeida, Hermione, ed. 1990. *Critical Essays on John Keats.* Boston: G. K. Hall.

Dickstein, Morris. 1972. "Coleridge, Wordsworth, and the 'Conversation Poems.'" *Centennial Review* 16: 367–83.

Dunbar, Georgia S. 1959. "The Significance of the Humor in 'Lamia.'" *Keats-Shelley Journal* 8: 17–26.

Dyck, Sarah. 1973. "Perspective in 'The Rime of the Ancient Mariner.'" *Studies in English Literature* 13: 591–604.

Dyer, Gary. 1989. "Unwitnessed by Answering Deeds: 'The Destiny of Nations' and Coleridge's *Sibylline Leaves.*" *The Wordsworth Circle* 20: 148–55.

Eco, Umberto. 1984. *The Role of the Reader: Explorations in the Semiotics of Texts.* Bloomington: Indiana University Press.

Evans, B. Ifor. 1935. "Coleridge's Copy of 'Fears in Solitude.'" *Times Literary Supplement,* 18 April, p. 255.

Finney, Claude Lee. 1936. *The Evolution of Keats's Poetry.* 2 vols. Cambridge: Harvard University Press.

Fish, Stanley. 1970. "Literature in the Reader: Affective Stylistics." *New Literary History* 2: 123–62. (Reprinted in Fish's *Is There a Text in This Class? The Authority of Interpretive Communities.* Cambridge: Harvard University Press, 1980, 21–67, 373–76.)

Fogle, Richard Harter. 1949. *The Imagery of Keats and Shelley: A Comparative Study.* Chapel Hill: University of North Carolina Press.

———. 1972. Review of *The Hoodwinking of Madeline. Key Reporter* 38 (Fall): 5.

Ford, George H. 1944. *Keats and the Victorians: A Study of His Influence and Rise to Fame, 1821–1895.* New Haven, Conn.: Yale University Press.

Garrod, H. W. 1926. *Keats.* Oxford, UK: Clarendon.

Gell-Mann, Murray. 1994. *The Quark and the Jaguar: Adventures in the Simple and the Complex.* New York: W. H. Freeman.

Genette, Gérard. 1980. *Narrative Discourse: An Essay in Method.* Ithaca, N.Y.: Cornell University Press.

Gérard, Albert. 1951. "Coleridge, Keats and the Modern Mind." *Essays in Criticism* 1: 249–61.

Gill, Stephen. 1983. "Wordsworth's Poems: The Question of Text." *Review of English Studies,* n.s., 34: 172–90.

———. 1989. *William Wordsworth: A Life.* Oxford, UK: Clarendon.

Gittings, Robert. 1968. *John Keats.* Boston: Little, Brown.

———. 1970. *The Odes of Keats and Their Earliest Known Manuscripts.* Kent, Ohio: Kent State University Press.

Green, E. M. 1917. "A Talk with Coleridge." *Cornhill Magazine* ser. 3, 42: 402–10.

Grigely, Joseph. 1995. *Textualterity: Art, Theory, and Textual Criticism.* Ann Arbor: University of Michigan Press.

Groom, Bernard. 1966. *The Unity of Wordsworth's Poetry.* London: Macmillan.

Halpern, Martin. 1966. "Keats and the 'Spirit that Laughest.'" *Keats-Shelley Journal* 15: 69–86.

Hardy, Barbara. 1952. "Keats, Coleridge and Negative Capability." *Notes and Queries* 197: 299–301.

Harlan, David. 1989. "Intellectual History and the Return of Literature." *American Historical Review* 94: 581–609.

Harper, George McLean. 1925. "Coleridge's Conversation Poems." *Quarterly Review* 244 (January–April): 284–98.

———. 1926. "Growth." *Saturday Review of Literature*, 2 October, p. 154.

Havens, Raymond Dexter. 1941. *The Mind of a Poet: A Study of Wordsworth's Thought with Particular Reference to "The Prelude."* Baltimore: Johns Hopkins University Press.

Haydon, Benjamin Robert. 1960. *The Diary of Benjamin Robert Haydon.* Ed. Willard Bissell Pope. 5 vols. Cambridge: Harvard University Press, 1960–63.

Hazlitt, Willliam. 1930. *The Complete Works of William Hazlitt.* Ed. P. P. Howe. 21 vols. London: J. M. Dent, 1930–34.

Hirsch, E. D., Jr. 1967. *Validity in Interpretation.* New Haven, Conn.: Yale University Press.

Hobsbaum, Philip. 1979. "The Essential Wordsworth." In Hobsbaum's *Tradition and Experiment in English Poetry,* 180–205. London: Macmillan.

Holland, Norman. 1968. *The Dynamics of Literary Response.* New York: Oxford University Press.

Homans, Margaret. 1990. "Keats Reading Women, Women Reading Keats." *Studies in Romanticism* 29: 341–70.

Houghton, Walter E. 1946. "The Meaning of Keats's *Eve of St. Mark.*" *ELH* 13: 64–78.

Hunt, Leigh. 1828. *Lord Byron and Some of His Contemporaries.* 2nd ed. 2 vols. London: Henry Colburn.

Iser, Wolfgang. 1974. *The Implied Reader: Patterns of Communication in Prose Fiction from Bunyan to Beckett.* Baltimore: Johns Hopkins University Press.

———. 1978. *The Act of Reading: A Theory of Aesthetic Response.* Baltimore: Johns Hopkins University Press.

Jack, Ian. 1967. *Keats and the Mirror of Art.* Oxford, UK: Clarendon.

Jackson, J. R. de J. 1980. *Poetry of the Romantic Period.* London: Routledge and Kegan Paul.

Jarvis, Robin. 1981. "The Five-Book *Prelude:* A Reconsideration." *Journal of English and Germanic Philology* 80: 528–51.

Johnson, Mary Lynn. 1975. "How Rare Is a 'Unique Annotated Copy' of Coleridge's *Sibylline Leaves?*" *Bulletin of the New York Public Library* 78: 451–81.

Johnston, Kenneth R., and Gene W. Ruoff, eds. 1987. *The Age of William Wordsworth: Critical Essays on the Romantic Tradition.* New Brunswick, N.J.: Rutgers University Press.

Jones, Elizabeth. 1995. "The Suburban School: Snobbery and Fear in the Attacks on Keats." *Times Literary Supplement,* 27 October, pp. 14–15.

———. 1996. "Keats in the Suburbs." *Keats-Shelley Journal* 45: 23–43.

Jones, Mark, and Karl Kroeber. 1985. *Wordsworth Scholarship and Criticism, 1973–1984: An Annotated Bibliography, with Selected Criticism, 1809–1972.* New York: Garland.

Jordan, Frank, ed. 1985. *The English Romantic Poets: A Review of Research and Criticism.* 4th ed. New York: Modern Language Association.

Jordan, John E. 1976. *Why the "Lyrical Ballads"? The Background, Writing, and Character of Wordsworth's 1798 "Lyrical Ballads."* Berkeley: University of California Press.

Keats, John. 1926. *The Poems of John Keats.* Ed. Ernest de Selincourt. 5th ed. London: Methuen.

———. 1938. *The Poetical Works and Other Writings of John Keats.* Ed. H. Buxton Forman, rev. Maurice Buxton Forman. 8 vols. New York: Scribner, 1938–39.

———. 1958. *The Letters of John Keats, 1814–1821.* Ed. Hyder E. Rollins. 2 vols. Cambridge: Harvard University Press.

———. 1959. *Selected Poems and Letters.* Ed. Douglas Bush. Riverside Edition. Boston: Houghton Mifflin.

———. 1970. *The Poems of John Keats.* Ed. Miriam Allott. London: Longman, 1970; 3rd impression, with corrections, 1975.

———. 1973. *The Complete Poems.* Ed. John Barnard. Harmondsworth: Penguin; 2nd ed., 1976.

———. 1978. *The Poems of John Keats.* Ed. Jack Stillinger. Cambridge: Harvard University Press.

———. 1982. *Complete Poems.* Ed. Jack Stillinger. Cambridge: Harvard University Press.

———. 1985a. *Endymion: A Facsimile of the Revised Holograph Manuscript.* Ed. Jack Stillinger. New York: Garland.

———. 1985b. *Endymion (1818): A Facsimile of Richard Woodhouse's Annotated Copy in the Berg Collection.* Ed. Jack Stillinger. New York: Garland.

———. 1985c. *Poems (1817): A Facsimile of Richard Woodhouse's Annotated Copy in the Huntington Library.* Ed. Jack Stillinger. New York: Garland.

———. 1985d. *Poems, Transcripts, Letters, &c: Facsimiles of Richard Woodhouse's Scrapbook Materials in the Pierpont Morgan Library.* Ed. Jack Stillinger. New York: Garland.

———. 1988a. *The Charles Brown Poetry Transcripts at Harvard: Facsimiles Including the Fair Copy of "Otho the Great."* Ed. Jack Stillinger. New York: Garland.

———. 1988b. *Manuscript Poems in the British Library: Facsimiles of the "Hyperion" Holograph and George Keats's Notebook of Holographs and Transcripts.* Ed. Jack Stillinger. New York: Garland.

———. 1988c. *The Woodhouse Poetry Transcripts at Harvard: A Facsimile of the "W2" Notebook, with Description and Contents of the "W1" Notebook.* Ed. Jack Stillinger. New York: Garland.

———. 1990a. *John Keats.* Ed. Elizabeth Cook. Oxford Authors. Oxford: Oxford University Press.

———. 1990b. *Poetry Manuscripts at Harvard: A Facsimile Edition.* Ed. Jack Stillinger. Cambridge: Harvard University Press.

———. 1995. *Selected Poems.* Ed. Nicholas Roe. London: J. M. Dent.

Kelley, Theresa M. 1995. "Keats, Ekphrasis, and History." In *Keats and History,* ed. Nicholas Roe, 212–37. Cambridge: Cambridge University Press.

Kermode, Frank. 1985. *Forms of Attention.* Chicago: University of Chicago Press.

Kernan, Alvin. 1990. *The Death of Literature.* New Haven, Conn.: Yale University Press.

King, Henry. 1926. "Wordsworth's Decline." *Adelphi* 4: 106–15.

Knapp, Steven, and Walter Benn Michaels. 1982. "Against Theory." *Critical Inquiry* 8: 723–42.

Kohli, Devindra. 1968. "Coleridge, Hazlitt and Keats's Negative Capability." *Literary Criterion* 8(2) (Summer): 21–26.

Kreuzer, James R. 1955. *Elements of Poetry.* New York: Macmillan.

Langbaum, Robert. 1957. *The Poetry of Experience.* New York: Random House.

———, ed. 1970. *The Modern Spirit: Essays on the Continuity of Nineteenth- and Twentieth-Century Literature.* New York: Oxford University Press.

Lau, Beth. 1987. "Keats's Reading of Wordsworth." *Studies in Romanticism* 26: 105–50.

———. 1991. *Keats's Reading of the Romantic Poets.* Ann Arbor: University of Michigan Press.

Levinson, Marjorie. 1986. *The Romantic Fragment Poem: A Critique of a Form.* Chapel Hill: University of North Carolina Press.

———. 1988. *Keats's Life of Allegory: The Origins of a Style.* Oxford: Blackwell.

Lindenberger, Herbert. 1963. *On Wordsworth's "Prelude."* Princeton, N.J.: Princeton University Press.

Lipking, Lawrence. 1977. "The Marginal Gloss." *Critical Inquiry* 3: 609–55.

Luke, David. 1970. "*The Eve of Saint Mark:* Keats's 'ghostly Queen of Spades' and the Textual Superstition." *Studies in Romanticism* 9: 161–75.

Lyon, Harvey T. 1958. *Keats' Well-Read Urn: An Introduction to Literary Method.* New York: Henry Holt.

MacGillivray, J. R. 1949. *Keats: A Bibliography and Reference Guide with an Essay on Keats' Reputation.* Toronto: University of Toronto Press.

Madonick, Michael David. 1993. "The Pirate Map." *Cimarron Review* 103 (April): 83–85. (Reprinted in Madonick's *Waking the Deaf Dog.* New York: Avocet, 2000, 31–33.)

Magnuson, Paul. 1988. *Coleridge and Wordsworth: A Lyrical Dialogue.* Princeton, N.J.: Princeton University Press.

———. 1991. "The Politics of 'Frost at Midnight.'" *The Wordsworth Circle* 22: 3–11.

———. 1998. *Reading Public Romanticism.* Princeton, N.J.: Princeton University Press.

Maier, Rosemarie. 1971. "The Bitch and the Bloodhound: Generic Similarity in 'Christabel' and 'The Eve of St. Agnes.'" *Journal of English and Germanic Philology* 70: 62–75.

Manning, Peter. 1983. "Reading Wordsworth's Revisions: Othello and the Drowned Man." *Studies in Romanticism* 22: 3–28.

Marquess, William H. 1985. *Lives of the Poet: The First Century of Keats Biography.* University Park: Penn State Press.

Matthews, G. M., ed. 1971. *Keats: The Critical Heritage.* New York: Barnes and Noble.

Mays, J. C. C. 1992. "Reflections on Having Edited Coleridge's Poems." In *Romantic Revisions,* ed. Robert Brinkley and Keith Hanley, 136–53. Cambridge: Cambridge University Press.

McFarland, Thomas. 1981. *Romanticism and the Forms of Ruin: Wordsworth, Coleridge, and Modalities of Fragmentation.* Princeton, N.J.: Princeton University Press.

———. 1985. *Originality and Imagination.* Baltimore: Johns Hopkins University Press.

McGann, Jerome J. 1981. "The Meaning of *The Ancient Mariner.*" *Critical Inquiry* 8: 35–67. (Reprinted in McGann's *The Beauty of Inflections: Literary Investigations in Historical Method and Theory.* Oxford, UK: Clarendon, 1985, 135–72.)

———. 1983. *A Critique of Modern Textual Criticism.* Chicago: University of Chicago Press.

McLaverty, James. 1984. "The Concept of Authorial Intention in Textual Criticism." *Library,* 6th ser., 6: 121–38.

Mellor, Anne K. 1980. *English Romantic Irony.* Cambridge: Harvard University Press.

Milnes, Richard Monckton, ed. 1848. *Life, Letters, and Literary Remains, of John Keats.* 2 vols. London: Edward Moxon.

Mitchell, W. J. T., ed. 1985. *Against Theory: Literary Studies and the New Pragmatism.* Chicago: University of Chicago Press.

Moorman, Mary. 1965. *William Wordsworth: A Biography,* Vol. 2, *The Later Years, 1803–1850.* Oxford, UK: Clarendon.

Motion, Andrew. 1997. *Keats.* New York: Farrar, Straus and Giroux.

Muir, Kenneth, ed. 1958. *John Keats: A Reassessment.* Liverpool: Liverpool University Press.

Murry, John Middleton. 1939. *Studies in Keats: New and Old.* Oxford: Oxford University Press.

———. 1955. *Keats.* London: Jonathan Cape.

Newton-De Molina, David, ed. 1976. *On Literary Intention: Critical Essays.* Edinburgh: Edinburgh University Press.

O'Rourke, James. 1998. *Keats's Odes and Contemporary Criticism.* Gainesville: University Press of Florida.

———, ed. 2003. *"Ode on a Grecian Urn": Hypercanonicity and Pedagogy.* In the University of Maryland's *Romantic Circles* Praxis series, www.rc.umd.edu/praxis/grecianurn.

Osgood, Charles Grosvenor. 1935. *The Voice of England: A History of English Literature.* New York: Harper.

Parker, Hershel. 1984. *Flawed Texts and Verbal Icons.* Evanston, Ill.: Northwestern University Press.

Parker, Reeve. 1972. "'Finer Distance': The Narrative Art of Wordsworth's 'The Wanderer.'" *ELH* 39: 87–111.

Parrish, Stephen Maxfield. 1957. "'The Thorn': Wordsworth's Dramatic Monologue." *ELH* 24: 153–63.

———. 1973. *The Art of the "Lyrical Ballads."* Cambridge: Harvard University Press.

———. 1976. "The Worst of Wordsworth." *The Wordsworth Circle* 7: 89–91.

———. 1983. "The Editor as Archeologist." *Kentucky Review* 4: 3–14.

———. 1988a. *Coleridge's "Dejection": The Earliest Manuscripts and the Earliest Printings.* Ithaca, N.Y.: Cornell University Press.

———. 1988b. "The Whig Interpretation of Literature." *TEXT* 4: 343–50.

Patterson, Charles I. 1954. "Passion and Permanence in Keats's *Ode on a Grecian Urn.*" *ELH* 21: 208–20.

Peckham, Morse. 1961. "Toward a Theory of Romanticism: II. Reconsiderations." *Studies in Romanticism* 1: 1–8.

Perkins, David. 1990. "The Imaginative Vision of *Kubla Khan:* On Coleridge's Introductory Note." In *Coleridge, Keats, and the Imagination: Romanticism and Adam's Dream,* ed. J. Robert Barth and John L. Mahoney, 97–108. Columbia: University of Missouri Press.

Perrine, Laurence. 1956. *Sound and Sense: An Introduction to Poetry.* New York: Harcourt, Brace.

Random House Webster's College Dictionary. 1991. New York: Random House.

Reed, Mark L. 1975. *Wordsworth: A Chronology of the Middle Years, 1800–1815.* Cambridge: Harvard University Press.

Reiman, Donald H., ed. 1972. *The Romantics Reviewed,* Part C, *Shelley, Keats, and London Radical Writers.* New York: Garland.

———. 1987. *Romantic Texts and Contexts.* Columbia: University of Missouri Press.

Renwick, W. L. 1963. *English Literature, 1789–1815.* Oxford, UK: Clarendon.

Rhodes, Jack Wright. 1984. *Keats's Major Odes: An Annotated Bibliography of the Criticism.* Westport, Conn.: Greenwood.

Ridley, M. R. 1933. *Keats' Craftsmanship: A Study in Poetic Development.* Oxford, UK: Clarendon.

Roe, Nicholas, ed. 1995. *Keats and History.* Cambridge: Cambridge University Press.

———. 1997. *John Keats and the Culture of Dissent.* Oxford, UK: Clarendon.

Rollins, Hyder Edward. 1946. *Keats' Reputation in America to 1848.* Cambridge: Harvard University Press.

———, ed. 1948. *The Keats Circle: Letters and Papers, 1816–1878.* 2 vols. Cambridge: Harvard University Press.

Rooke, Barbara E. 1974. "An Annotated Copy of Coleridge's 'Christabel.'" *Studia Germanica Gandensia* 15: 179–92.

Rosenbaum, Barbara, and Pamela White, compilers. 1982. *Index of English Literary Manuscripts,* Vol. 4, 1800–1900, Part 1. London: Mansell.

Rosenblatt, Louise M. 1938. *Literature as Exploration.* New York: Appleton-Century; 5th ed., New York: Modern Language Association, 1996.

———. 1978. *The Reader, the Text, the Poem: The Transactional Theory of the Literary Work.* Carbondale: Southern Illinois University Press.

Rossetti, William Michael. 1887. *Life of John Keats.* London: Walter Scott.

Routh, James. 1910. "Parallels in Coleridge, Keats, and Rossetti." *Modern Language Notes* 25: 33–37.

Ryan, Robert M., and Ronald A. Sharp, eds. 1998. *The Persistence of Poetry: Bicentennial Essays on Keats.* Amherst: University of Massachusetts Press.

Schell, Richard. 1975. "Wordsworth's Revisions of the Ascent of Snowdon." *Philological Quarterly* 54: 592–603.

Schulz, Max F. 1985. "Samuel Taylor Coleridge." In *The English Romantic Poets: A Review of Research and Criticism,* 4th ed., ed. Frank Jordan, 341–463. New York: Modern Language Association.

Schwartz, Lewis M. 1973. *Keats Reviewed by His Contemporaries.* Metuchen, N.J.: Scarecrow.

Searle, John R. 1983. *Intentionality: An Essay in the Philosophy of Mind.* Cambridge: Cambridge University Press.

Sharp, William. 1892. *The Life and Letters of Joseph Severn.* London: Sampson Low, Marston.

Shillingsburg, Peter L. 1986. *Scholarly Editing in the Computer Age: Theory and Practice.* Athens: University of Georgia Press.

Simpson, David. 1979. *Irony and Authority in Romantic Poetry.* London: Macmillan.

Siskin, Clifford. 1983. "Revision Romanticized: A Study in Literary Change." *Romanticism Past and Present* 7(2) (Summer): 1–16.

Slatoff, Walter J. 1970. *With Respect to Readers: Dimensions of Literary Response.* Ithaca, N.Y.: Cornell University Press.

Smith, Barbara Herrnstein. 1968. *Poetic Closure: A Study of How Poems End.* Chicago: University of Chicago Press.

Smith, G. C. Moore. 1926. Review of *The Prelude.* Ed. Ernest de Selincourt. *Modern Language Review* 21: 443–46.

Sperry, Stuart M. 1971. "Romance as Wish-Fulfillment: Keats's *The Eve of St. Agnes.*" *Studies in Romanticism* 10: 27–43. (Revised in Sperry's *Keats the Poet.* Princeton, N.J.: Princeton University Press, 1973, 198–220.)

Spurgeon, Caroline F. E. 1928. *Keats's Shakespeare: A Descriptive Study.* Oxford, UK: Clarendon.

Stevens, Wallace. 1966. *Letters of Wallace Stevens.* Ed. Holly Stevens. New York: Knopf.

Stillinger, Jack. 1960. Review of Wordsworth's *Prelude.* Ed. Ernest de Selincourt. *Journal of English and Germanic Philology* 59: 161–64.

———. 1961. "The Hoodwinking of Madeline: Skepticism in *The Eve of St. Agnes.*" *Studies in Philology* 58: 533–55. (Reprinted in Stillinger's *The Hoodwinking of Madeline and Other Essays on Keats's Poems.* Urbana: University of Illinois Press, 1971, 67–93.)

———, ed. 1966. *The Letters of Charles Armitage Brown.* Cambridge: Harvard University Press.

———. 1968a. "The Meaning of 'poor cheated soul' in Keats's 'The Eve of Saint Mark.'" *English Language Notes* 5: 193–96. (Reprinted in Stillinger's *The Hoodwinking of Madeline,* 1971, 94–98.)

———, ed. 1968b. *Twentieth Century Interpretations of Keats's Odes: A Collection of Critical Essays.* Englewood Cliffs, N.J.: Prentice Hall.

———. 1971. *The Hoodwinking of Madeline and Other Essays on Keats's Poems.* Urbana: University of Illinois Press.

———. 1974. *The Texts of Keats's Poems.* Cambridge: Harvard University Press.

———. 1985. "John Keats." In *The English Romantic Poets: A Review of Research and Criticism,* 4th ed., ed. Frank Jordan, 665–718. New York: Modern Language Association.

———. 1991a. *Multiple Authorship and the Myth of Solitary Genius.* New York: Oxford University Press.

———. 1991b. "Multiple Authorship and the Question of Authority." *TEXT* 5: 283–93.

———. 1994. *Coleridge and Textual Instability: The Multiple Versions of the Major Poems.* New York: Oxford University Press.

———. 1999. *Reading "The Eve of St. Agnes": The Multiples of Complex Literary Transaction.* New York: Oxford University Press.

Stone, C. F., III. 1974. "Narrative Variation in Wordsworth's Versions of 'The Discharged Soldier.'" *Journal of Narrative Technique* 4: 32–44.

Strand, Mark. 1969. *Reasons for Moving.* New York: Atheneum.

Thayer, Mary Rebecca. 1945. "Keats and Coleridge: 'La Belle Dame sans Merci.'" *Modern Language Notes* 60: 270–72.

Thorpe, Clarence D. 1926. *The Mind of John Keats.* New York: Oxford University Press.

———. 1927. "Wordsworth and Keats—A Study in Personal and Critical Impression." *PMLA* 42: 1010–26.

———. 1944. "Coleridge as Aesthetician and Critic." *Journal of the History of Ideas* 5: 387–414.

Thorpe, James. 1965. "The Aesthetics of Textual Criticism." *PMLA* 80: 465–82.

———. 1972. *Principles of Textual Criticism.* San Marino, Calif.: Huntington Library.

Twitchell, James B. 1978. "Porphyro as 'Famish'd Pilgrim': The Hoodwinking of Madeline Continued." *Ball State University Forum* 19(2) (Spring): 56–65.

———. 1981. *The Living Dead: A Study of the Vampire in Romantic Literature.* Durham, N.C.: Duke University Press.

Valdés, Mario J., and Owen Miller, eds. 1985. *Identity of the Literary Text.* Toronto: University of Toronto Press.

Wall, Wendy. 1987. "Interpreting Poetic Shadows: The Gloss of 'The Rime of the Ancient Mariner.'" *Criticism* 29: 179–95.

Wallen, Martin. 1986. "Return and Representation: The Revisions of 'The Ancient Mariner.'" *The Wordsworth Circle* 17: 148–56.

Ward, Aileen. 1963. *John Keats: The Making of a Poet.* New York: Viking.

Wasserman, Earl R. 1953. *The Finer Tone: Keats' Major Poems.* Baltimore: Johns Hopkins University Press.

———. 1964. "The English Romantics: The Grounds of Knowledge." *Studies in Romanticism* 4: 17–34.

Watkins, Daniel P. 1989. *Keats's Poetry and the Politics of the Imagination.* Rutherford, N.J.: Fairleigh Dickinson University Press.

Webb, Charles Harper. 1999. "Byron, Keats, and Shelley." In Webb's *Liver,* 68–69. Madison: University of Wisconsin Press.

Webster's Ninth New Collegiate Dictionary. 1983. Springfield, Mass.: Merriam-Webster.

Wheeler, K. M. 1981. *The Creative Mind in Coleridge's Poetry.* London: Heinemann.

Wimsatt, W. K., Jr., and Monroe C. Beardsley. 1946. "The Intentional Fallacy." *Sewanee Review* 54: 468–88. (Revised in Wimsatt's *The Verbal Icon.* Lexington: University of Kentucky Press, 1954, 3–18.)

Wolfson, Susan J. 1984. "The Illusion of Mastery: Wordsworth's Revisions of 'The Drowned Man of Esthwaite,' 1799, 1805, 1850." *PMLA* 99: 917–35.

———. 1986a. *The Questioning Presence: Wordsworth, Keats, and the Interrogative Mode in Romantic Poetry.* Ithaca, N.Y.: Cornell University Press.

———, ed. 1986b. "Keats and Politics: A Forum." *Studies in Romanticism* 25: 171–229.

———. 1990. "Feminizing Keats." In *Critical Essays on John Keats,* ed. Hermione de Almeida, 317–56. Boston: G. K. Hall.

———. 1995a. "Keats Enters History: Autopsy, *Adonais,* and the Fame of Keats." In *Keats and History,* ed. Nicholas Roe, 17–45. Cambridge: Cambridge University Press.

———. 1995b. "Keats and the Manhood of the Poet." *European Romantic Review* 6: 1–37.

———, ed. 2001. *The Cambridge Companion to Keats.* Cambridge: Cambridge University Press.

Woof, Robert, and Stephen Hebron. 1995. *John Keats.* Grasmere: Wordsworth Trust.

Wordsworth, Jonathan. 1969. *The Music of Humanity: A Critical Study of Wordsworth's "Ruined Cottage."* London: Nelson.

———. 1970. "'The Climbing of Snowdon.'" In *Bicentenary Wordsworth Studies in Memory of John Alban Finch,* ed. Jonathan Wordsworth, 449–74. Ithaca, N.Y.: Cornell University Press.

———. 1977. "The Five-Book *Prelude* of Early Spring 1804." *Journal of English and Germanic Philology* 76: 1–25.

———. 1982. *William Wordsworth: The Borders of Vision.* Oxford, UK: Clarendon.

———. 1985. Editorial note introducing 1984 Wordsworth Conference papers. *The Wordsworth Circle* 16: 45.

Wordsworth, William. 1940. *The Poetical Works of William Wordsworth.* Ed. Ernest de Selincourt and Helen Darbishire. 5 vols. Oxford, UK: Clarendon, 1940–49.

———. 1959. *The Prelude or Growth of a Poet's Mind.* Ed. Ernest de Selincourt (1926). 2nd ed., rev. Helen Darbishire. Oxford, UK: Clarendon.

———. 1965. *Selected Poems and Prefaces.* Ed. Jack Stillinger. Riverside Edition. Boston: Houghton Mifflin.

———. 1967. *The Letters of William and Dorothy Wordsworth: The Early Years.* Ed. Ernest de Selincourt. 2nd ed., rev. Chester L. Shaver. Oxford, UK: Clarendon.

———. 1970. *The Prelude or Growth of a Poet's Mind (Text of 1805).* Ed. Ernest de Selincourt. New ed., corr. by Stephen Gill. London: Oxford University Press.

———. 1971. *The Prelude: A Parallel Text.* Ed. J. C. Maxwell. Harmondsworth, UK: Penguin.

———. 1975. *The Salisbury Plain Poems of William Wordsworth.* Ed. Stephen Gill. Ithaca, N.Y.: Cornell University Press.

———. 1977. *"The Prelude," 1798–1799.* Ed. Stephen Parrish. Ithaca, N.Y.: Cornell University Press.

———. 1979a. *The Letters of William and Dorothy Wordsworth: The Later Years.* Ed. Ernest de Selincourt. 2nd ed., rev. Alan G. Hill, Part 2. Oxford, UK: Clarendon.

———. 1979b. *The Prelude, 1799, 1805, 1850.* Ed. Jonathan Wordsworth, M. H. Abrams, and Stephen Gill. Norton Critical Edition. New York: Norton.

———. 1979c. *"The Ruined Cottage" and "The Pedlar."* Ed. James Butler. Ithaca, N.Y.: Cornell University Press.

———. 1981. *Benjamin the Waggoner.* Ed. Paul F. Betz. Ithaca, N.Y.: Cornell University Press.

———. 1982. *The Borderers.* Ed. Robert Osborn. Ithaca, N.Y.: Cornell University Press.

———. 1983. *"Poems, in Two Volumes," and Other Poems, 1800–1807.* Ed. Jared Curtis. Ithaca, N.Y.: Cornell University Press.

———. 1984a. *Descriptive Sketches.* Ed. Eric Birdsall. Ithaca, N.Y.: Cornell University Press.

———. 1984b. *An Evening Walk.* Ed. James Averill. Ithaca, N.Y.: Cornell University Press.

———. 1984c. *William Wordsworth.* Ed. Stephen Gill. Oxford Authors. Oxford: Oxford University Press.

———. 1985a. *The Fourteen-Book "Prelude."* Ed. W. J. B. Owen. Ithaca, N.Y.: Cornell University Press.

———. 1985b. *Peter Bell.* Ed. John E. Jordan. Ithaca, N.Y.: Cornell University Press.

———. 1991. *The Thirteen-Book "Prelude."* Ed. Mark L. Reed. 2 vols. Ithaca, N.Y.: Cornell University Press.

———. 1992. *"Lyrical Ballads," and Other Poems, 1797–1800.* Ed. James Butler and Karen Green. Ithaca, N.Y.: Cornell University Press.

Wright, Herbert G. 1945. "Has Keats's 'Eve of St. Agnes' a Tragic Ending?" *Modern Language Review* 40: 90–94.

Young, Robert. 1982. "A Reply: To 'Prelude and Prejudice,' by Jeffrey Baker." *The Wordsworth Circle* 13: 87–88.

Zeller, Hans. 1975. "A New Approach to the Critical Constitution of Literary Texts." *Studies in Bibliography* 28: 231–64.

Credits

Index

JACK STILLINGER is Center for Advanced Study Professor Emeritus of English at the University of Illinois at Urbana-Champaign. Stillinger, a Fellow of the American Academy of Arts and Sciences, is widely recognized as a distinguished scholar of nineteenth-century British literature. He is the author of many books, articles, and reviews, including *The Hoodwinking of Madeline and Other Essays on Keats's Poems*, *The Texts of Keats's Poems*, *Multiple Authorship and the Myth of Solitary Genius*, *Coleridge and Textual Instability: The Multiple Versions of the Major Poems*, and *Reading "The Eve of St. Agnes": The Multiples of Complex Literary Transaction*.

The University of Illinois Press
is a founding member of the
Association of American University Presses.

———————————————————

Composed in 10.5/13 Minion
with Minion display
by BookComp, Inc.
Manufactured by Thomson-Shore, Inc.

University of Illinois Press
1325 South Oak Street
Champaign, IL 61820-6903
www.press.uillinois.edu